Utopia Gesamtkunstwerk

Edited by Agnes Husslein-Arco
Harald Krejci, Bettina Steinbrügge

21

Verlag der Buchhandlung Walther König,
Köln 2012

Utopia Gesamtkunstwerk

Edited by Agnes Husslein-Arco
Harald Krejci, Bettina Steinbrügge

Deconstruction

Technologies of the Unconscious

Correlations

Appendix

Prologue

Agnes Husslein-Arco

Utopie Gesamtkunstwerk is the first group exhibition to take place at the new 21er Haus. 28 years ago, in his exhibition *Der Hang zum Gesamtkunstwerk* Harald Szeemann presented a variety of different models of the *Gesamtkunstwerk* at the former Museum of the 20th Century in Vienna: from Kurt Schwitter's Merzbau and Antoni Gaudí's cathedral Sagrada Família to the life reform movement of Monte Verità near Ascona. The exhibition assembled European utopias from 1800 onwards, that refused to limit themselves to merely aesthetic aspects, intending instead a transformation of social reality towards a renewed society. *Utopie Gesamtkunstwerk* resumes this project in a contemporary context. The curators Harald Krejci and Bettina Steinbrügge focused on the questions what Gesamtkunstwerk means today and how the socio-political project of the Gesamtkunstwerk has actually lived on beyond the utopian models of the "life reform" movement. The desire to make our society more liveable, and the question of which models of living are still or again valid, have been central topics ever since the beginning of modernism. After Szeemann's epochal exhibition projects like *Utopia Station* (2004) curated by Hans Ulrich Obrist, Rirkrit Tiravanija and Molly Nesbit, as well as numerous publications have shown that the topic Gesamtkunstwerk can give fresh impetus anytime. The new political order subsequent to the fall of the Iron Curtain, the events of 9/11 2001 and the financial crisis of the recent past have majorly affected social dynamism and caused great anxiety. Looking back further on the history of the Gesamtkunstwerk, one of the pioneers dealing with contemporary life was Richard Wagner, whose revolutionary socio-political concern has been underestimated since.

The exhibition as well as the publication *Utopie Gesamtkunstwerk* present a new view—from a contemporary position—on the historically transmitted ideas of the Gesamtkunstwerk and thus the beginning of Modernism in art. Contemporary Art has been performing a re-reading of modernism for some time now. Although it is an aspect that has been long neglected, the Gesamtkunstwerk intrinsically linked to modernism.

One aim of the exhibition is to emphasise this connection: showing works of more than 50 artists and collectives, *Utopie Gesamtkunstwerk* takes a tour de force from the 1950s up to today. In the exhibition generations, working on similar topics but whose approach to the Gesamtkunstwerk could not be any more divergent, clash, with no claim to completeness and sometimes willingly against chronological order.

It is about a lively discussion on the topic, about approximation and distance, about illustrating how art and artistic ideas dynamise and develop through the work of an individual artist. Moreover, the exhibition shows the responsibility of the 1960s, generation of artists, who felt they had to leave an artistic message for their successors. These important positions of post-war avant-garde will have to adopt future generations, concerning the question of the social relevance of art and a contemporary artistic self-conception in times of worldwide financial crisis, nuclear disasters and endangered democratic movements.

First and foremost I have to thank all artists involved. Their unceasing commitment and especially their enthusiasm for the project have largely guaranteed the realisation of this exhibition. I want to thank Esther Stocker in particular, who has developed an innovative and well-conceived display, which excellently reflects the qualities of the institution as well as the topic of the exhibition, while being an autonomic sculpture at the same time.

Harald Krejci and Bettina Steinbrügge are responsible for the concept of this exhibition, and I would hereby like to thank them for their great commitment and their personal dedication for this complex project. They were actively supported by Véronique Aichner and Nina Herlitschka. Moreover, I would like to thank Oswald Oberhuber, who provided us with crucial inputs and hints during the development phase of the project. I am particularly delighted about our authors, who have applied themselves to this topic cross-generationally. Special thanks to Werner Hofmann, who has written a replication on his text roughly twenty years after Harald Szeemann had published it in the exhibition catalogue to *Der Hang zum Gesamtkunstwerk* (1983). All loans were provided by public or private collections whose support was vital to realise such a comprehensive exhibition. Thus, I am very grateful to all museums, collectors and galleries for their cooperation. Last, but not least, I would like to thank my dedicated on-scene team, who has spared no efforts to realise ideas and concepts successfully, but who has also continuously brought in new ones.

Das Gesamtkunstwerk gibt es nicht. **(Harald Szeemann)**

[…] denn im Kunstwerk werden wir Eins sein […] **(Richard Wagner)**

Das große Gesammtkunstwerk, das alle Gattungen der Kunst zu umfassen hat, um jede einzelne dieser Gattungen als Mittel gewissermaßen zu verbrauchen, zu vernichten zu Gunsten der Erreichung des Gesammtzweckes aller, nämlich der unbedingten, unmittelbaren Darstellung der vollendeten menschlichen Natur, – dieses große Gesammtkunstwerk erkennt er nicht als die willkürlich mögliche That des Einzelnen, sondern als das nothwendig denkbare gemeinsame Werk der Menschen der Zukunft. **(Richard Wagner)**

[…] we should employ all the elements which the other arts have to offer and fuse them to produce a concerted effect on the audience […] **(Wsewolod Meyerhold)**

There's always also the totalitarian danger that comes with the Gesamtkunstwerk. **(Hans Ulrich Obrist)**

Der totalisierte Kunstbegriff, das ist ja das Prinzip, was ich mit diesen Materialien ausdrücken wollte […] Alle Fragen können nur Fragen der Gestaltung sein und das ist der totalisierte Kunstbegriff. **(Joseph Beuys)**

Toxische Atmosphäre **(Peter Sloterdijk)**

Für das Gesamtkunstwerk ist die fixierte Vision, Utopie oder Systemkonstruktion – also das gestaltete Werk – der Träger des Anspruchs auf Darstellung eines Ganzen. **(Bazon Brock)**

Yet as a model of artistic interrelation, the Gesamtkunstwerk both supports and inverts modernist principles as they have been traditionally understood. **(Juliet Koss)**

Das Verschwinden des Gesamtkunstwerks ist, wie die Suche nach ihm, als ästhetisches Problem zugleich ein soziales, oder vielmehr ein Hinweis auf ein solches; wobei sich zeigt, dass die Kunst auch dann etwas sagt, wenn sie sich versagt; dass sie auch dann vom anderen, besseren Leben spricht, wenn sie schweigt. **(Johannes Werner)**

„Der Hang zum Gesamtkunstwerk", der Wunsch nach dem Ganzen als äußerste Herausforderung an den schöpferischen Menschen **(Ingrid Rein)**

[…] ein Gesamtkunstwerk wird es nie geben. Es zu schaffen ist so unmöglich wie die Quadratur des Kreises oder das Perpetuum mobile unmöglich sind. **(Wieland Schmied)**

Kraftwerk der Gefühle **(Alexander Kluge)**

Damit das Ganze mehr als seine Teile, muss jeder Teil zunächst ein Ganzes sein. Je später die Verbindung, desto mehr an Realität und Individualität wird eingebracht. Je später die Bauteile ihre Selbstständigkeit behaupten, desto komplexer das Gesamtkunstwerk. **(Heiner Müller)**

[…] eine geschlossene und festgefügte Weltanschauung bzw. ein in unterschiedlicher Weise, etwa gesellschaftstheoretisch, geschichtsphilosophisch oder metaphysisch-religiös akzentuiertes Bild vom Ganzen **(Roger Fornoff)**

Kandinskys Gesamtkunstwerk, in dem sich alle Künste treffen, um sich zu neuen Möglichkeiten der Wirkung und der Aussage zu vereinigen, entspricht den Zielen der Dadaisten, die in ihren Veranstaltungen eine „Synthese der modernen Kunst" nicht alleine stilistisch sondern auch im Hinblick auf ein Zusammenwirken der Künste anstreben. **(Hugo Ball)**

Ich fordere die restlose Zusammenfassung aller künstlerischen Kräfte zur Erlangung des Gesamtkunstwerkes. **(Kurt Schwitters)**

Wenn wir vom Gesamtkunstwerk sprechen, verstehen wir darunter ein Gesamt-Kunstwerk oder ein Gesamtkunst-Werk? **(Anke Finger)**

One cannot embrace in a single epic, the entire world of the single past […] But this is no great loss, because the structure of the whole is repeated in each part, and each part is complete and circular like the whole. **(Michail M. Bachtin)**

The pressures of the transitory affect the monumental itself: the only monument that counts is the one already imagined as ruin. **(Andreas Huyssen)**

Mein Ziel ist das Merzgesamtkunstwerk, das alle Kunstarten zusammenfasst zur künstlerischen Einheit. Zunächst habe ich einzelne Kunstarten miteinander vermählt. Ich habe Gedichte aus Worten und Sätzen so zusammengeklebt, dass die Anordnung rhythmisch eine Zeichnung ergibt. Ich habe umgekehrt Bilder und Zeichnungen geklebt, auf denen Sätze gelesen werden sollen. Ich habe Bilder so genagelt, dass neben der malerischen Bildwirkung eine plastische Reliefwirkung entsteht. Dieses geschah, um die Grenzen der Kunstarten zu verwischen. Das Merzgesamtkunstwerk aber ist die Merzbühne, die ich bislang nur theoretisch durcharbeiten konnte […] **(Kurt Schwitters)**

Wir haben die Sehnsucht nach dem Ganzen und dem Einen, nach der Versöhnung von Begriff und Sinnlichkeit teuer bezahlt. **(Jean-François Lyotard)**

Gesamtkunstwerk: New Art from Germany **(Saatchi Gallery)**

Als Zeichen kommt das Wort an die Wissenschaft; als Ton, als Bild, als eigentliches Wort wird es unter die verschiedenen Künste aufgeteilt, ohne dass es sich durch deren Addition, durch Synästhesie oder Gesamtkunst je wiederherstellen ließe. **(Theodor W. Adorno/Max Horkheimer)**

Als totalisierendes Medium erfordert Gesamtkunst zugleich die „Wiedergewinnung einer Totalität der Wahrnehmung": „Alle Sinne sind am Ende ein Sinn." **(Marshall McLuhan)**

Wagner sucht hier in seinem ästhetischen Kontext einzuholen, was die gescheiterte Revolution von 1848 ihm verweigert hatte: das Umdenken aller bestehenden religiösen, politischen, gesellschaftlichen und kulturellen Verhältnisse, die revolutionäre Erneuerung einer moralisch wie institutionell als Bankrott erachteten Welt. **(Udo Bermbach)**

Kein Nebeneinander, sondern eine organische Verbindung, kein Zusammenwürfeln der einzelnen Künste, sondern eine neue Kunst mit eigenen Möglichkeiten, eigenen Wirkungen, eigenen Gesetzen [...] **(Max Reinhardt)**

In Wilsons Theater äußert sich in letzter Konsequenz nicht die Überwindung der Korrespondenzen, sondern ihre Verortung in der Rezeption. **(Guido Hiß)**

Scheitern als Chance **(Christoph Schlingensief)**

Diskursverknappungsbekämpfung und negatives Gesamtkunstwerk **(Diedrich Diederichsen)**

In Zukunft wird mit einem anderen Gesamtkunstwerk zu rechnen sein [...] mit dem der kapitalistischen Ökonomie, einem Gesamtkunstwerk, das zwar mit den Differenzierungsphänomenen und Pluralitätsanforderungen der postmodernen Welt kompatibel ist, seinen suggestiven und manipulativen Charakter aber keineswegs verloren hat. **(Roger Fornoff)**

[...] zum Gesamtkunstwerk gehört die Tendenz zur Tilgung der Grenze zwischen ästhetischem Gebilde und Realität. **(Odo Marquardt)**

If this truly was a Gesamtkunstwerk, suddenly it seemed alarmingly feasible that every detail of the entire "live" event might have been prescripted. **(Catherine Wood)**

Die höchste Form der Kunst ist das Gesamtkunstwerk, in dem die Grenzen zwischen Kunst und Nichtkunst aufgehoben sind. **(Kurt Schwitters)**

Essays

There is no Decay of Art History

Werner Hofmann

"Only with the end of the Gesamtkunstwerk the program of the 'Gesamtkunstwerk' begins." Three decades ago, I put this statement at the beginning of my essay on the "Gesamtkunstwerk Vienna" for Harald Szeemann's exhibition *Der Hang zum Gesamtkunstwerk. Europäische Utopien seit 1800*, which was held at the Museum im Schweizergarten. In nearly all of these world concepts the isolation of the arts is seen as a lack, which the Gesamtkunstwerk should remedy by restoring a state in which all art genres collaborate equally in a synthesis. In these artistic "wholes" gathered by Szeemann the design process is stylised to a factor of order, which frees arts from their isolation, their conflicts and contradictions, and reduces them to common denominator, which makes everything seem reasonable and necessary. This notion of consent was expressed exemplary in the cult of beauty of the Vienna Secession, which categorised any design idea—from a tea cup to a wall painting—according to the belief that the artist gave our world meaning, and whose work represented the idealisation of all raison d'etre. In this completely consistent harmony the material world is covered with an aura of consecrational gestus.

Thus the Secession, which at first only wanted to give new impetus to the arts, returned to the pedestal of festive enactments of salvation, e.g. displaying Klinger's Beethoven sculpture in the Beethoven exhibition of 1902. It acted on the strict maxims St. Thomas Aquinas had elaborated. Thus three things are vital for beauty: integritas (perfectio), proportio (consonantia) and claritas. They led to the development of the formal rules of the Renaissance (Alberti).[1]

This thinking in coherence omitted that there was an early religious thinker, who had proposed another, unconditional, and thus open discourse between the formal possibilities of an art work—St. Augustine. His "aesthetics" were rediscovered by Alois Riegl: When Klimt painted his frieze for the Beethoven exhibition, Riegl set a caesura with the wall of monsters and seductresses—"The Hostile Powers" (Fig.)—between both longitudinal walls, on which the quest for happiness is illustrated in hieratic constancy before it leads to the apotheosis of embracement. The Hostile Powers represent a gritty "interval" to this quest. Precisely back then Alois Riegl published his main work: *Die spätrömische Kunstindustrie nach den Funden in Österreich-Ungarn*.[2] In its final chapter, he refers to the theological vindications for the countervailing forces, whom Klimt's arrangement on "The Hostile Powers" wall allows the rank of necessary discords. Riegl regards such an "emancipation of intervals" as a fundamental principle of Augustine's ethics and aesthetics. In this text on music, he finds the relativity of beauty and ugliness visualised in the contrast between light and shade. Bright light and impenetrable shades may not please us humans, but are indeed liked by other beings. In *De civitate Dei* Augustine stands up for the use of black paint, which (according to Riegl) represents "the shade, the intangible, the immaterial, the formless, the void, and the non-being". The art historian based his theory on a passage from volume XI. *Gottesstaat*: „Denn wie ein Gemälde mit der schwarzen an rechter Stelle angebrachten Farbe, so ist das Weltall, könnte man es nur überschauen, auch mit den Sündern schön, wie sehr ihnen auch für sich allein betrachtet, ihre Häßlichkeit Schande macht [...]" Riegl added: "Is black, however, used at the right spot in the painting, it appears—in combination with the brightly painted textual individual forms—beautiful from a distance. The function of the relocation to the perfect spot is—according to Augustine's teachings—carried out by Ordo, which is basically an expression of rhythm; this means that Augustine also eyed the rhythmical allocation of dark and bright, shade and light in painting as the artistic aim."[3]

Riegl was neither interested in a monosensual synthesis, nor in a solely coherent harmony. He wanted a coexistence of opposites. This view is in accord with the image that Augustine sketched from the world. It is a wonderful, with *posita* and *contraposita*[4] vested poem, to make everything in our world have its perfect place.[5] This leads to the multipolar structure of the Gesamtkunstwerk, which does not behave monofocally, but polyfocally to the world. To illustrate this fact, Riegl has created a seemingly unpretentious parable: the chamois and the Alpine panorama.[6] The art historian placed himself in a solitary Alpine landscape. What his contemplating distant view descries creates a "nameless feeling of ensoulment, easing, and harmony in him"[7]. He senses a cosmic law. Suddenly, he catches a sound: A chamois has jumped onto its feet destroying the perfect idyll. Chaos disrupts this harmony. The art historian draws the complementary categories of close-up view and distant view from the incident. He will put them in coexistence in his famous analysis of the relief of the Arch of Constantine.[8]

Riegl uses, what Nietzsche has called the „dual-object view"[9], to unveil its opposite in *one* phase only. The respective location of the observer influences this process, it decides on the viewpoint of the verdict. This means that the art work is calculated for several spectator angles. In the reliefs of the Arch of Constantine two phases are contained, one of which become accessible to the close-up view of the observer, the other to his distant view. The close-up view discovers the lawful beauty in the strictest form of "crystallinism", which turns into "truth of life", when regarded from a distance, expressed in the extreme form of the momentary optical effect.[10] Thus, timelessness and temporalisation are opposing each other. With this bi-polar view Riegl has eradicated the flaws of a decline of ugliness and vapidity. He earned applause from Hermann Bahr, who discovered an epochal turn of the aesthetic scale of values in Riegl's anti-decay-theory. His text *Expressionismus* (1916) contains the following lead: Riegl "has uttered the relieving phrase that there is actually no decay in history', and he has declared that there was neither a regression in the development, nor a stop'."[11]

The competence of judgement is handed over to the subject, who approaches the art work trying out several viewpoints. This partnership discov-

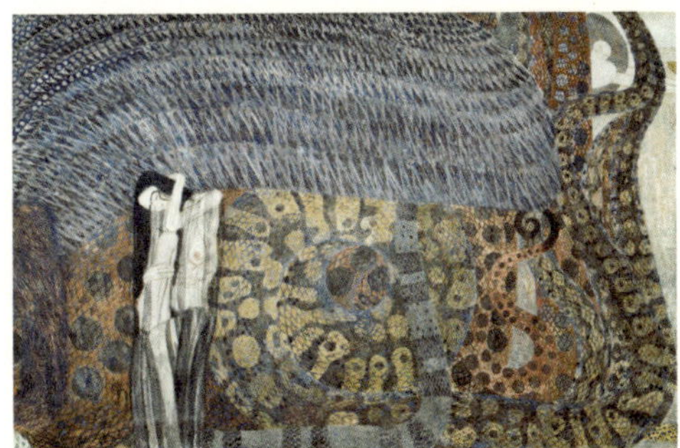

—Fig. 1
Gustav Klimt, *Beethovenfries*,
detail, 1901/02

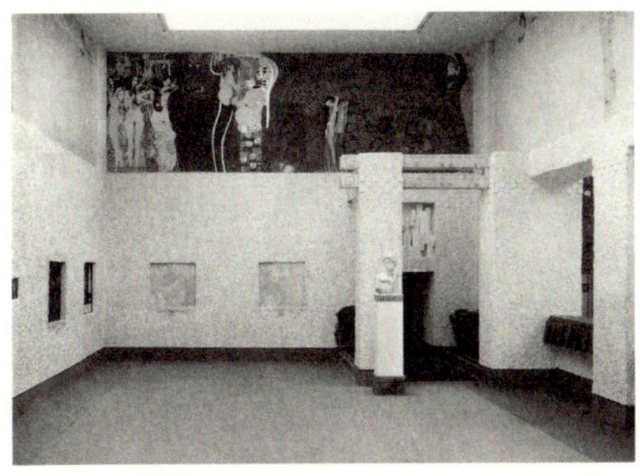

—Fig. 2
Interior view of the Secession with
Beethovenfries, 1901/02

ers that each distance from the art work, each viewpoint contains potentially new statements, but also new questions. The judgement sums up experiences, whose result is a palimpsest of meanings.

Therefore, also in Klimt's work multi-polarity supports multiple meaning, causing and thematising contrasts. Dissonances are allowed for as possibilities. The dual focus describes stylisation and its correlate amorphisation. It stands for the ornament as an exquisite decor and as a conglomerate of fragments. Klimt develops labyrinths in all levels, which extract life substance from their bodies. Doing justice to Klimt, we would have to examine his version of the Gesamtkunstwerk as a continual Gesamtkunstwerk. In this context the golden cage which celebrates his women, changes into the paralysis of pseudo-life. His actions become rituals of escape and withdrawal, in which the physical surrender turns into obsessive self-satisfaction. His views on nature show growth in rampant disguise, organic life as a collapsing backdrop. These images developed, when Adolf Loos denounced the beauty of the ornament as perversion and depicted an art crime.

If several, often contrary phases meet in the Gesamtkunstwerk—to preserve it as a productive challenge, as I define it—our confrontation with the art work as well as our judgement loose the Pathos of uniqueness and finality. In spontaneous experience and judgement opposites clash which are questioning each other. These tensions are the bread and butter of our argumentation. Unveiling and bringing them into revocable dialogues is an equally challenging and difficult task for the recipient. If the Gesamtkunstwerk, today more than ever, illustrates complexes with open contours (also palimpsests), it is the perfect site for testing the repeated interaction with the observer. Richard Wagner's hope for a community of a collective togetherness, which celebrates the "Feasts of Humanity" and gathers around the altar of the future, never took place.[12] The multiple meanings of the current Gesamtkunstwerk result from the interaction of several levels of reflection. It stems from the poly focus, which holds the conditions of his perception ready for the spectator. Already Riegl knew that this requires an intellectual effort, which the broad audience would only hesitantly be ready to undergo. Maybe it is enough for the time being to waive all theoretical constructs and to place art matters, as Wittgenstein had proposed it for our entire item inventory: "All that we can see could also be different. All that we can describe could also be different. There is no order of things a priori."[13]

1 "Beauty is a kind of accordance and coherence of parts to one whole, which according to a certain number implemented a particular relation and array, as symmetry, i.e. the perfect and highest law of nature, demands." (Leon Battista Alberti, *Zehn Bücher über die Baukunst*, hg. and übers. von Max Theuer, Buch IX, chap. 5, Vienna/Leipzig 1912, p. 492.)
2 cf. Werner Hofmann, „Der Betrachter ist im/das Bild", in: Steffen Bogen/Wolfgang Brassat/David Ganz (ed.), *Bilder—Räume—Betrachter. Festschrift für Wolfgang Kemp zum 60. Geburtstag*, Berlin 2006, p. 140f.
3 "Sicut pictura cum colore nigro, loco suo posita, ita universitas rerum, si quis possit intueri, etiam cum peccatoribus pulchra est, quamvis per se ipsos consideratos sua deformitas turpet." (Alois Riegl, *Spätrömische Kunstindustrie*, Wien 21927, p. 399f. cf. German version in the version of *City of God* by Hans Urs von Balthasar, *Augustinus. Der Gottesstaat*, Einsiedeln 1996, p. 49.)
4 Balthasar 1996, p. 56f. (XI, 18).
5 cf. Balthasar 1996, p. 48–50 (XI, 22).
6 cf. Werner Hofmann, „Die Gemse and das Alpenpanorama", in: *Wiener Schule. Erinnerung and Perspektiven* (*Wiener Jahrbuch für Kunstgeschichte* 53), Vienna/Cologne/Weimar 2004, p. 92–94.
7 Alois Riegl, „Die Stimmung als Inhalt der modernen Kunst", in: *Graphische Künste* XXII, 1899, p. 47–49; also in Karl M. Swoboda (ed.), *Alois Riegl. Gesammelte Aufsätze*, Vienna 1928, p. 28.
8 cf. Hofmann 2004, p. 90.
9 cf. Friedrich Nietzsche, *Ecce homo*, in: Karl Schlechta (ed.), *Friedrich Nietzsche. Werke in drei Bänden*, Vol. 2, Munich 1955, p. 1123.
10 Riegl 21927, p. 91: "Already these brief implications distil that in the Constantan reliefs both artistic aims- beauty and truth of life—are strived for and actually reached like in classical art; as they were united in the latter to a harmonic equation ("Schönlebendigkeit"), they have now been parted into their extremes again: on the one hand the highest lawful beauty in its strictest form of crystallinism, and on the other as truth of life in its most extreme form of the momentary optical effect."
11 Hermann Bahr, *Expressionismus*, München 1916, p. 80. Hermann Bahr refers to Alois Riegl, *Die spätrömische Kunstindustrie nach den Funden in Österreich-Ungarn im Zusammenhange mit der Gesamtentwicklung der bildenden Künste bei den Mittelmeervölkern*, Vienna 1901, p. 7.
12 Szeemann has assembled Wagner's ideas to the Gesamtkunstwerk for the exhibition catalogue: Harald Szeemann (ed.), *Der Hang zum Gesamtkunstwerk. Europäische Utopien seit 1800*, Aarau 1983, p. 166–178.
13 Ludwig Wittgenstein, *Tractatus logico-philosophicus*, 5.634, in: *Ludwig Wittgenstein. Schriften*, Frankfurt/Main 1960, p. 66.

Fantasies of Fusion
Alice on Her Way Through the Birth Canal (for the Second Time)

Holger Birkholz

The need for de-limitation of one's Self, for fusion with the other and thus becoming one with the world persistantly affects us humans when meeting with others or when facing the "world" in its the broadest possible sense, and art in particular. While succumbing to such desires, we can also view them from a distance and regard them as exaggeratedly idealistic or romantic. We emotionally protect ourselves by approaching this wish with scepticism, even while simultaneously succumbing to it. Fantasies of fusion only seem possible in the context of bygone naive worldviews, exaggerated in images of antique Arcadia, or the Christianity of medieval times. We distance ourselves from these by observing them critically because we fear the loss of our own sovereignty, which seems more important to us than enhancing our Self through fusion with the bigger picture.

Novalis and the Night

The breach, still valid today, took place at the turn of the 17th century and the intellectual movement of Romanticism. Novalis, a contemporary poet and philosopher, was a theoretician in whose overall world outlook motives of fusion were realized in combination with prose, poetry and reflective texts. He was driven by fantasies of "merging" wherein borders became increasingly blurred. He searched for unity in religion at a time during which the feeling of the individual being at home in state and church seems lost forever. His essay "Christianity or Europe," written in 1799, speaks of the views of a lost era, and sees itself as a vision for the future. Novalis imagined a universalistic social utopia that named God its metaphysical authority. It legitimated, and furthermore, constituted its entirety without need for questioning. This image of a macro cosmos corresponds with the inward way. The author's investigations of Self seek to access unknown territories by overcoming all perimeters. The starting point of this poetic research was the death of his young bride. Instead of loosing her to death, he endeavored to draw even more closely to her than when she was living. During the night at the grave of his beloved, the material world dissolved, uniting physical and metaphysical worlds, "Away fled the glory of the world, and with it my mourning; the sadness flowed together into a new, unfathomable world. Thou, soul of the Night, heavenly Slumber, didst come upon me; the region gently upheaved itself, and over it hovered my unbound, new-born spirit."[1]

The night, the seclusion of the impenetrable forest, and deep secret caves are the settings for his fantasies of fusion. In such remote locations our "mind" seems entirely alone, secluded, capable of unfurling itself in its own world. Here, where our imagination begins its voyage into our inner Self, it reveals its own richness in images and ideas. For Novalis these are erotically motivated, and use sexual linguistic images by emulating divergent speech-forms, such as prose and poetry, description and allegory.

In his poem *Astralis*, Novalis evokes sexual coalescence while describing an all-embracing worldview synthesis in which everything organically merges and borders dissolve. This repudiation of boundaries and its related principle of totality have a strongly libidinous resonance.[2]

"For each other all must strive, / One through the other must ripen and thrive; / Each is shadowed forth in all, / While itself with them is blending, / And eagerly into their deeps doth fall, / Its own peculiar essence mending, / And myriad thoughts life doth call. [...] Life and death, rapture and sadness, / Are here in inmost sympathy,—/ Who yieldeth himself to love's deep madness, / From its wounds is never free."[3]

Remoteness and the cave like darkness draw select objects to the fore and unite the literary space of Novalis through a method similar to that utilized in a number of contemporary art installations.. The location for Novalis's experience must have pleased Ilya Kabakov, for it resembles the settings he discusses as suitable venues for the conveyance of an artistic world outlook in his on-the-*"Total"-Installation*. Without any windows, and thus without any relation to the outside world, these spaces provide him with a remoteness in which he can emphasize objects and sounds by plucking them from the silent darkness. He turns this fusion with the artistic space into a sort of stage direction that determines the posture of the spectator, "Each venue forces us to be 'different,' as it tells us clearly what it is and what it means." Kabakov draws this conclusion from observing venues like his own home, public offices or public transportation and applies these principles to his installations.[4] Consequently, he proposes a list of artistic means of spectator guidance, including the exclusion from the exhibition space, the use of specific colors and object arrangements, and the dramaturgical use of light and sound. This resembles the "total" installation of sacred rooms.[5] He shrinks however, therefore prefers the concept of immersion, which he links to the old tradition of "contemplation" in the face of religious images or works of art. Kabakov wants to create a semi-dream or semi-illusion, "in which you are dreaming despite being awake and thus keeping control of yourself and your current state."[6] Blending and reflecting oppose each other, and at the same time become components of his new alliance. Basic skepticism regarding the imminent fusion forces him to keep distancing reflections as a necessary possibility on hand.

Desire for De-limitation

We dream of merging with objects in our vicinities in order to outgrow them, and thus the significance of the individual is abolished in favor of the whole. We attempt to compensate the finiteness of our lives and our influence, which are often regarded as imperfect, by dedicating and connecting them to greater causes.

This raises the issue of straightforwardness. It is impossible, with our limited means, to entirely perceive complex and comprehensive pieces of art.

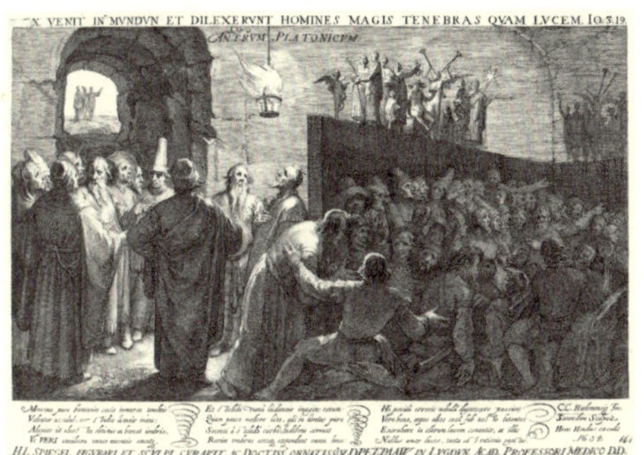

—Fig. 1
Jan Pietersz Saenredam,
The Cave of Plato, 1604

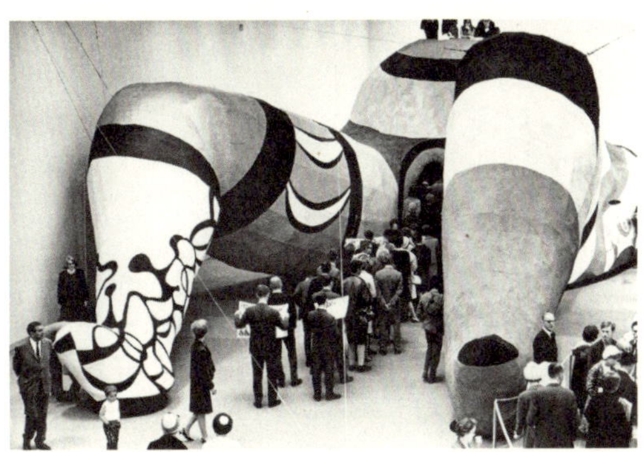

—Fig. 2
Niki de Saint-Phalle,
Hon, 1966

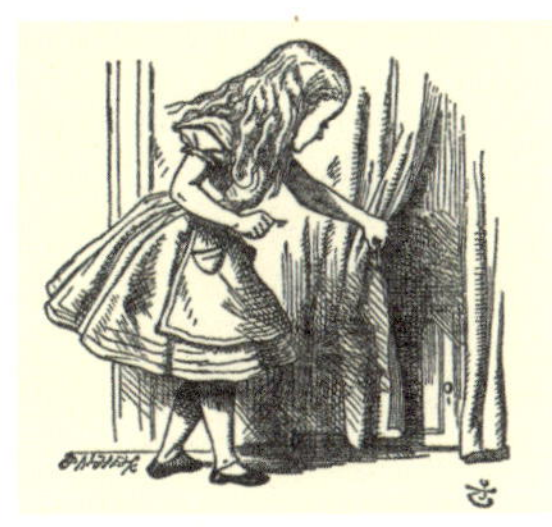

—Fig. 3
John Tenniel, *Alice Finding Tiny Door Behind the Curtain*, 1941

We can only focus on the single part of the whole that draws our interest, making us concentrate on it, and wish to remain in contact with it. The whole is only sketched in our imagination.

The desire for fusion and empathy is a major characteristic of the confrontation with art. Interest in a piece of art is pleasant, creates affection. We can only analyze something that we have previously grasped.

Even encounters with gross works of art cause some sort of empathy. Strong aversion and disgust are, like excitement, also forms of identification.

These fantasies of fusion are always phantasms, as we veil the actual possibilities with our wishes and "fusion" with the artwork can occur only gradually. As an object, the work usually remains static and uninfluenced by our attention to it unless we are engaging so-called "interactive" art, which expands the aspect of the *Gesamtkunstwerk* to another level, and actively involves the user. This however, only happens seemingly, as the basic structure in which the user interaction is embedded remains unchanged by these intrusions.

The crux of modernity is a longing for something that we already know will not be achieved. We believe that in pre-modern societies the status of the individual was defined in an undisputed manner. The *Gesamtkunstwerk* ceases to exist if it is named as such, because the consciousness of its form and its theoretical examination create a distance in which the feeling of totality is suspended. The social factor is lacking. Participants in religious masses or the representative state act of courtly feasts form an entity in which individuals do not question their roles in the overall structure because these undoubtedly resemble their socially appropriate status.

Such delimitating desires of integration in totalitarian concepts became highly suspicious to our ancestors. We contemporarily regard them as not only characteristic of mid 20th century Fascist abuses, but also as contraposed to a self-perception whose own totality defines itself in relation to other individuals, which is obviously difficult in a society of prefabricated identities.

Thus "comprehensive stagings"—to use more neutral terminology—often face skepticism from their audience as well as their creator. Doubt and criticism are essential structural approaches to modern art, which make it particularly difficult to live out fantasies of fusion in that field. (Where "final traces" are discovered, "merry original states" are oftentimes not far behind.)

They have however kept their function in other parts of culture. They continue to have a meaningful function at the monumental Olympic Games opening ceremonies, exclusive fashion shows such as Vienna's "MQ Fashion Week," and in general at stagings with large audiences such as state visits from the Pope and the corresponding masses. The pure presence of the spectator, along with his contribution of any kind whatsoever, create a form of dignity that is based on the value of participation, or taking on a role within the structure of a system. This aspect of presence is particularly made use of by Hermann Nitsch in his "Mysteries."

Even demonstrations can achieve the quality of the *Gesamtkunstwerk* today. The staging of rituals, banners, clothing and make-up, chanting and so on, or less unintentional dramaturgical procedures caused by the confrontation of groups with divergent interests (for example demonstrators and police), creates a synaesthetic framework.[7] This occurs not only on site, but also as a result of the broadcast of an event, thus lending it an additional aesthetic dimension. The degree of reality of these events, which take place in the framework of social turmoil, may well be compared to that of artworks, and recurring accusations that the events were not real but only staged for the media, can impact both equally.

It is not cynical to call these events Gesamtkunstwerke.[8] The "accusation of being cynical" only proves that there is hardly any readiness in our society to assign artmaking any responsible, societal roles that could produce real consequences.

In his works Christoph Schlingensief utilizes the concepts of political representation and the integration of self-perception within the context of the army or the church, applying totalitarian forms of physical pain and expression, only to have them collapse afterward into absurdness. It becomes apparent that he cannot leave the for salvation promises of such philosophies alone. He digs tunnels into the structure of total worlds or concepts such as the church or the opera with every artistic tool available.

The Cave as a World

Borders and de-limitation are also important for the appearance of the *Gesamtkunstwerk*, because these manifest themselves in its various formal solutions. They become evident in, for example, a plain formal moment that is supposed to dim the borders of the piece and render them invisible. This proves true not only for Richard Wagner, the creator of the *Gesamtkunstwerk*, who set his plays on darkened theatre stages and hid the orchestra to render the delimited music free from its instruments. This is also applicable to the spatial theatrical stagings of artists like Kabakov, Schlingensief, Meese and Schneider. Heimo Zobernig, too dimmed the entire Kunsthalle Zürich for one of his latest exhibitions there. In order to accentuate his video projects and sculptures, he turned the entire space into a burrow of tunnels and storage rooms that was only possible to view in a modified manner from without through magenta colored filters on the window panes.[9]

De-limitation is manifested aplenty. The installations of these artists consist of—at first sight, and perhaps at second as well—a confusing accumulation of individual objects arranged more or less replicably. In the arrangements, certain items are placed closer to the spectator while others stand at the back, forming a background of similarly aligned objects. In this was the objects themselves create a type of cave.

As a model the "cave" unites two systems of reference. It is the place for the development of a world scheme. At the same time it symbolizes a proto-entity, emotional security and a return to the womb. This zone became an ideogram of a worlview as early as Plato's "Allegory of the Cave."[10] Plato portrayed a group of prisoners who had only ever seen the shadows of objects, and had thus taken these to be forms themselves. The seclusion of the location and the specific conditions of its limited world outlook unite Plato's cave with the world of art exhibition, regardless of whether we are referring to the "Blackbox" of video projections or the "White Cube" of object presentations. Both create conditions to replace reality by assigning their presentation a comprehensive definitional character. Plato was a committed art critic for a reason; he understood art as merely an image of an image, and as such an impediment to the world of ideas. In this context, the philosopher proceeded from a purely mimetic understanding of art, and did not consider the reflexive power of artistic positing. In his "Allegory of the Cave" however, he makes use of this closed form of philosophical argumentation, creating if you will, his own "text cave."

The enthusiasm for caves is particularly high among children, who let their imagination run wild while turning all available furniture, woolen blankets, and large—preferably opaque—clothing into shelters where they store items like small treasures. This becomes an initial form of property and the value through which they define themselves. Seclusion in this small confined world, and concentration on a beloved item likewise become an entanglement of one's Self and the world.[11]

Total installations often resemble such "shelters." They are carefully arranged worlds of their own that close themselves off to the outside world.

Kabakov emphasizes the importance of dark painted walls, "[…] as the over coating creates a world of its own once and for all […]."[12] The dark paint of his preference directs the viewer's attention to the illuminated objects, while the walls move to the back like those of a dark cave. Thomas Hirschhorn likes to use simple materials for his "rooms." Corrugated cardboard, tarpaulin and roofing battens are affixed with adhesive tape to form numerous landscapes that contain an unimaginable richness of objects, melding in similar manner to a unit using adhesive tape. Contextual nexuses are realized palpably through the simple gluing together of objects. They protrude like stalactites and stalagmites from everywhere into these caves of thoughts, drawing nearer to each other, referring to one another and leaving space in which we move between and come perhaps to understand some kind of link between them.

Jonathan Meese's installations—like every one of his paintings, sculptures and collages—exhibit a nearly impenetrable range of motives that are intertwined by an expressively moved flow of painting and equality in all components. Terms evolve from these mergings that claim totality and world outlook in an allegorically pointed meaning. Meese-typical composites such as *Staatsbürgerkundaddy*,[13] *Erzspielraum*,[14] or *Dr. Parfumeesex*,[15] align artistic belief in almightiness with the respective historic and cultural fantasies of totalitarian absoluteness. Meese inflates them to such a degree that one fears they will burst. The bugaboo may collapse because he cannot cope with his own size, neither meeting, nor enduring his own aspiration. His figures often have ostentatiously extraposed sexuality, exhibiting oversized genitals. He appears in women's clothes at performances and kisses male co-actors. This type of ambisexuality is not to be understood in terms of androgyny but rather as exponentiated sexuality. Its ostentation through penetration emphasizes its programmatic function, the artistic approach of a simultaneously allegoric and brutal commingling of the diverse.

The wish to fuse with the Other by overcoming one's own boundaries falls in with, among others, the concept of a primal and lost unity that serves as a philosophical model of love. In *Symposium* Plato describes the androgynyes, whose feeling of omnipotence leads them to revolt against the Gods and are subsequently punished by being halved.[16] According to the story's narrator, comic playwright Aristophanes, we have been searching for our original lost unity with the other ever since then. The lost androgynous shape stands for the physical totality. The sphere is the shape that, above all other sculptural forms, has the highest degree of completeness and self-reference, and exudes a form of perfection that wants to be regarded as universal.

It is not surprising that Plato puts this story into the mouth of a comic playwright, as the myth thus becomes literary fiction. As comedy the myth stands beside itself, and both narrator and listener seek an empathic fusion with the myth while at the same time distancing themselves from it with a relieved laugh. The unique ambivalence of the desire for fusion and a simultaneous distanced view from the outside are therefore both present in this narration and narrative structure. The same is true for Plato the art critic who, in this part of his *Symposium*, presents a literary piece of art from which he actually distances himself by drawing it forth from somebody else's mouth. Furthermore, the fact that eroticism and sexual fusion are the piece's actual subjects, proves the close relation between the notions of totality and sexuality.

Upon entering this "unknown world," the sexually stylized entrance to the *Gesamtkunstwerk* underlines the erotic aspect of a fusion with artwork. Like many sexual moments, it is linked with primal experiences and thus the topos of the wish for a return to the womb is realized as sexual penetration when entering the exhibition room. Meese's pink MOR-Festung seems to entwine us in swollen labia.[17] To travel from one room to another in Gregor Schneider's house one must worm their way through a small tunnel underneath the sink, as if through a birth canal. Schneider has applied the hidden entry motif in combination with a narrow cave-like tunnel in his design for the entrance to the exhibition rooms at the Museum Abteiberg in Mönchengladbach.[18] In this case, the hidden portal is a rather mangy looking back-alley garage. These are the emblems of transition from one world into another. In terms of fine art they can be found in Niki de Saint Phalle's Stockholm piece *Hon* (1966),[19] and in literature, when Lewis Carroll's curious Alice enters the subterranean caves of a rabbit burrow and tumbles through a hole into Wonderland.[20]

The *Gesamtkunstwerk* and sexual fantasies of fusion are closely related both structurally and emotionally. The libidinous recharging causes a certain arousal and agitation in experiencing the art works of a comprehensive aspiration and forces us—apart from experiencing an offer of integration—to defend this call. Fantasies of fusion irritate us or convey a anguorous feeling that may even lead to the discharge of pent-up energy from the center of the art work. We capitulate and deny ourselves, and like the artists, dig exit holes into their pieces. Cracks, breaches and shifts, if allowed, can only become visible if one knows that an entity was destroyed there.

1 Novalis, *Hymns to the Night*. George MacDonald (trans.), first published in: George MacDonald. Rampolli, Growhts from a Long-Planted Root. London, 1897; quoted here from Sergei O. Prokofieff (ed.), *Novalis, Hymns to the Night, Spiritual Songs*. London, 1992, p.7f.
2 Cf. Martina Steinig, "Wo man singt, da lass' dich ruhig nieder ..." in: *Lied- and Gedichteinlagen im Roman the Romantik*. Berlin, 2006, p. 250f.
3 Novalis, *Henry of Ofterdingen, A Romance, From the German*. Cambridge: John Owen, 1842, pp. 194, 195.
4 Cf. Ilya Kabakov, *On the "Total Installation."* Cologne: Cantz, 1992, p. 12.
5 Cf. Kabakov 1992, p. 109.
6 Cf. Kabakov 1992, p. 47.
7 Artists like the Reinigungsgesellschaft (The Readymade Demonstration, Columbus, Ohio, 2009, cf. www.reinigungsgesellschaft.de Accessed on: Dec. 19 2011) or Jacob Dahlgren (Demonstration December 5 2007, Stockholm 2007, cf. www.jacobdahlgren.com Accessed on: Dec 19 2011) use the formal structures

of demonstrations as artistic re-enactments or—freed from political content—as "pure" aesthetic forms.
8 For example, the comments by Karlheinz Stockhausen must be understood in the context of the events of September 11, 2001, which he described as, "the largest piece of art ever created in our cosmos." Press meeting on September 16, 2001 at the Senatszimmer of the Hotel Atlantic in Hamburg with Karlheinz Stockhausen", in: *MusikTexte* 91, 2002, pp. 69-77, cf. p.76f.
9 Heimo Zobernig, *Ohne Titel (In Red)*. Kunsthalle Zurich, exhibiton catalogue, 2011
10 Cf. Platon, *Politeia*, Book 7 (514a-517a), in: Gunther Eigler (ed.), *Platon. Werke in acht Bänden*. Friedrich Schleiermacher (trans.), Vol. 4, Darmstadt, 1990, pp. 555-563.
11 "Jeder geliebte Gegenstand ist der Mittelpunkt eines Paradieses," from: Novalis. "Blütenstaub," Fragment Nr. 50, in: Richard Samuel (ed.), *Novalis. Werke, Tagebücher und Briefe*. Vol. 2, Munich/Vienna, 1978, p. 246.
12 Cf. Kabakov, 1992, p. 64.
13 Cf. Jonathan Meese, *Mama Johnny*, Deichtorhallen Hamburg, exh. cat., Hamburg 2006, p. 10f.
14 Cf. Meese. 2006, p. 144.
15 Cf. Meese. 2006, p. 226f.
16 Cf. Platon, *Gastmahl*. Ch. 5.1, "Das ursprüngliche Menschengeschlecht und die Entstehung der Liebe," (89d-193d), in: Gunther Eigler (ed.), *Platon. Werke in acht Bänden*. Friedrich Schleiermacher (trans.), Vol. 3, Darmstadt, 1990, pp. 266-283.
17 Jonathan Meese and Tal R., *MOR*, Statens Museum for Kunst, Kopenhagen, 2005
18 Gregor Schneider, *Garage 2009*, Museum Abteiberg, Mönchengladbach, 2009
19 Niki de Saint Phalle, *Hon (Sie)*, Moderna Museet-Stockholm, 1966
20 Cf. Martin Gardner (ed.), *The Annotated Alice*, Hamburg 2000, p. 13f. Gardner points out that a fall into earth is a recurring motif in children's books and fantasy novels that represents entrance into another world.

Designers of the Unconscious and Their Audience

Boris Groys

The brief consideration of the Russian culture of the pre-Stalin and post-Stalin periods presented here enables us to define more precisely the nature of Stalinist culture itself. Stalinist culture brought out into the open the myth of the demiurge, the transformer of society and the universe, which, although it was presumed by the avant-garde, was not explicitly expressed in avant-garde artistic practice, and it set this myth in the center of its entire social and artistic life. Like the avant-garde, Stalinist culture continues to be oriented toward the future; it is projective rather than mimetic, a visualization of the collective dream of the new world and the new humanity rather than the product of an individual artist's temperament; it does not retire to the museum, but aspires to exert an active influence upon life. In brief, it cannot simply be regarded as "regressive" or pre-avant-garde.

At the same time, Stalinist culture is interested above all in the creator of this new utopian world, who in the art of the avant-garde remained outside the project he had created in "the present," which was merely a prelude to the future. In this sense the avant-garde may be said to be "Old Testament": its God transcends the world he has created, and the prophet does not enter the Promised Land. Stalinism overcomes this excessively one-sided iconoclastic spirit and makes a new icon using the realistic devices of secular painting. Socialist realism does not need stylizations of historical icons or the classics of antiquity, because it is based upon the thesis that sacred history takes place here among us, and the gods and demiurges—Stalin and his "Iron Guard"—constantly work their world-transforming miracles in the here and now of the everyday.

It is for this reason that the "realism" element of socialist realism is so deceptive. It is merely a means of indicating the contemporaneity, novelty, and relevance of a demiurgic process of transformation which, although it is clothed in visible symbols, for the most part takes place outside the visible world. In this sense, Stalinism, like Christianity, liberates the inhabitants of utopia from blind obedience to the laws handed down by unseen creators—Malevich, Rodchenko, Khlebnikov, and others—but inspires in them love for their creator and the creator of their world: Stalin. The withdrawal beyond the space of history that this entails allows history to be regarded as an allegory of the present that need not be negated so completely as the avant-garde had demanded. "Progressive" phenomena of the past and the accompanying artistic styles can then also be viewed as anticipating the creation of the new world and the figure of its creator, the "positive demiurge" Stalin, whereas "reactionary" social movements, figures, and styles anticipate the negative, demonic, destructive impulses of the avant-garde that were incarnated during the Stalin years in the figure of Trotsky and other "enemies of the people." Again, this reinterpretation of the past as a multitude of allegorical figures illustrating the present represents not a return to the past but the final overcoming of the "historical," real past which, for the avant-garde that strove to break free of it, constituted the horizon and background of contemporaneity.

Stalinist culture considered that it represented the only escape from history and that the rest of the world had not yet entered the realm of pure mythology but remained historical. And it was here that Stalinist culture encountered its limits—it was swept away by the forces of history, because unlike Christianity it had failed to establish itself in the superhistorical; and when the extrahistorical competes with the historical, it inevitably loses, because it is fighting on alien ground. Modern Russian post-utopian art uses the lesson it has learned to make this defeat obvious and final, overcoming the Stalinist period by remythologizing and aestheticizing it. At the same time, the art that continues actively and virulently to polemize with and demythologize Stalinism fails, for it shares with Stalinism the inadequately articulated utopian impulse. Indeed, the meaning of post-utopian art is to show that history is nothing other than the history of attempts to escape history, that utopia is inherent in history and cannot be overcome by it, that the postmodernist attempt to consummate history merely continues it, as does the opposite aspiration to prove that historical progress is infinite. Post-utopian art incorporates the Stalin myth into world mythology and demonstrates its family likeness to supposedly opposite myths. Beyond the historical, this art discovers not a single myth but an entire mythology, a pagan polymorphy; that is, it reveals the nonhistoricity of history itself. If Stalinist artists and writers functioned as icon painters and hagiographers, the authors of the new Russian literature and art are frivolous mytho*graphs*, chroniclers of utopian myth, but not mytho*logists*, that is, not critical commentators attempting to "reveal the true content" of myth and "enlighten" the public as to its nature by scientifically demythologizing it. As was already stated above, such a project is itself utopian and mythological. Thus the post-utopian consciousness overcomes the usual opposition between belief and unbelief, between identifying with and criticizing myth. Left to themselves today, artists and writers must simultaneously create text and context, myth and criticism of myth, utopia and the failure of utopia, history and the escape from history, the artistic object and commentaries upon it, and so on. Just as Keyserling predicted when he said that he was not worried about Stalin and Hitler, because eventually all Europeans would enjoy the rights reserved to these two men alone, the death of totalitarianism has made us all totalitarians in miniature. As these rights spread, of course, they also became obligations: only for a limited time can the loss of totality be referred to indirectly, through a "difference" or negative utopia. In the final analysis, it must be privately restored, as Kabakov says in each successive reenactment of the sacred history of the avant-garde and its defeat.

Since the myth of Stalin as the demiurge of the new life is at the center of Stalinist culture, and since it has its source in the avant-gardist myth, it is appropriate by way of conclusion to say a few words about myth in general and define the notion of myth as such. It is commonly thought that myth and the avant-garde are opposites, or rather that the avant-garde struggles with myth and that because Stalinism generates myth it cannot be the heir of the avant-garde.

Especially useful in a discussion of the notion of myth is Roland Barthes's *Mythologies*, which both marks the beginning of the systematic study of modern myths and can itself be regarded as mythological. For Barthes, myth is "depoliticized speech," history made Nature, or the inversion of *anti-physis* into *pseudo-physis*.[1] In other words, myth describes that which exits as eternal and "natural;" it is directed toward the preservation of the status quo and conceals the historical "madness" of a world that can also be historically remade. Thus for Barthes myth is always rightist, always on the side of the bourgeoisie (Proudhon's "property is theft" comes to mind here).

Myth is the opposite of revolution, which returns language to its immediate function of "making" things and the new world as a whole. As Barthes notes: "There is … only one language which is not mythical, it is the language of man as a producer: wherever man speaks in order to transform reality and no longer to preserve it as an image … myth is impossible."[2] Revolution, therefore, which is a "making" of the world, is "antimythological": "Revolution announces itself openly as revolution and thereby abolishes myth."[3] The alternative to the language of myth is thus political language directed toward political action. Opposition to myth comes from the left. Although Barthes acknowledges the existence of myth "on the left" and takes the Stalin myth as an example, he does not attach any particular importance to it. He maintains that left-wing myths are merely invented on the analogy of and in order to combat those on the right. There is nothing so terrible about this, for the artificiality and clumsiness of left-wing myths renders them relatively harmless.[4] Barthes also considers that avant-garde poetry is opposed to myth because it "works with language" and does not use it merely to convey a figurative content.

On the level of refined structural analysis, Barthes to some extent reproduces here the structure of Stalinist culture itself: myths are divided into right and left, "theirs" and "ours," and are judged accordingly. At the same time, however, he obviously sympathizes more with the aesthetic theory and practice of the avant-garde and its aspiration to remake the world, and he is reconciled to the myth on the left as merely an inescapable transitory evil. What is surprising about his contrasting of myth and the making of transforming of the world, however, is that it contradicts the obvious fact that what all significant known myths tell about is the creation and transformation of the world: a static, unchanging, unhistorical world cannot be narrated in myth. The reason for Barthes's strange reasoning becomes understandable if it is realized that he regards myth as the metalanguage that describes the "object-language." That is, for him myth is a theoretical entity. In actual fact, however, if myth does have any relevance to the theory, it is only as a narrative about the creation of theory; it thus has a legitimizing function, especially in our age, when new descriptions of the world are in effect equated with its creation and are themselves incorporated into traditional mythology.

If, contrary to Barthes, myth has to do with the creation and transformations of the world, however, then it is precisely the avant-garde and leftist politics that are mythological, since by casting the artist, the proletariat, the party, the leader in the role of demiurge, they provide for their natural integration into world mythology. This is now acknowledged to some extent by Western Marxists, who are prepared to admit parallels between Marxist narrative, Christian historicism, and ancient magical practices.[5] Because people are incorporated by Marxism in a unified mythological narrative about the creation of the objective world through labor, they can transcend the bounds of their earthly determinacy and, by altering the conditions of their existence, change themselves, become the "new humans." Marxism seems antimythological when it insists that human existence must be understood in its social relationship. However, revolutionary Marxism—and in another respect, avant-garde art—are placed in a mythological context by the very possibility of such a description (which presuppose a view from "outside" the world) and the fact that this description can be used to replace the context with another through revolution. We would not escape myth even if we were to follow the current fashion which rejects the principle of creation as bourgeois and mythological and declares the social, linguistic, etc. context of human existence to be unlimited and not subject to transformation. Reference to the world as a whole is still preserved, as is the possibility of relating one's practice to it, even if this practice is no longer "constructive" like that of the avant-garde, but is "deconstructive" and relativizes every creative effort. This, as has already been mentioned, is in turn a new postmodern utopia, a new attempt to leave history and enter the eternal extrahistorical play of codes.

The above, of course, should not be taken to mean that myth is in actual fact entirely on the left rather than on the right. Wittgenstein has shown that the essentially "rightist" demand to abandon "metaphysical questions" results in a kind of mythologization of the everyday as the sole area of action (contrary to Barthes, who obviously has Wittgenstein in mind, it is the object-language rather than the language of description that Wittgenstein regards as mythological). Thus there is no escaping myth, least of all in the avant-garde, revolution, remaking the world, and so on. This circumstance does not seem to be directly related to Stalinist culture. Yet in a situation in which there has been an external break with mythological tradition, through its obvious objective of revealing a new mythology, this culture enables at least those who have experienced it to relate in a new way to myth as such. In a situation where the context has changed even more decisively than the text, and where world history has been told anew, Soviet artists and writers can no longer naively believe that the history of their own liberation is reality rather than mythological ritual.

It provided impossible to break free of Stalin without reiterating him at least aesthetically. Consequently modern Russian art has approached Stalin as an aesthetic phenomenon in order to repeat him and thus liberate itself from him. By constructing both text and context, practicing both construction and deconstruction, simultaneously projecting utopia and transforming it into anti-utopia, it is attempting to enter the mythological family so that it may relate to Stalin not with *ressentiment* but with a feeling of superiority: every family has its black sheep.

Revealed in this frivolous, irreverent play is the colossal potential of desire and the unconscious that was inherent in the Russian avant-garde but was insufficiently recognized because it was encoded in a rationalistic, geometric technical, constructive form. The machines of the avant-garde, however, were in reality machines of the unconscious, machines of magic, machines of desire—they were meant to process the artist's and viewer's unconscious in order to harmonize and save them through union with the cosmic unconscious. It was not until the Stalin years, however, that their true purpose began to become apparent, and then only partially. The term "machine of desire" suggested by Deleuze and Guattari is in fact defined by them very much in the spirit of Wittgenstein and Barthes: "The unconscious poses no problem of meaning, solely problems of use. The question posed by desire is not *"What does it mean?"* but rather "How does it work?" … The greatest force of language was only discovered once a *work* was viewed as a machine, producing certain effects, amenable to a certain use."[6]

Deleuze and Guattari, of course, think that they are once and for all rid of the "subject" and of all "consciousness" and mythology. All they are doing in reality is repaving the way for the "engineers of human souls," the designers of the unconscious, the technologists of desire, the social magi and alchemists that the Russian avant-gardists aspired to become and that Stalin actually was. The privilege of the context over the text, the unconscious over the consciousness, the "other" over the subjective, or all that is known as the "unsaid" (non-dit) and "unthought" (impensé) over the individual human being merely means the dominance of the person who speaks about, or even more precisely, the person who actually works on, this context, this unconscious, this other, this unsaid. If such work succeeds in creating an artificial unconscious, an artificial context, and new and as yet unseen machines of desire called, say, "Soviet people," then these persons will suddenly be able to lead lives and generate texts that do not differ from natural ones, rendering irrelevant both distinction between natural and artificial and all the effort expended on it. And these amazing beings with an artificial unconscious but a natural consciousness will also be capable of deriving aesthetic pleasure from contemplating this unconscious of theirs as a work of art created by someone else. In the most tasteless pretty-bourgeois tradition, they will thereby transform the avant-garde's unique and horrible feat—the creation of Stalinist art—into an object of frivolous amusement.

1 Roland Barthes, *Mythologies*. Annette Lavers (trans.), New York, 1987, p. 142.
2 Ibid., p. 146.
3 Ibid., p. 147.
4 Ibid., pp. 147-48.
5 Frederic Jameson, The Political Unconscious. Ithaca, N.Y., 1981, p. 285.
6 Gilles Deleuze and Felix Guattari, The "Anti-Oedipus." New York, 1977, p. 109.

Before all, Keep That Unfortunate "Gesammtkunst" out of the Title!!! Enough of this!!!

Bettina Steinbrügge

Before all, Keep That Unfortunate "Gesammtkunst" out of the Title!!! Enough of this!!!

Richard Wagner declared the above in a letter to Franz Liszt already in 1853[1] thereby giving air to his grievances that, for one, he was never really understood correctly, and for another, the significance of the term was overrated in his work, as: "[o]therwise it would be quite impossible that this wretched 'separate art' and 'universal art' should be the upshot of all my disquisitions."[2] Wagner never considered the Gesamtkunstwerk programmatic, and ultimately could also have certainly gotten by without it. His statement already anticipates current discomfort with the term quite early on: a discomfort that exists even though the Gesamtkunstwerk has maintained a large presence in modern discourse through to our "postmodern" times. Seriously, though, THE Gesamtkunstwerk has never existed, does not exist, and most likely will never exist. It is a utopian concept that is worked toward; that is filled with desires, and for precisely this reason, remains legitimate until today. The term was ultimately discredited by its proximity to Wagner, without recognizing the origins of the Gesamtkunstwerk idea in German Romanticism.

The term correspondingly surfaces as a vague and confusing concept in art and architectural history, in theater, film, and music, in contemporary critique, as well as in the arts section, with entirely different emphases in each case, and often in ways that could easily be misunderstood. It is used with reference to milieus as diverse as the Cabaret Voltaire 1915 in Zürich, Kandinsky's influence, futurist theater, Berlin's *Kinopaläste* in the 1920s, Andy Warhol's *Factory* in New York of the 1960s, and even Christoph Schlingensief's actions in contemporary art and theater. It is described, in abridged terms, as a seamless melding of a variety of art forms that overcomes the beholders with emotion, thus thwarting the possibility of critical thinking as a group of individuals dissolves into a powerless mass. Yet the Gesamtkunstwerk is much more than the sum of a number of individual parts; it answers for a model for artistic contexts that pursues modernist principles, as well as reversing them.[3]

The design of this holistic concept is, primarily, no more than a "mental construct of higher connections as a visual or epic idea, or a scientific system or political utopia."[4] The Gesamtkunstwerk is a fictive magnitude that subsumes various points of view running as streams of thought from modernity through to today. Szeemann wrote: "The term Gesamtkunstwerk, first used by Richard Wagner in his Zurich writings for his artistic ambitions and his visions of the unity of the arts in the 'artwork of the future,' has never been theoretically defined and has become an empty concept that is used randomly, not only in art literature."[5] The Gesamtkunstwerk in its original form is a utopia, but in every utopia is a certain legitimacy, which persists and thereby also influences art production. Concern here is with these influences as they continue to function or are carried forward in a contemporary form.

The present text aims to cast a contemporary glance at the Gesamtkunstwerk by returning to its revolutionary ideas, and for the present day, emphasizing its emancipatory potential, or perhaps merely the remains that are still significant, which, when related to the present, illuminate new perspectives and chances. The idea is to make various aspects of the Gesamt-kunstwerk useful for the current discussion without, however, making a case for the total artwork, or attempting to create a Gesamtkunstwerk for the exhibition *Utopie Gesamtkunstwerk*. Consequently, for the exhibition archi-tecture we invited the artist Esther Stocker who designed a sculptural object that creates a seemingly holistic stage of sorts, and in its simultaneous frag-mentation or division of a formal unit poses the question of what the "whole" actually is. Stocker develops a walk-in sculptural group. The fictive images that arise within correspond with an imaginary world capable of making the conceptual construct Gesamtkunstwerk more than just visibly tangible.

Modernity

The Gesamtkunstwerk is often seen as the counterpart to advanced European modernism, especially when concern is with principles, such as the purity of art, autonomy, or media specificity. Innate to the concept are synes-thesia, phantasmagoria, and psychedelic art, which often represent a nega-tive temptation of the beholder.[6] This "anti-modern" quality is by no means a characteristic of the Gesamtkunstwerk. Instead, this idea can be seen as a key component of European modernism when one starts from the premise that a striving for a teleology, that is, certain goal states, finds expression within it. These goals might be completely thought out, but are not completely carried out and perhaps cannot be.[7] This begins already with Wagner. After all, he aes-thetically pre-structured the ancient model of a democratic society in his Gesa-mtkunstwerk in that he wanted to bring the ancient ideal of a citizens' society into the modern era and combine it with the ideas of anarchists and socialists to a social and artistic model for the future: a model in which art and politics are inseparable. Similar thoughts can be found in the artists' group WochenKlausur, which has carried out social interventions since 1993. In the style of twentieth-century avant-garde movements that wanted to take an active part in shaping society, WochenKlausur considers art as a place in which it is possible to inter-vene in societal structures to achieve a long-term change in social conditions such as the improvement of medical care for the homeless, the creation of citi-zen participation models, or the building of a senior center. "Theoretically, there is no difference between artists who do their best to paint pictures and those who do their best to solve social problems with clearly fixed boundaries. The individually selected task, like the painter's self-defined objective, must only be precisely articulated."[8] Concealed in the Gesamtkunstwerk's main features is the intention of a socio-cultural revolution, which stands beside subjectivity and the revolution or liberation of the individual.

In his work *Das gequälte Quadrat*, Peter Weibel draws attention to the fact that polar opposites do not have to be resolved, and instead, contradictory situations can be made the object of productive interplay. Malewitsch painted his first *Black Square* in 1913 on the curtain of *Victory over the Sun*, an opera in which all conventional terms had to be destroyed to enable the start of a new social order. Boris Groys draws attention to a further aspect of the *Black Square*: "Every image made in the context of any imaginable culture is also a black square, because it will look like a black square if it is erased. And that means that—to a messianic gaze—it always already looks like a black square. This is what makes the avant-garde a true opening for a universalist, democratic art. But the avant-garde's universalist power is a power of weakness, of self-erasure, because the avant-garde only became so universally successful by producing the weakest images possible."[9] Weibel now takes Malevich's modern square and dissolves it, shatters it to fragments. Here, the deconstructive aspect begins, after classical modernity, which maintains the forms but lets the space collapse, to question analytical meanings, reveal and thwart contradictions, and, in the new composition, to create new connections through paradoxes. The Gesamtkunstwerk distinguishes itself to then return to the plurality of its possibilities. In *Monumental and Personal Modernism*, Marjetica Potrč investigates structures, mechanisms, and methods in the area of contemporary architecture and urbanism. She is concerned with models for life that are based on handed down, modernist ideas of architecture and urban planning, which she opposes with an up-dated modernism conceived for the individual. Art does not appear as a mere model, but instead, takes on an active social role. Art and life enter a unity, which for its part, approaches what Malevich had hoped to achieve with Suprematism.

I agree with Wolfgang Welsch when he writes that the postmodern is a radicalized continuation of Modernism.[10] The contemporary era draws on the experiences of Modernism in that it denies the autonomy of art. It dismisses ideas about the originality of the artist, innovation in art production, as well as all stylistic hierarchies. The bottom line is, Modernism's utopias have proved to be repressive. In the view of sociologists Luc Boltanski and Eve Chiapello, beginning in the 1960s, more important than social critique for the regeneration of capitalism was "artistic critique" rooted in Romantic philosophy, opposing standardization, bureaucratization, and stereotyping and promoting autonomy, emancipation, and the transgression of borders.[11] The need for authenticity and freedom had to be rethought as the methods of Modernism and its avant-garde were no longer effective. A similar form of the loss of utopia was played out in the theater installation *Der Ring—Fünfter Tag. Der Tag danach*, which Christian Boltanski, Ilya Kabakov, and Jean Kalman conceived as an "adding of a post-utopian perspective to the Bayreuth Festspiel program."[12] In this project, they turned against Wagner's goal of an anthropological, aesthetic, and political totality by joining the composer's aesthetic utopia with the sanatorium's social utopia and communism's political utopia, which they declared failures. The installation was designed to be participatory, as a stroll, and itself had characteristics of a Gesamtkunstwerk aesthetic.

At the turn from the eighteenth to nineteenth century, German and English Romanticism supplemented the concept of nature previously degraded by modern science to an object of study, with the components passion and fear. Being "modern" meant dividing the world along the dualistic separation of mind and matter, considered valid since Descarte. In the era of modernism, nature lost all of the mysterious, wild attributes of the sublime that the Romantics had acclaimed in their day. Thiago Rocha Pitta's series *Heritage* takes up these ideas and suggests an adventure in the high seas as an event that combines the romantic concept of natural powers with scientific discoveries. On the contrary, with *Die Planierung der Alpen*, Hermann Painitz creates the utopia of a new, democratic nature. For Painitz, nature becomes a cultural landscape that emanates from a political concept of space. The clearest step against modernism's concept of nature was taken by Joseph Beuys with his project *7000 Eichen*, in which he promoted urban forestation in Kassel. As much as 60 percent of the city had been destroyed in World War II, and was rebuilt in the 1950s along modernist precepts. Beuys wrote: "I wish to go more and more outside, to be among the problems of nature and the problems of human beings in their working places. This will be a regenerative activity."[13] Beuys attempted to create an artistic intervention for eternity here, an intervention capable of changing an entire city. And, in fact, he succeeded. Throughout the entire modern era, traditions and lifestyles were cast away and lost, which has led to the situation that today, one no longer even believes in the present as fashions and models fluctuate at an even greater speed. Securities are lost, adding an apocalyptic aspect to contemporary life whereby we almost automatically anticipate impending decline in all that is new.[14] How can contemporary artists avoid this destruction, how can art remain timeless, tied with temporal claims set far (over)stretched in the future, in the sense of Beuys, and escape permanent change? According to Groys, this seems to be the question with the greatest utopian potential.[15]

Correspondences

From 1938, Friedrich Kiesler worked on his theory of Correalismus, a holistic design concept that was meant to dissolve the borders between all of the sciences and art. He based his theory on the observation of human behavioral forms, sequences of movement, and physiological conditions: their precise analysis was meant to ultimately improve human living conditions. The latest technological standards and discoveries in the natural science together with Kiesler's psychological, sociological, and philosophical dispositions, formed universal models for the world. The different artistic fields of action ultimately flowed into the idea of the *Endless House*, a biomorphic house, the equivalent of a living unit designed by the powers of life. In 2009, Heinz Emigholz conveyed the concept in a film that analyzed ideas that had become reality—visible as writing, drawing, photography, architecture, and sculpture—as a quasi-reversed process of seeing. The eye becomes an interface between brain and outside world, the gaze a composing power that turns an inside outward and is, in reality, presented as a mirror image.

Since the beginning of the modern era, the significance of the beholder has risen steadily. With regard to the idea of the Gesamtkunstwerk, the role of the audience tends to be conceived as one-sided. Terms such as synesthesia, phantasmagoria, and psychedelic represent an artistic environment or performance in which a dark and strong creative power is able to masterly maneuver the beholder into passivity. A passive aesthetic reaction is assumed, as formulated so concisely by Guy Debord in *Die Gesellschaft des Spektakels* in 1968, and again by Theodor W. Adorno. At that historical moment, this may have been justifiably identified implicitly or explicitly as fascist, proto-fascist, or neo-fascist, but today, when the relational has become a topic of contemporary art production, it is necessary to take another look at this crucial aspect of the modern conception of art. Although the paradigm change in art from a relationship between objects to one between subjects has only become obvious in recent years, it has a long history behind it. Perception studies have offered a base for new life practices through to the definition of the viewer's role as a component of artistic production, which should steer reflection about social, political, and scientific content. In the exhibition, this is reflected in Bernhard Cella's work *Salon für Kunstbuch im 21er Haus*, a communication system and a dramaturgy, which is concerned with more than simply the production and distribution of artworks. From the start, this location was designed as a model space at a scale of 1:1, within which a unique play of relations between objects, people, and artworks can develop. Bruno Latour is likewise interested in the tracks that the social realm leaves behind. The clearer the separation of nature and society was carried out in modernism, the easier it was for "quasi objects" to spread between the separated areas, which are both naturally and socially determined. These hybrid "quasi objects" that modernism ignored, must be recognized. Only then, namely, is it possible to dismiss the meanwhile dubious credo of modernism: that economic rationality, scientific truth, and technology are, in fact, guarantors of a sensible progress, without simultaneously falling into a postmodern depression.[16] Ralo Mayer has worked on the research project Biosphere 2 since 2007, which as a perhaps "failed" materialization of a utopia, has become a microsystem. The ability to objectify modernist beliefs in progress is deconstructed in various media here in order to expose the creating of myth by precisely these media and playfully rehearse a new scientific, screenplay-like historiography.

The interdisciplinary or mutual illumination of the arts in a Gesamtkunstwerk is based on the assumption that the individual arts would develop their full potential precisely when they define themselves through differentiation from one another. Thus here, each individual art form maintains the autonomy and freedom that can be found in the dictates of modernism. Gerhard Rühm is interested in the conjuncture of text and image, in the way it was first analyzed within concrete poetry. Text serves as an expansion of the complex of content and form. At the moment it is instrumentalized, its use becomes a balancing act. The juxtaposition in an artistic work makes demarcation possible, which is what comprises the interdisciplinary element of the Gesamtkunstwerk.

Technologies of the unconscious

Running like a red line through the entire history of conceptual ideas and practices of the Gesamtkunstwerk is the formation of new life models with various empirical points of view. Richard Wagner associated the collaboration of individual art forms with a social utopia meant to overcome the gap between art and society in the future. There was and still is a need for a sense that one is in safe hands in the world, for something that points the way, which can be redeemed in art. The reformers around 1900 also approached the idea of a Gesamtkunstwerk as a model for life. Art and life forms should be united as one whole through dance, whereby esoteric currents created the spiritual backdrop against which these ideas could be lived out. This movement emerged from the protagonists themselves, from their individuality and the emancipation from social constraints. Rudolf von Laban, pioneer of modern expressive dance, had already developed a mystical dance cult during his student days, which was meant to relate all aspects of being; material, spiritual, and mental, as a basic cosmic movement. The dance cult experienced its heyday on Monte Verità. Una Szeemann focuses on this era in the film *Montewood Hollyverità* by uniting Monte Verità, the mountain of truth, with Hollywood and a genealogy that extends from the utopists ca. 1900 through to the illusion machine Hollywood. New-age philosophies, American body culture, and esoteric trends join with turn-of-the-century counter-culture movements such as pacifism, anarchism, and theosophy. Szeemann lets music, film, and art collide here; she brings together original historical material with fictional stories, allowing moments of personal authenticity and personal wishes to appear, in which the fictions of one's own likeness can be found. Seb Patane places a different emphasis in his work *Patrons Papers*. Here, four archetypical figures stand before us gesticulating like actors and seem to be taken by the writing above Alejandro Jodorowsky's Tarot. Like in Tarot, called for here, too, are the fortune-teller's, and the viewer's precise gaze and willingness to engage in associative thinking: Everything has a meaning, from the way that the figures are set up on the patterns through the unidentifiable costumes, to the gestures. Yet here, concern is not with future prophesies. Instead, these figures serve to allow beholders to fathom themselves, to discover the situation and alternatives of the moment. The cards are reflections of the soul and are closely related to what Schopenhauer works out in *The World as Will and Representation* when he epistemologically recognizes the principles of will and representation as the factors that define our world,[17] to consequently reveal irrationality as the basic principle of the world and describe how only negation of individual will offers a way out. Schopenhauer recognized the sole possibility for a temporary negation of will in art. Wagner begins from precisely this point in his metaphysics and music dramas when he conjures up the innards of music and sets dream theory at the center of his observations. In contemporary art, while the beholder is seen as an accomplice in the work, the postmodern world's differentiation phenomenon and demands for plurality accompany the suggestive moments in front of and with the work, for example, with Seb Patane. "Although it was still valid four decades ago to use art as a means to point out life forms and physically represented identity formations not recognized politically and not visible publicly or in the media, today, after an increasing opening of the visual world through media and the internet, there is less inquiry into the physically invisible as there is into the mental state of the individual behind that, which is, no least, the result of a steadily accelerating social transformation."[18] An occupation with non-normative mental models of behavior can be detected in art beginning in the 1960s. The works of VALIE EXPORT are among the early examples of those in the 1960s that tied pathological forms of behavior with social conditions. In *Restringierter Code,* EXPORT takes up the division of society into different classes and analyses them. By imitating the panting of a dog or the behavior of a small child, she attempted to overcome social divisions and analyze medial translation mechanisms. In *Dictio Pii*, Markus Schinwald evokes various worlds of psychopathic expressive power that put the reality principle to the test. Similar to VALIE EXPORT, he repositions gender issues whereby at the forefront is each individual self and its positioning in a hostile environment. The actors, constrained in artificial expansions of the body, form the perfect image of the incongruence of personal and social worlds.

Motivated by the search for a scenic Gesamtkunstwerk meant to deliver a new center to a collapsed world, the stage further developed in the twentieth century and differentiated itself in connection with other art forms. The Bauhaus stage in particular, can be identified in this context as a multiple Gesamtkunstwerk in which various theatrical Gesamtkunstwerk models were developed. "The work of the stage, as an orchestral unity, is inherently related to architecture; both receive and give to each other mutually. Just as, in the work of building, all members leave their own ego behind in favor of a higher mutual liveliness of the total work of art [*Gesamtwerk*], so too, in the work of the stage, do a variety of artistic problems come together according to this transcending law, to a new, greater unity."[19] In theater, people are understood and treated as social beings. This was expressed in the Bauhaus stage in that, like Bauhaus architecture, the stage's collective spatial symbols were capable of providing a superordinate metaphysical idea. Hermann Nitsch's *Orgies Mysteries Theater* on the contrary, used a complex language of organic materials and religious symbols that brought together cult, theatrics, and human psychic constitution in a quasi-religious, existential experience, thus releasing a liberation already proclaimed by Antonin Artaud. Bauhaus theater and the *Orgies Mysteries Theater* share a cult-like act of liberation of an active subject from all constraints, and a testing out of the didactic potential of art, beginning from theater. Paul McCarthy releases the desired catharsis spatially. The video *Bunker Basement* shows a labyrinth in McCarthy's Los Angeles studio that is constantly changing in theatrical settings, thus generating a claustrophobic spatial experience. It is surpassed only by Gregor Schneider's *Haus u r, Rheydt 1985 – today (Nacht – Video)*, a process-based work developed over the course of many years, which lines the original house to become theater, performance, sculpture, installation, Gesamtkunstwerk, and social practice. The space itself becomes performative here, and in the end, examines identity and difference. Likewise, Tom Burr dramatizes props to point out hidden power structures within society, Julia Hohenwarter, turns the exhibition space into a two-level *Catwalk*, and Liam Gillick constructs a seemingly modernist installation, *Volvo Bar*, which ultimately serves as the theater setting for an educational play. The stage—a site predestined for the synthesis of the arts—now finds in the fine arts, an expansion of its possibilities and forms characterized especially by the deliberate release of differences.

Unity and fragment

The dream of wholeness has remained current throughout the eras, styles, and ideologies. The utopias, desires, and plans go all out, but what one is able to see today are only the fragments, leftovers, and relics of a complex, monumental machine. Contemporary art emerges in the logic of division that is translated into differences. Historical narrations often develop through montage, harsh cuts, condensing, and culmination—forms to interlace disparate elements and counter the discontinuity of our lives. The tendency toward fragmentation in the fine arts can first be pinpointed with the emergence of the historical avant-garde. This development occurred alongside a science, a philosophy, and a literature that achieved ultimate alignment at the beginning of the twentieth century. In Vienna in particular, this relation condensed through to Otto Neurath's scientific view of thought and the Vienna Circle around Ernst Mach, whose main goal was to serve as a type of umbrella organization for thought, which should also be applied didactically in cultural spheres of values: A knowledge-machine of sorts, which should result in a community of solidarity. At this time, art also established itself as a unique social value sphere, removed from the intentions of state and religious authorities, which obeyed primarily the laws of aesthetic subjectivity. The new discourse about the Gesamtkunstwerk arising from that was a reaction to the disruption of the Christian world view and was now built from a new mythology based on a solidarity-based human community, or an individual artist genius or universal artist. The avant-garde's social tendencies toward differentiation and dissociation provoked opposing utopian-synthetic models. In contrast to the earlier, socially-conformist Gesamtkunstwerk, the modern Gesamtkunstwerk negated the divided society of its era and countered it with a new, social Leitbild in which art, in particular, should be set in socio-political and life practice contexts. After World War II, these wholeness movements were discredited and especially in Europe, artists took up the ideas of the avant-garde for redefining art after this caesura. In the 1950s, a development began in the area of art whose dynamics remain strong until today: music, painting, sculpture, and architecture began to push beyond their traditional borders and combine with elements from other arts. At the same time, the individual artistic genres became fragmented to then reorganize themselves in a "postmodern" way.

Today, the aesthetic, art-inherent definition of the Gesamtkunstwerk has given way to the idea of a unity of art, science, and philosophy, with relational artistic strategies. This can be seen particularly well in *Utopia Station* by Hans Ulrich Obrist, Molly Nesbit, and Rirkrit Tiravanija. More than 200 artists, architects, writers, musicians, and performers contributed to the project in its various phases and versions. The term has been elevated to an inapproachable level of reflection in order to tackle its being turned into an absolute, and the concept of 'total.' At the same time, new levels of meaning of the Gesamtkunstwerk have opened up through concepts of the relational, complexity, and heterogeneity in artistic strategies since 1968. Christoph Schlingensief and Gerwald Rockenschaub are but two artists who provoked a unity through a formal and conceptual game of deception of the relations of complex artistic networks of meaning with the help of scientific methodologies and relations to lived reality. In place of artistic practices related to the Gesamtkunstwerk, discontinuities and differences, hybrids and eclectic elements appeared; one made do with practices of irritation, deconstruction, and subversion. Nowadays we understand the concept of the Gesamtkunstwerk as a cultural symptom arising from the modern subject's experiences of dissociation. An attempt is made to overcome differences through a new assemblage of the fragments, for example, Isa Genzken's use of heterogeneous trash material in *empire vampire*, which then, in the form of a B movie, becomes the site of shifted perspectives. The gothic cathedral, an early example of the Gesamtkunstwerk, both combines architecture, sculpture, painting, and arts and crafts, and stands for the Christian belief in which humans are striving for a universal whole. Interestingly, it also experienced a renaissance in the second half of the nineteenth century, at a time of increasing discussion of the Gesamtkunstwerk. In *Grey Cloth Project*, Ian Kiaer refers to Bruno Taut's expressionist futuristic cathedral, which is understood as a "utopian-crystalline transformation of the earth and universe."[20] Taut tied the creative process to the religious and saw himself as a chosen one "with a mission in world history and privileged relationship to the absolute."[21] In *Innenblick Kirche*, Tillman Kaiser transforms this cathedral through its arrangement together with objects related to fishing, to generate new levels of meaning. The "Menschenfaenger" steps to the foreground and quizzically inquires if this life model can be discussed as unbrokenly as the church would like it to be. In *Ground Zero Bagdad*, Klaus Auderer encounters globalism and the wars that accompany it with a similar skepticism, whereby he considers it important to meld the artistic sphere of activity and the warlike political sphere to a totality that goes far beyond the documentary level. A complete picture of this situation cannot be produced, but it is possible to show fragments. These fragments offer insight into the complexity of the situation and remain open in such a way as to make available the plurality of levels of meaning of each. Global, intercultural life forms are apparently not possible, yet are, indeed, subliminally desired.

The Will to Change the World

The current concept of Gesamtkunstwerk culminates in the work of Christoph Schlingensief. The networking of the arts and the subsequent medial compactions and collisions are most closely related to a Gesamtkunstwerk working method. It is no coincidence that Schlingensief also managed the stage in Bayreuth. The border crossings of art and life, of staging and reality, of stage and public space attained an intensity within which latent social conflicts surfaced, and mechanisms of public agitation were examined. Yet, *Eine Kirche der Angst vor dem Fremden in mir*, about Schlingensief's lung cancer, which he staged in 2008 for the RuhrTriennale, is far from the salvation tale of Parzival.

"…[C]atastrophic space and catastrophic time are absolutely modern; they are modern in their irrationality, and their logical systems; in fact, they are the underside of modernity, the other world that lies behind the mirror…" wrote artist Tony Chakar in 2007.[22] Giorgio Agamben identified this at the start of the new millennium as a state of emergency.[23] Towards the end of the twentieth and onset of the twenty-first centuries, the world had great difficulties grasping the meaning of the accumulation of cultural forms outside of the economic and other power complexes. Surprisingly, the Gesamtkunstwerk always surfaces in such crisis situations, as a thoroughly modern relict that refuses such situations and attempts to formulate new approaches.

It is about the whole after the loss of the great context that must have once been present. The political reorganization after the fall of the Iron Curtain, 11 September 2001, and the increasing economization of all layers of society evoke insecurities and have effects on social dynamics. When the members of the artists' group gelatin set up a balcony on the 91st floor of the World Trade Center in New York in *B-Thing*, in the form of a performance, and in extreme secrecy, no one could image that this work would be seen in an entirely different way after 2001. In their research, they found out that the World Trade Center's outside sculptures served not only as aesthetic elevation of the public space, but also, at the same time, as camouflaged road blocks to guard against terrorist attacks, and the art covering the World Trade Center served to mislead and camouflage. gelatin's approach offered a disarming counter-image to the prevention of a terrorist attack of the building by means of camouflaged art, which simply became stronger when this work was subjected to a new view after the events of 9/11. Today, it seems to have become established that "the multimedia connection of all arts within one artwork cannot be seen as the only special characteristic of the Gesamtkunstwerk, but instead, also another connection: that of art and reality; as the Gesamtkunstwerk also has the tendency to expunge the borders between aesthetic construct and reality."[24] Artistic interest today focuses on the wish for a society worth living in and the question of which models for life are still or once again possible. Claire Fontaine shows this quite simply and effectively. To the dismay of beholders, she destroys an iPhone and asks if we need it and all others. Thomas Hirschhorn's chaos works in a similar way in that it can be interpreted as a reaction to the random behavior in a world in crisis controlled by capitalism and globalization, mourning the increasing loss of its culture. Monica Bonvicini returns to modernism via architecture and thereby to the life models that were developed during this era. For years, she collected quotations that are now aired in the installation *We Finally Built Walls*. While Charles Bukowski's excerpt describes his subjective view ("I've been in a room—I've felt suicidal"), other quotes are from critical texts about the role of transparency in modernist architecture, a transparency that in most cases promises far more than it is capable of delivering. All of these examples indicate that today and in the future we must reckon with a different Gesamtkunstwerk; one that is more highly differentiated and that equally considers a non-belief in the big entity.

Despite all initial skepticism, the world and the human community can be viewed as a Gesamtkunstwerk. Concepts usually exist for a reason, especially when they have been discussed for generations. In Constanze Ruhm's *Crash Site / My_Never_Ending_Burial_Plot* a new version of Hari, from Andrej Tarkowskij's *Solaris*, encounters two other undead beings from film history:

Godard's Nana from *Vivre sa vie* and Antonioni's Giuliana from *Il deserto rosso*. Lost in a forsaken clearing in the woods, the three characters attempt to come to terms with their pasts: "to reach an end," "to bury the past," to kill themselves, kill one another. It is about a never-ending funeral, with the three characters perpetually trapped in a present that repeats in different variations …[25]

1 Richard Wagner/Franz Liszt, *Briefwechsel zwischen Wagner und Liszt—Vom Jahre 1841 bis 1853*, Vol. 1, Leipzig 1887, p. 270. English, see: http://www.gutenberg.org/cache/epub/3835/pg3835.html (viewed 13 December 2011)
2 Wagner/Liszt 1887, p. 269. English: Ibid.
3 Cf. Juliet Koss, *Modernism after Wagner*, Minneapolis/London, 2009, p. 11.
4 Bazon Brock, "Der Hang zum Gesamtkunstwerk," in: Harald Szeemann (ed.), *Der Hang zum Gesamtkunstwerk. Europäische Utopien seit 1800*, exh. cat. Museum des 20. Jahrhunderts, Vienna, Frankfurt/Main, 1983, pp. 21–39.
5 Harald Szeemann, "Vorbereitungen," in: Ibid. (ed.), *Der Hang zum Gesamtkunstwerk. Europäische Utopien seit 1800*, exh. cat. Museum des 20. Jahrhunderts, Vienna, Frankfurt/Main, 1983, p. 16.
6 Cf. Juliet Koss, "Mythos Gesamtkunstwerk," in: *Der Tagesspiegel*, Online edition, September 14 2008, www.tagesspiegel.de/zeitung/mythos-gesamtkunstwerk/1323434.html (last viewed on December 9 2011).
7 Cf. Anke Finger, *Das Gesamtkunstwerk der Moderne*, Göttingen, 2006, p. 8.
8 Pascale Jeannee, "WochenKlausur," http://eipcp.net/transversal/0102/jeannee/en, 01/2002 (last viewed on December 15 2011).
9 Boris Groys, "The Weak Universalism," in: *e-flux journal*, no. 15, 4/2010, www.e-flux.com/journal/view/130 (last viewed on December 9 2011).
10 Wolfgang Welsch, "Rückblickend auf einen Streit, der ein Widerstreit bleibt, ein letztes Mal: Moderne versus Postmoderne," in: Armin Wildermuth/Ulrike Klein (eds.), *Postmoderne*, Heiden, 1990, pp. 1–25.
11 Luc Boltanski/Eve Chiapello, *The New Spirit of Capitalism*, London, 2007.
12 Barbara Gronau, *Theaterinstallationen—Performative Räume bei Beuys, Boltanski und Kabakov*, Munich, 2010, p. 149.
13 Joseph Beuys in an interview with Richard Demarco, in: Fernando Groener/Rose-Maria Kandler (eds.), *7000 Eichen—Joseph Beuys*, Cologne 1987, p. 16. (English, see http://www.publicartscotland.com/features/10-Between-Conversation-and-Memory-Collaborative-Conversation-Making- last viewed December 15 2011)
14 Cf. Groys, 2010.
15 Cf. Groys, 2010.
16 Cf. Bruno Latour, *We Have Never Been Modern*, transl. Catherine Porter, 1993.
17 Arthur Schopenhauer, *The World as Will and Representation*, transl. E.F.J. Payne, Dover, 1966.
18 Walter Seidl, "Modelle psychischer Realitätsverhältnisse in der Kunst," in: *Journal für Neurologie, Neurochirurgie und Psychiatrie*, vol. 9, no. 3, 2008, pp. 53–56.
19 Walter Gropius, "Idee und Aufbau des Staatlichen Bauhauses," in: Karl Nierendorf (ed.), *Staatliches Bauhaus Weimar 1919-1923*, Munich, 1980, p. 17. Quoted in English by Matthew Wilson Smith in *The Total Work of Art: From Bayreuth to Cyberspace*, New York, 2007, p. 51
20 Roger Fornoff, *Die Sehnsucht nach dem Gesamtkunstwerk*, Hildesheim, 2004, p. 425.
21 Fornoff, 2004, p. 420.
22 Tony Chakar, "Bis ans Ende der Welt" in: *Documenta Magazine*, no. 1, Cologne, 2007, p. 211. (English: http://www.slashseconds.org/issues/001/004/articles/03-tchakar/index.php, last viewed on December 15 2011)
23 Giorgio Agamben, *Means without Ends: notes on politics*, Minnesota, 2000.
24 Odo Marquard, "Gesamtkunstwerk und Identitätssystem. Überlegungen im Anschluss an Hegels Schellingkritik," in: Harald Szeemann (ed.), *Der Hang zum Gesamtkunstwerk. Europäische Utopien seit 1800*, exh. cat. Museum des 20. Jahrhunderts, Vienna, Frankfurt/Main, 1983, p. 40. (own translation)
25 I would like to thank Nina Herlitschka, Annette Grigoleit, and especially Harald Krejci for their corrections and valuable advice while writing this text.

Display

A wonderful, but insolvable Question
Harald Krejci and Bettina Steinbrügge in conversation with Esther Stocker

Harald Krejci You are working on the display for the exhibition *Utopie Gesamtkunstwerk*. What is your idea of the Gesamtkunstwerk?

Esther Stocker At first the term sounded somehow sinister to me, it had the character of totality. As I had always been interested in Donald Judd, in the beginning the Chinati Foundation in Marfa constantly came on my mind. Walking through the city I often thought "Oh, not again!" when I saw things related to Judd. It is kind of spooky if a single thought dominates everything. In this exhibition it is more about a shelter or the playful character of the idea. To me the Merzbau seems more processual, like the totality of incompleteness.

Bettina Steinbrügge What is your approach to the Gesamtkunstwerk within this exhibition, especially regarding the display?

ES There are different aspects in the idea of a Gesamtkunstwerk I am interested in. Central question is the meaning of "Totality". It sounds like a wonderful, but insolvable question, and of course this fact is interesting about it. The exhibition is different to the sum of its parts, an aspect I also see in the idea of the Gesamtkunstwerk.

BS Concepts closely linked to Wagner's opera, the theater, stage and stage design are initial ideas thinking about Gesamtkunstwerk. Is there a connection between these topics and your exhibition display?

ES Painting is the background for my work on the display, not theater. I am interested in pictorial concepts, the attempt to integrate the human being in the image. On the other hand the image is a virtually accessible imaginary world. Within this context I don't want to limit myself on two- or three-dimensional levels.

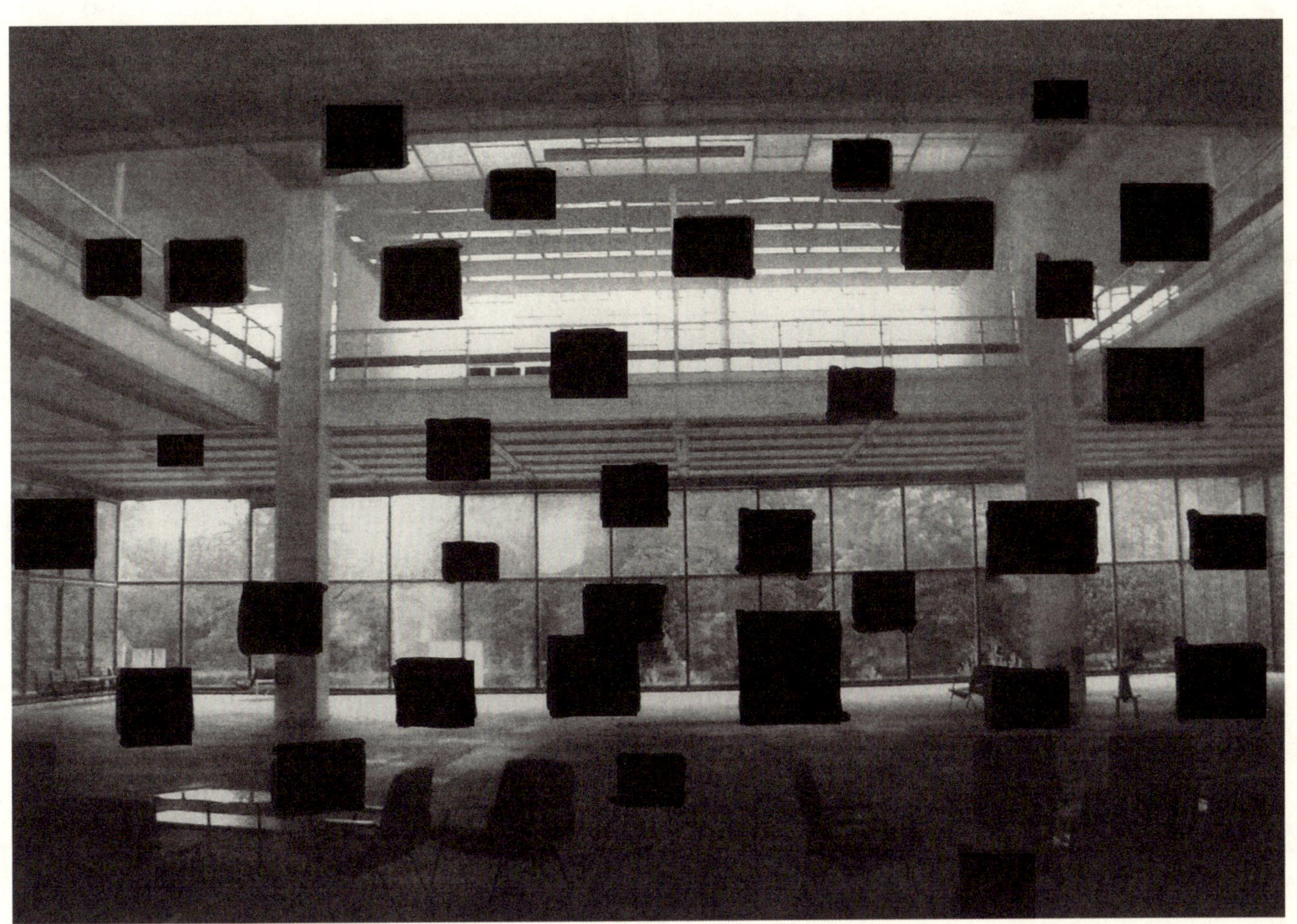

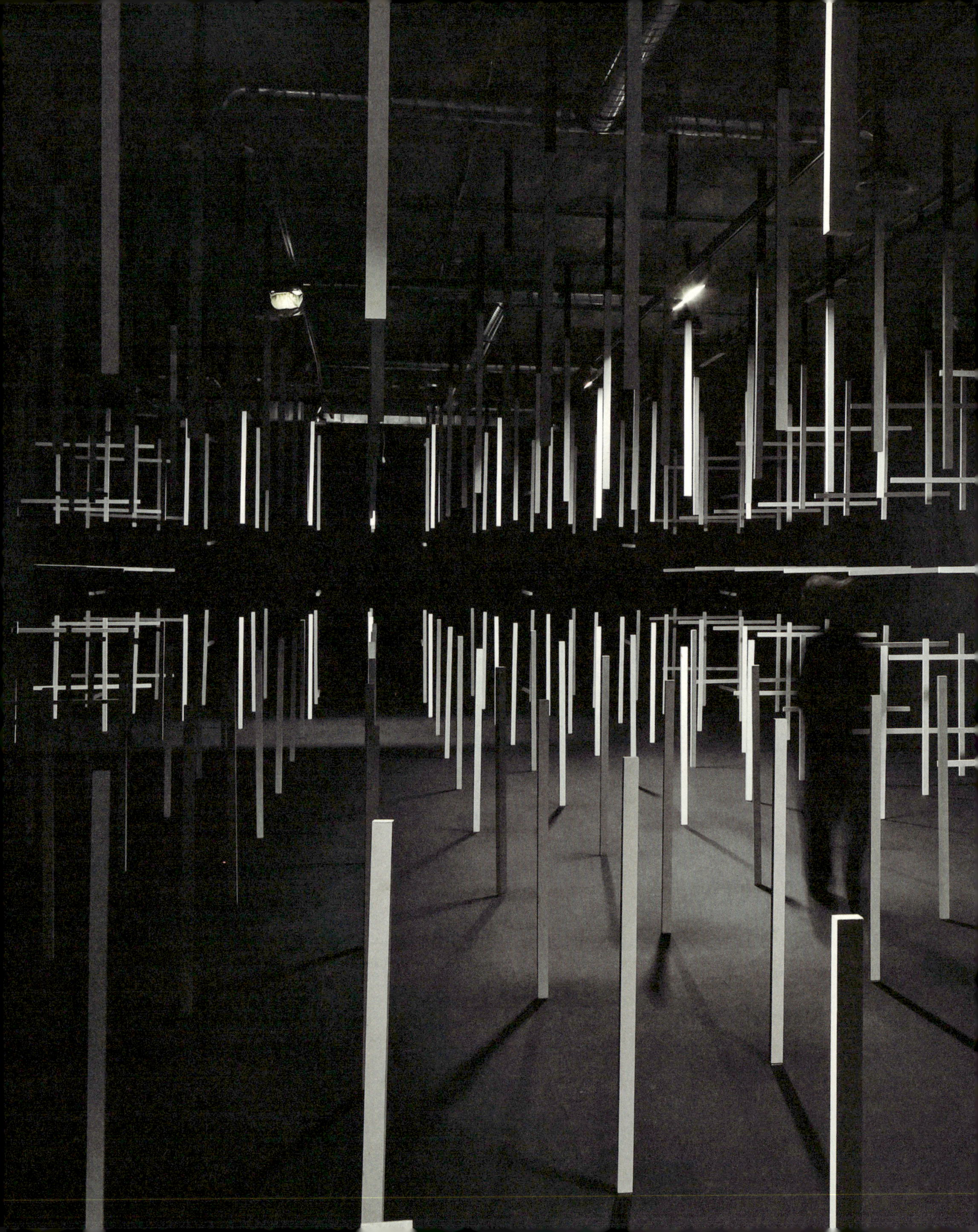

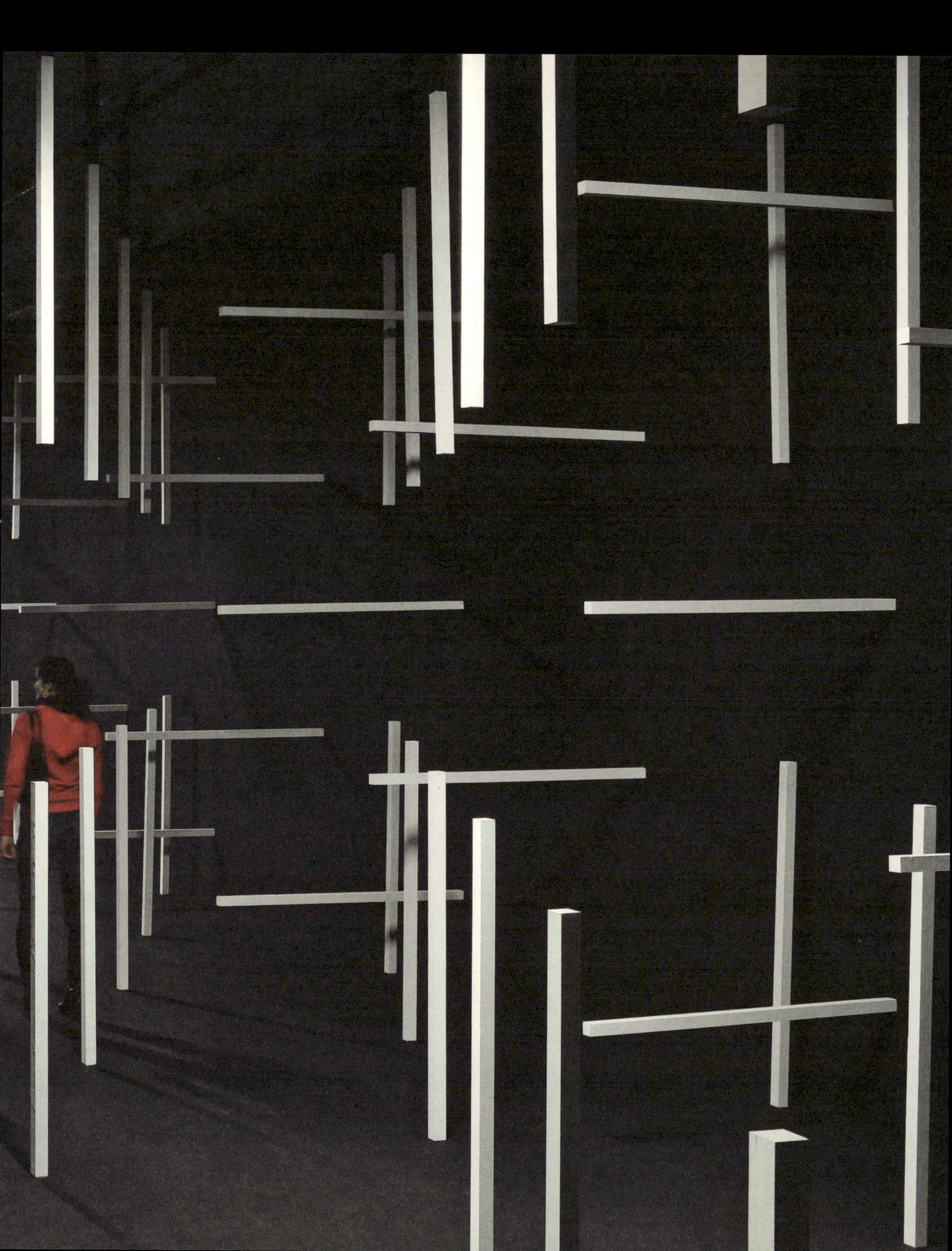

BS You mentioned the term of Gesamtkunstwerk to seem somehow sinister to you, that you find the idea of totality irritating. Is it the idea of the uniform space, the total space as it was realized by the Vienna Secession discomforting you? Your draft of the display for this exhibition appears to be the alternative draft, the fragmentation of a formal unity emphasising on the relational character of the art works.

ES As for me the Gesamtkunstwerk still is a „free" concept to be evolved, relational and processual aspects were definitely central ideas. I wanted to advance on this uniformity as the extensive Gesamtkunstwerk wouldn't work, back then and nowadays. It would be a cohesive cube no one could enter, no room to gain experience, there would have been no use for me.

HK The building itself with its heterogeneous structure can't be referred to as total space. Especially the different structures of the glass front work against the homogeneity of the uniform space. What's your perception of the display in proportion to the architecture?

ES In this display, relating with the architecture is very important. The building itself with its straight shape is very consistent; it opens up to the beholder in its totality as it almost seems to float. I was particularly interested in the open, non-hierarchical space. The space unveils numerous diagonal perspecives in all dimensions, a fact I considered and emphasized in the concept of the rotation of some cubes.

HK Can you tell us something about your artistic work in relation to the exhibition display?

ES In my work I am interested in limiting methods, the freedom of not having to get lost in variation is a quite relief. I usually work with one shape in minimal variations I achieve through the respective position. With minimal variations in shape or position I try to find possibilities to break the underlying system and change it. Applied on the display this means expanding the

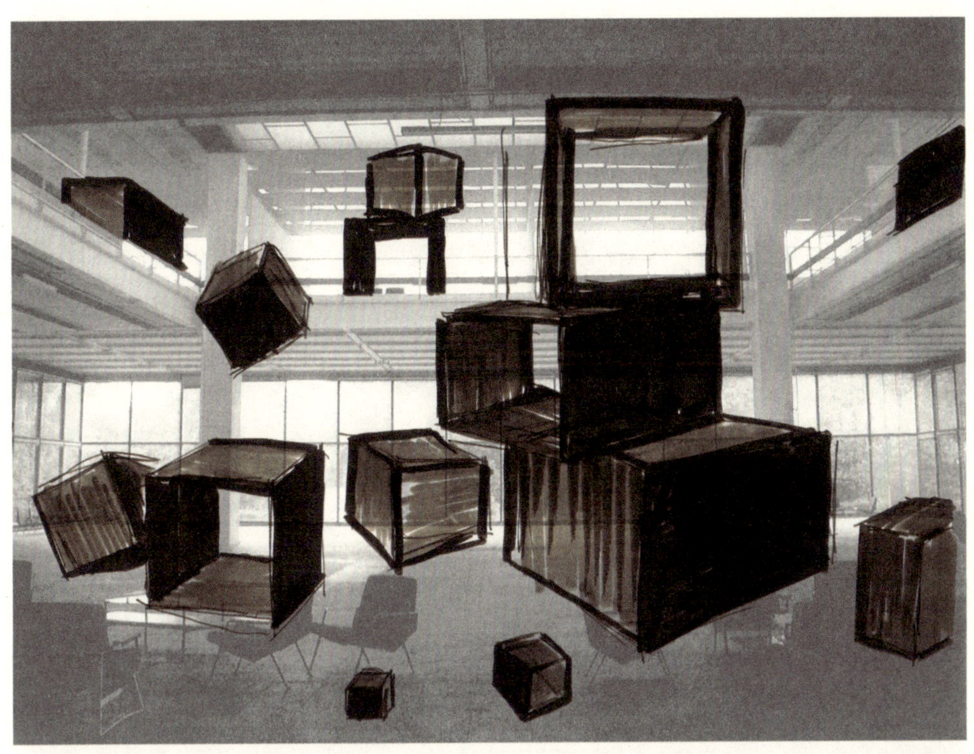

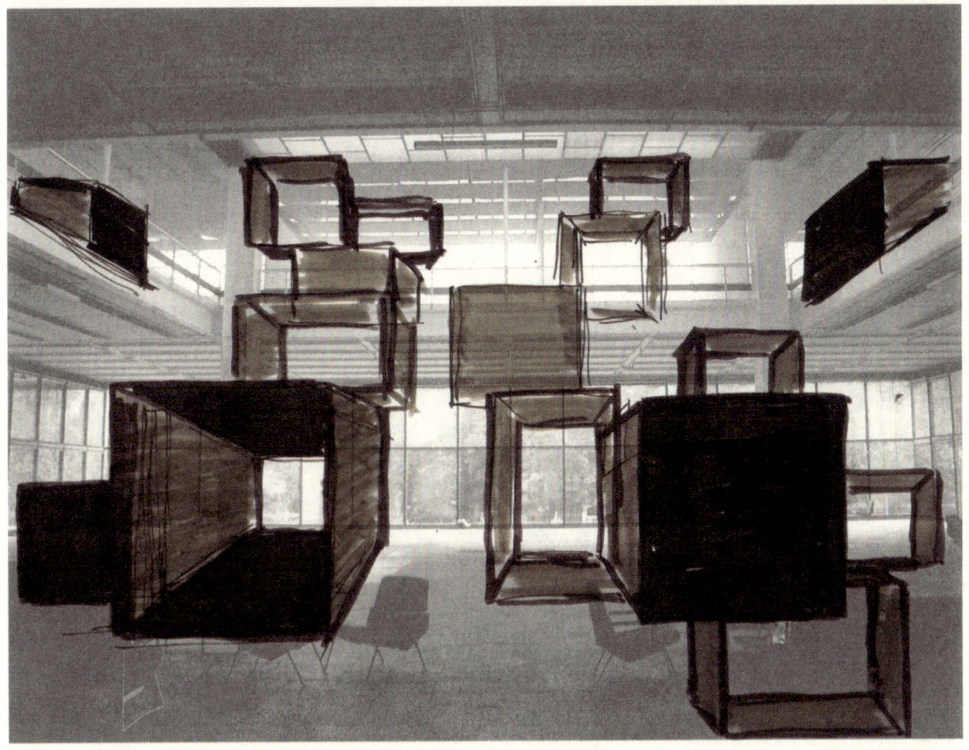

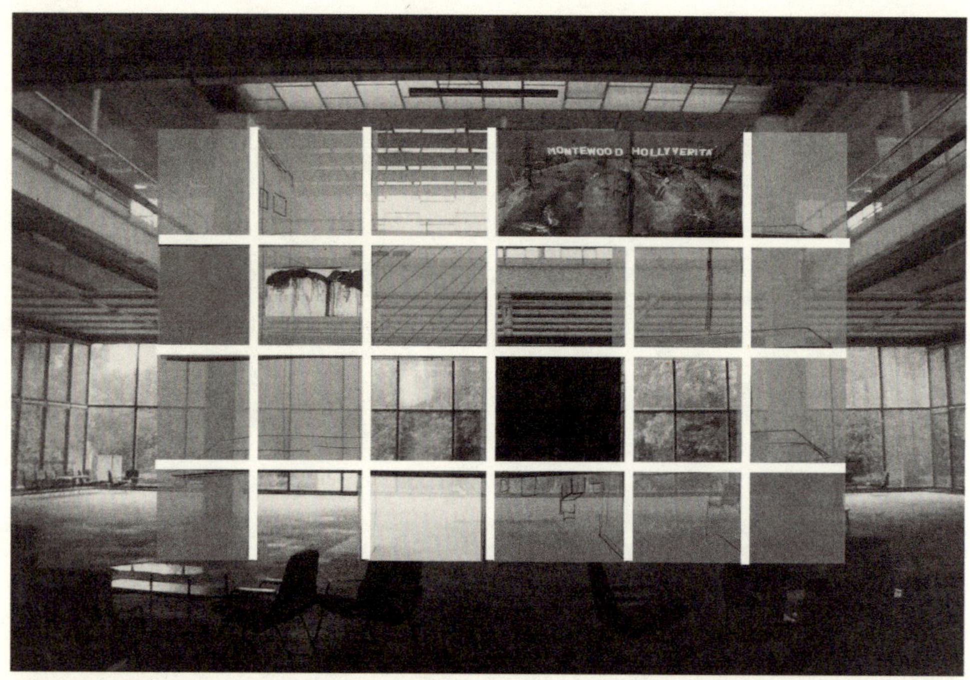

MONTEWOOD HOLLYVERITA

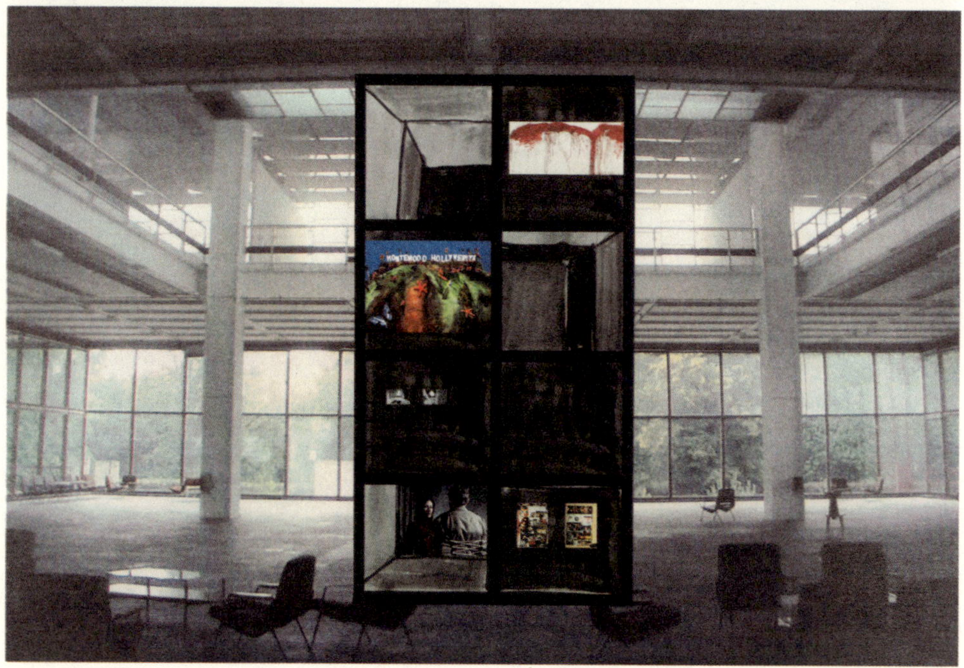

MONTEWOOD HOLLYVERITA

system through minimal formal mutation, in this particular case the rotation of a cube or by leaving out a wall. This corresponds to my approach in painting as well as installation.

BS Let's go back to the beginning. What was your initial thought working on the display?

ES I was interested in portioning the space; in dispersion as well as in bundling precisely, because the room is so open. These two contrary formal criteria led to the central concentration of the cubes. I was particularly interested in the contradiction of fragmentation and concentration of space at the same time: the dispersal of space over 14 cubes, their repetition in the four small showcases and the final summery of all elements.

HK You started the project experimenting with some kind of a letter case, a structure far more stringent than the final exhibition display. Why was that?

ES The initial concept resembled a letter case, monotonous and broken by perforations. It was some kind of "total display", everything should have been perceptible at a glance. An image is captured at a glance as well, but somehow you have to enter the image in order to grasp its entirety. This idea made the display much more intimate.

HK In theater, systems similar to letter cases are applied in order to illustrate concurrent plots. You destroyed your initial idea by fragmenting the case and installing the cubes in the exhibition space …

ES I hope so! The display gains temporary character and breaks the architecture. The shape of the cubes is the reference to the architecture of the 21er Haus. As the cubes are not incorporated in the architectonic pattern, the display breaks but doesn't work against it, it rather assimilates to the architecture. Besides exhibitions are temporary events where art works often appear to be thrown into the exhibition space. I would appreciate people to realize the humorous dimension of the display.

BS The White Cube, a neutral, almost sterile space, had been predominant in the 20th century. Your display is far away from being neutral thus connotes the room. Display and artworks merge. What does it mean to you?

ES I believe the display to gain expression by losing its neutral character. I want the display to approach and absorb the beholder; this is why the top floor is quite open and clear: there are more ways to get in.

BS Your display matches excellently our approach to the Gesamtkunstwerk. It takes up the moment of fragmentation, the expressiveness in the movement towards the beholder, just like Wagner's opera it is anything else but neutral. This leads us back to the beginning. Is it about contradictions?

ES On the one hand I like the character of totality; on the other hand my work attempts to provoke irritation or infection, some kind of transition, which is contradictory. By "irritation" in this sense I mean the conflict between figure and the background, a distinction that allows us to create relations: one thing (figure) shadows the other (background). I am not able to change the perceptional process, but I can interfere with it: as soon as it remains uncertain whether art or the beholder is figure or ground, it becomes fascinating to me.

HK The intention to create references, to relate art works and force certain legibility is the antipode to neutrality.

ES Possibly my display is some sort of infection, something, that spills over…

BS The longer I work on the project, the more I see the term Gesamtkunstwerk in the context of subjectivity, exuberance, and assumptions thrown in just like the cubes. You throw in something and wait whether it is accepted or not.

ES Testing theories is one peculiarity of art. I am particularly interested in this exemplary character in art.

BS Your display emphasizes on perspective and the links between the art works. It's the opposite of a labyrinth …

ES I kept asking myself the same question: do I force confusion, or do I force the overview? The display remains quite transparent, with a plain basic structure. It opens perspectives, and though—as some walls remained empty—it creates a sense of irritation. I believe it's the rotation of the cubes as they suddenly literally cross one's perception. The cubes evoke a dramatic sensation, emphasized by their black color. The black square and the black cube are absolute shapes to me, passing them shall unveil new worlds of experiences. The beholder experiences the entire exhibition on a physical and intellectual level.

The Will for Changes of World

r

f the

The Contemporary Gesamtkunstwerk

Eva Kernbauer, Simon Baier

In the Vastness of the Exhibition Space

The unification of the arts into a single comprehensive piece: the intellectual design of the *Gesamtkunstwerk* shows that its traces are most clearly evident where the borderlines between the skills, scenes and mechanisms of artistic genres exist. In the current ubiquity of intermedial and collaborative art projects it seems inevitable that such a unification of artistic forces must disappear unnoticed, like an aberration within the realms of experience, discursive machines, social projects and design.[1]

This anachronistic momentum is precisely what, in terms of contemporary art, can make the *Gesamtkunstwerk* interesting. Richard Wagner derived the necessity of collaboration from the inevitable need for artistic technical expertise. As Friedrich Nietzsche and Thomas Mann have remarked however, the megalomaniac aspiration of the *Gesamtkunstwerk* and its "sensual aggression" are less the result of successful division of labor and professionalization, than they are of Wagner's artistic dilettantism.[2] We are presently a long way from interlacing such genius and amateur practices in an analogue practice, such as conceptualist deskilling[3] or the institutional critical practice "in and out of place."[4] Closer to this in its truest sense of the word is the amateurish approach of Jason Rhoades', whose installations force the world into the personal order of the artist and in return claims international recognition. It was not without good reason therefore, that Rhoades' personal reference system was published in a comprehensive dictionary—a perfect world of B-movies, donuts and cordless screwdrivers he affixed in the exhibition space with a hammer and nail—it chopped its way through the impenetrable thicket of references and proclaimed its universal right[5]. The value of personal approaches to which the public is at times denied access not only undermines the obvious significance of artistic setting, but also creates new ways of interpretation, and is perfectly illustrated in Tom Burrs' installations. Colored by his own autobiography, his often seemingly arbitrary sub- and pop cultural associations confound the neutralisms of minimal art and retroactively unveil their spectacularly theatrical moments as complicit with lifestyle and corporate culture.[6]

Such productively dilettante approaches are probably more important than the perfect enactment of intermedial experience, which today is found in film rather than theatre. Still, when searching for a contemporary *Gesamtkunstwerk* it is advisable to turn towards the inside of the exhibition space, this space, the post-war avant-gardists have increasingly considered a stage. Thus, Christoph Schlingensief's elective affinity with Richard Wagner is less apparent in planned projects, such as the opera village in Burkina Faso, than in the repatriation of Schlingensief's will to change the world inside the exhibition space. The latter is where the "last remnant" of holistic concepts of contemporary aesthetics must be sought. The *Gesamtkunstwerk* amounts to much more than just the synaesthetic mental overload of the spectator; it remains a promise for: postulation, mysticism, utopia and ultimately theatre. And thus, as Wagner already knew, the audience plays a key role within the *Gesamtkunstwerk*, within the concept of which it is firmly established. Therefore the audience must create a unity: the collective of visitors of an exhibition doesn't necessarily have social relevance, but they build up relations by aesthetic references. **EK**

Is there a future in the Gesamtkunstwerk?

Is the *Gesamtkunstwerk* not, precisely as Richard Wagner said, the "Art-Work of the Future"?[7] The question seems redundant. Does it not paradigmatically stand for the unfulfilled promise of modernist art, a form whose totality has not become reality and perhaps never will? Is the *Gesamtkunstwerk* not simply the "contrary" of our present that gives a future to the exhausted art? Its relevance in contemporary art seems obvious. What else than an unceasing mixture of the arts is our contemporary common sense? Rosalind Krauss characterizes this "international fashion of installation and intermediary work" as *post-*

medium condition, which, in her opinion, entirely subdues today's art.[8] According to Krauss, what became apparent in the art of the 1960s, and took centre stage with conceptual art and video projections in the 70s, at the end of the 20th century has lost its starting point—a system of the arts, in relation to which such a movement could actually be interpreted as a transgressive. The tendency to disband the arts has been abandoned. On the contrary: Its liquidation initiates that art defrauds itself of its own difference, which distinguishes it from the world in which it is produced: "art essentially finds itself complicit with a globalization of the image in the service of capital."[9]

Adorno and Horkheimer, whose arguments Krauss implicitly follows, depicted this situation, not only in 1970s art, but as early as the 1940s in the context of mass media. Inside the commercial media complex of television the *Gesamtkunstwerk* is both announced and realized: "Television aims for a synthesis of radio and film [...] whose unlimited possibilities promise to increase the loss of aesthetic materials so radically that the hastily disguised identity of all industrial products may triumph openly tomorrow, the cynical fullfilment of Wagner's dream of the *Gesamtkunstwerk*."[10] Television thus represents the synthesis of all arts replacing theatre and film. The *Gesamtkunstwerk* therefore marks a sensitive interface at which the art forms are erased, and at the same time,maintained in a peculiar way.[11] What differentiates the *Gesamtkunstwerk* from all other forms of combining different art genres is that it is not obliged to conform to one art form—theatre, film, music or even television. It simultaneously arranges all other arts "in the name" of one form. Thus, as for Adorno and Horkheimer, television only initially seems to be a particular form within which all other forms are united and organized.

So what is the difference between television and an opera by Richard Wagner? These authors clearly seem to regard it as superior to Wagner's operas: "The accordance of word, image and music are so much more perfect [on television] than in Tristan, because all sensual elements [...] are basically produced in the same technical process[12] and whose unity expresses their actual substance."[13] This part is strange: The division of labor, that dominates the *Gesamtkunstwerk* as well as Wagner's operas, and by which art forms within the *Gesamtkunstwerk* remain differentiated, abruptly dissolves. The actual synthesis, which the 19th century artist could not achieve because his own skill and capacity were not sufficient and for which he was dependent on other artists, suddenly seems possible. But is it not television that divides into several techniques? And does it not continuously integrate new ones? Is it not television that absolutizes the method of specialization and division of labor?

Here the text surprisingly changes course. The principle mentioned is not just a method or an art: "This process integrates all elements of the production, from the novel concept until the final sound effects. It is the triumph of the invested capital."[14] The method—which is the decisive use of the elliptic argumentation in the end—is no longer separable from the invested capital. Every art genre and every device has a different approach on investment. The *Gesamtkunstwerk* is realized in an unexpected manner and even: Television is the form of art that no other form succeeds. It does not only mark a technical, but also an economic deflection in media history, after the transgression of which it is of no significance to refer to various forms of art because the perspective of the exchange value rates them as secondary. Thus the message of television must be the voice of economy, a voice which sensu stricto does not speak, but communicates through the withdrawal of language: a muteness, which surpassed modernist art itself.

Is such a historic description for our situation still relevant today? Hasn't the monomania of television, as it is described here, already been dissolved by the manifold openness of the blogosphere in which none of us are merely recipients, and each of us is a producer? Still, what remains beyond the rhetoric of participation and inclusion, is that today everything we regard as a *cultural commons* is privatized in the name of economy, and in a way that would have been unthinkable in 1940. A *Gesamtkunstwerk*, which does not interrupt everyday monotony as it would a Dionysic frenzy, but marks the extension of events with which our own ability to communicate is handed over to private companies beyond the boundaries of all media, and by whom it is schematized for us: Google, Microsoft, Apple, Facebook, you name it. What has become reality is that a what-you-will-method that has inscribed itself onto our lives beyond television, whose specific character had begun to dissolve long ago before our very eyes, and whose limits remain unforeseeable.

What has all that got to do with the situation of contemporary art? Shouldn't we simply insist on the "inexhaustible" differences that art, with its particular language, can provide beyond commercially occupied space? Isn't it the future of the *Gesamtkunstwerk* to conceive another form of universality? Two things that contradict such revisionism seem decisive. For one, what would this "other" *Gesamtkunstwerk* be, an idea worth elaborating or worth thinking further? That we cannot fall back on a system of arts today, arts that claim their own history or tradition, and which—regardless of the "aberrations of the time" –speak their own particular tongue, raises doubts regarding whether a reversal of such separate art forms would be interesting, new or even possible. If the *Gesamtkunstwerk* is only conceivable to us as a paradoxical combination—using the arts on the verge of their dénouement—then it is actually inaccessible today. Whether or not we agree to an entire leveling of the differences between the arts at exchange value does not alter the fact that our art forms are only available as hollow codes—so many essences of painting and sculpture have passed that we can only take their lack of essence seriously.

Secondly, if the present itself bears the signature of the *Gesamtkunstwerk*—which in the 20th century has paid for its propensity toward universality by being forced to equivalence—then it is equally wrong to want to suggest a return to a separation of the arts. Rosalind Krauss sees this as a reaction to the present, the only way out: Arts that, because they no longer exist, must be either reinvented or reactivated as obsolete techniques from the past.[15] The materials of art, its techniques and media are inseparable from their historic situation. This also means accepting that there is neither another past we can participate in, nor a private language of a new art form. If contemporary art includes all materials and skills then this means: The arts are an object of speculation for privatization. Even as I write, I am participating in the programs that I am using, simply by making the text readable. This immanence must therefore strip the perspective from modernism, which wants to claim an individual field per art form— an escape, if only to the infinite spaces of a fold. Moreover, it must break free from the perspective of the historic avant-garde, who believe the *Gesamtkunstwerk* must be overcome in order to unite art and life. What we dispose of is neither a utopian outlook, nor a *retour à l'ordre*. What remains, and this to me seems the major task of contemporary art, is the elaboration of this destruction, a destruction that refuses to unveil its exterior form and its essential core.[16] This may not be the future of the *Gesamtkunstwerk*, but it is certainly a rule of its present. SB

1 Cf. Theodor W. Adorno. "Die Kunst and die Künste," in: *Ohne Leitbild. Parva Aesthetica*, Frankfurt/Main, 1968, p. 189.
2 Cf. Thomas Mann. "Leiden and Größe Richard Wagners," in: *Gesammelte Werke in 13 Bänden*, vol., IX: *Reden and Aufsätze I*, Frankfurt/Main: Please insert publisher, 1960, p. 375f.

3 Cf. in detail: John Roberts. *The Intangibilities of Form. Skill and Deskilling in Art After the Readmade*, London/New York, 2007.
4 Cf. Andrea Fraser. "In and Out of Place," in: Alexander Alberro (ed.), *Museum Highlights. The Writings of Andrea Fraser*, Cambridge, 2005, pp. 17–27.
5 Eva Meyer-Herrmann (ed.), *Volume. A Rhoades Referenz*. Nuremburg, 1988.
6 Cf. Sabeth Buchmann. "Dialektiken des Potentiellen," in: Nikola Dietrich, Matthias Mühling (ed.), *Tom Burr* (exh. cat. Städtische Galerie im Lenbachhaus and Kunstbau München/Kunstmuseum Basel, Museum für Gegenwartskunst), Cologne 2009, p. 41f.
7 Cf. Richard Wagner. *Gesammelte Schriften und Dichtungen*, Vol. III: *Die Kunst und die Revolution. Das Kunstwerk der Zukunft. Oper und Drama* pt. 1. Boston: 2001.
8 Rosalind Krauss. *A Voyage on the North Sea: Art in the Age of the Post-Medium Condition*. London: 2000, p. 56.
9 Cf. Krauss. 2000, p. 56.
10 Max Horkheimer, *Theodor W. Adorno. Dialektik der Aufklärung. Philosophische Fragmente*, Frankfurt/Main, 2002, p. 132. Rosalind Krauss actually also considers the breakthrough of television as one of the decisive historic events that drove the system of the arts to a fundamental borderline. In reference to Guy Debord, Jonathan Crary has emphasized that Debord's dating of the birth of spectacle to 1928 might be linked to the technical facilitation of television: cf. Jonathan Crary, "Spectacle, Attention, Counter-Memory," in: *October* vol. 50. 1989, pp. 97–107.
11 László Moholy-Nagy criticized the problem of the division of labor in the 1920s from the perspective of constructivism, as the *Gesamtkunstwerk* would not only pass down the individuation of the arts, but also its separation from other sectors of society. Thus, he suggests a concept for the *Gesamtwerk* as a counter model. Cf. László Moholy-Nagy, *Vom Material zur Architektur*, Münster, 1968.
12 Ibid.
13 Horkheimer, Adorno 2002, p. 132.
14 Horkheimer, Adorno 2002, p. 132.
15 Krauss develops this model based on Walter Benjamin in connection with a discussion of Marcel Broodthaers' opus; cf. Krauss, 2000, p. 45.
16 For an example of ontology of destructive plasticity cf. Catherine Malabou. *Ontologie des Akzidentiellen*, Berlin, 2011.

<u>Bernhard Cella</u>
Salon für Kunstbuch im 21er Haus,
since 2011 (ongoing project)

"This salon is an art space on two accounts, a communication system and a dramaturgy, that does not only focus on the production and distribution of art works. Right from the start this place was set up as a model space on a 1:1 scale in which a relational game of its own between objects, people and art works could unfold." (Bernhard Cella)

The *Salon für Kunstbuch im 21er Haus* is an artificial label for a range of products, a sculpture in which people gather for discourse and in which existing forms of organization are tested. The artist creates an image of reality that mirrors our habits, revealing and transforming them. At the *Salon für Kunstbuch im 21er Haus* the gap between living and art space collapses. The spectator is actually in the image, art is no longer assigned a separate space. It is a hull in which the spectator impersonates the artist or the artist is present as an absence. The borderline between interior and exterior become blurred, distances are curtailed. Cella places himself as an artist on an economic terrain; he stages service and entrepreneurship as basics of his own artistic practice. Well connected with art book publishers and the protagonists of the field of theoretical art, he organizes book presentations and discussions, which coexist equal to the aesthetic form in order to to get to the bottom of the interrelations in current art production. The salon does not become a theatrical room of illusion, because one can buy the pieces on display, but it turns into a room of possibilities that highlights questions of identity and difference. **BS**

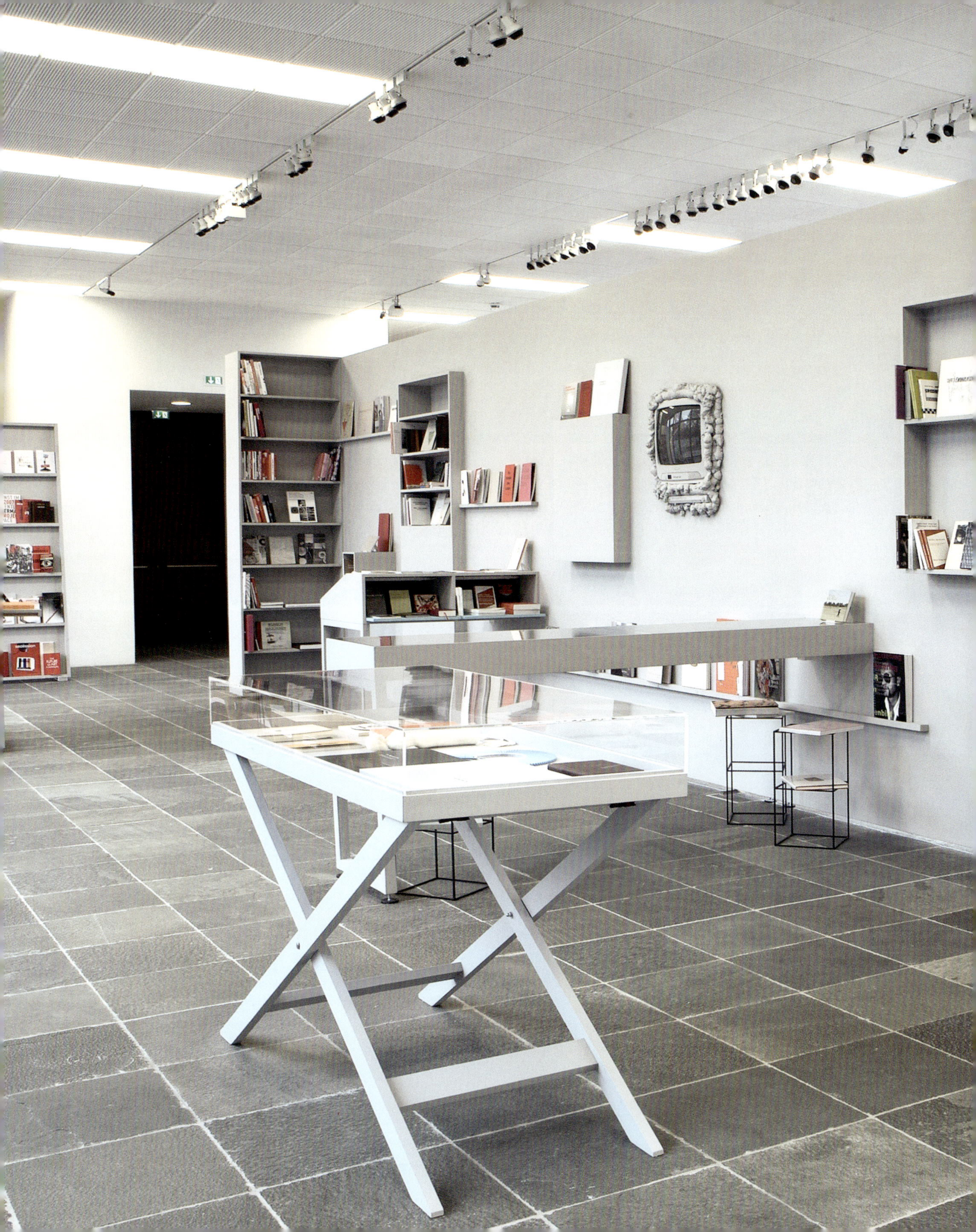

<u>Thomas Hirschhorn</u>
Tool Family, 2007

With his works—apart from assemblages, installations and video projects, he particularly focuses on art in public spaces—Thomas Hirschhorn takes a socio-critical position and points out social, cultural and political deficits. His use of simple materials like adhesive tape, panels etc. and items of everyday life is programmatic. The ordinariness of his materials and the deliberate rough workmanship of his pieces seek to abolish the exclusive air and elitist effect of art and thus its delimitation from the spectator.

Tool Family appears to be a persiflage on presentation and communication methods in the consumer industry, as the impression is given that products are advertised; bright, colorful, and in capital letters catchy slogans are announced. Alongside mannequins and tools, like a reference to the loss of the culture of thinking amidst this consumer landscape, literature by authors and philosophers like Immanuel Kant and Georges Bataille can be found. *Tool Family* faces the spectator with an archaic chaos, but through the seemingly confused composition of various elements a wide field of thoughts and associations opens up. Chaos and sensory overload dominate the scene; however, chaos is more of a design concept in this context, some sort of reaction to the chaotic conditions in the global crisis, in a world led by capitalism and globalisation, which has to bemoan the increasing loss of its culture. **VA**

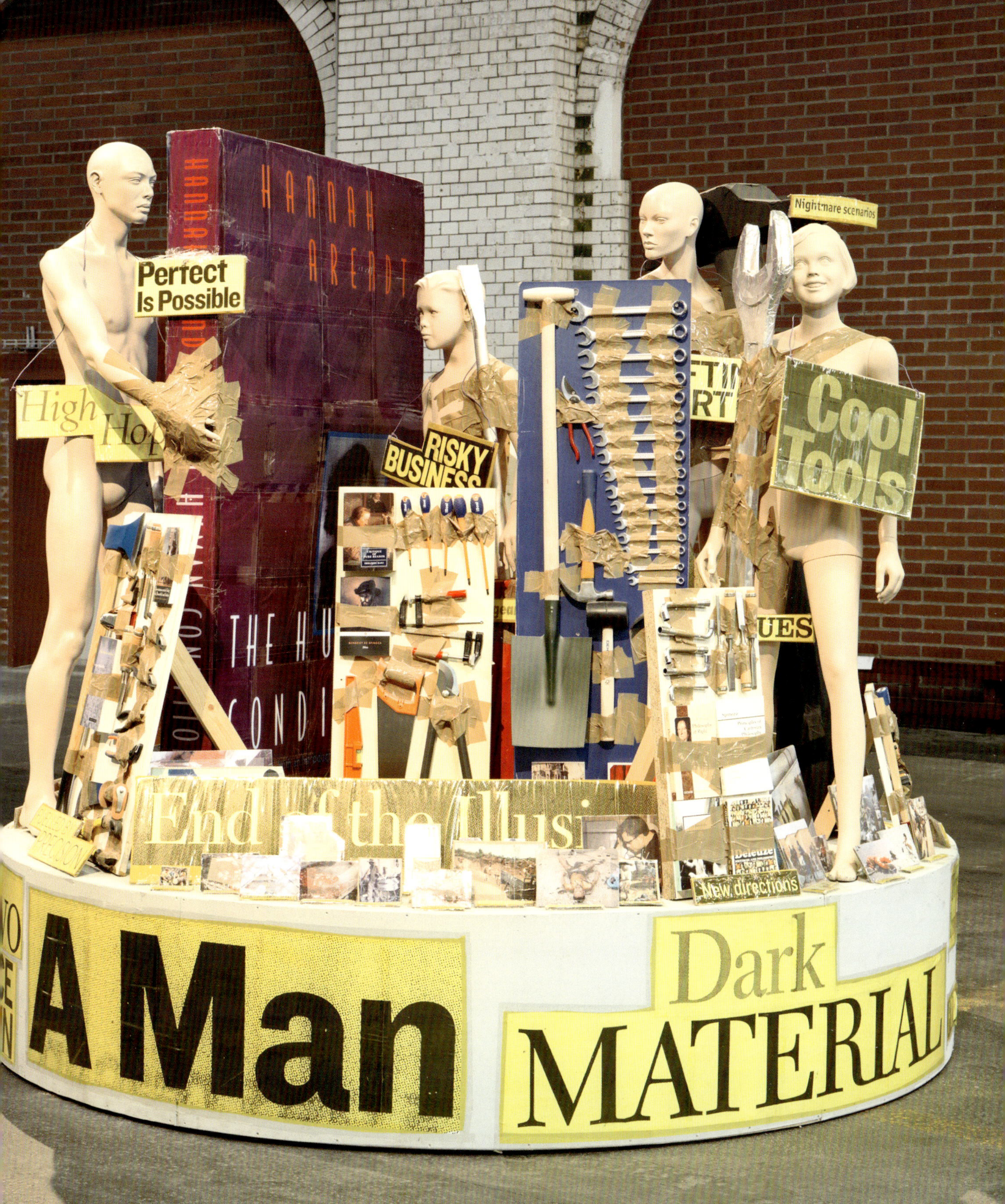

HANNAH ARENDT
Perfect Is Possible
High Hop
RISKY BUSINESS
Nightmare scenarios
Cool Tools
THE HUMAN CONDITION
End of the Illus
New directions
A Man
Dark MATERIAL

Hans Hollein and Walter Pichler
Architektur, Exhibition at Galerie nächst St. Stephan, 1963

When Walter Pichler and Hans Hollein made the exhibition *Architektur* at Galerie nächst St. Stephan in 1963, the artistic discourse was heavily characterised by dissolution strategies of the individual art genres. Yona Friedman realised his socio-utopian discursive urban strategies, Cedric Price worked on dynamic space structures adaptable to the respective demands, and Japanese architects planned mega cities. All this was also a reaction to the heavily media-hyped project of the new town Brasília, which led the rationalist architectural myth of Bauhaus to its climax. For long time architects had included the social relevance of architecture in their planning strategies. The attempt to reintegrate art and life much more strongly in the planning process was coined by a new historical awareness that also questioned the contents of architecture. In their exhibition project, Pichler and Hollein pursued an approach of dissolution at simultaneous new conscience, of creating art and architecture on the basis of human parameters, and of accepting the complexity of spatial patterns of human activity. Pichler's sculptural space concept shaped the architectonic strategies to an innovative spatial perception, whereas Hollein's architectonic approach examined the sculptural qualities of technology. Hollein's montage of everyday objects in unreal architectonic-spatial nexuses offensively relied on the connection of several levels of reality of heterogenic picture elements and in the end problematised the functional relations between man, architecture and sculpture. Moreover, in his collages Hollein quoted the architectural fantasies of Le Corbusier, who had linked the sculptural quality of technological production, e.g. of ships or cars, with architectonic concepts in the publication *L'Architecture d'Aujourd'hui* dating from 1925. In their exhibition project Pichler and Hollein merged two different artistic concepts by adapting each others' methods and thus defining this utopian new space, which should lead to the renewal of architecture and art.[1]

1 Cf. Matthias Boeckl, *Komprimierte Weltanschauung. Ein motivgeschichtlicher Versuch über das Werk des Plastikers, Zeichners and Architekten Walter Pichler,* diploma thesis, Vienna, 1987.

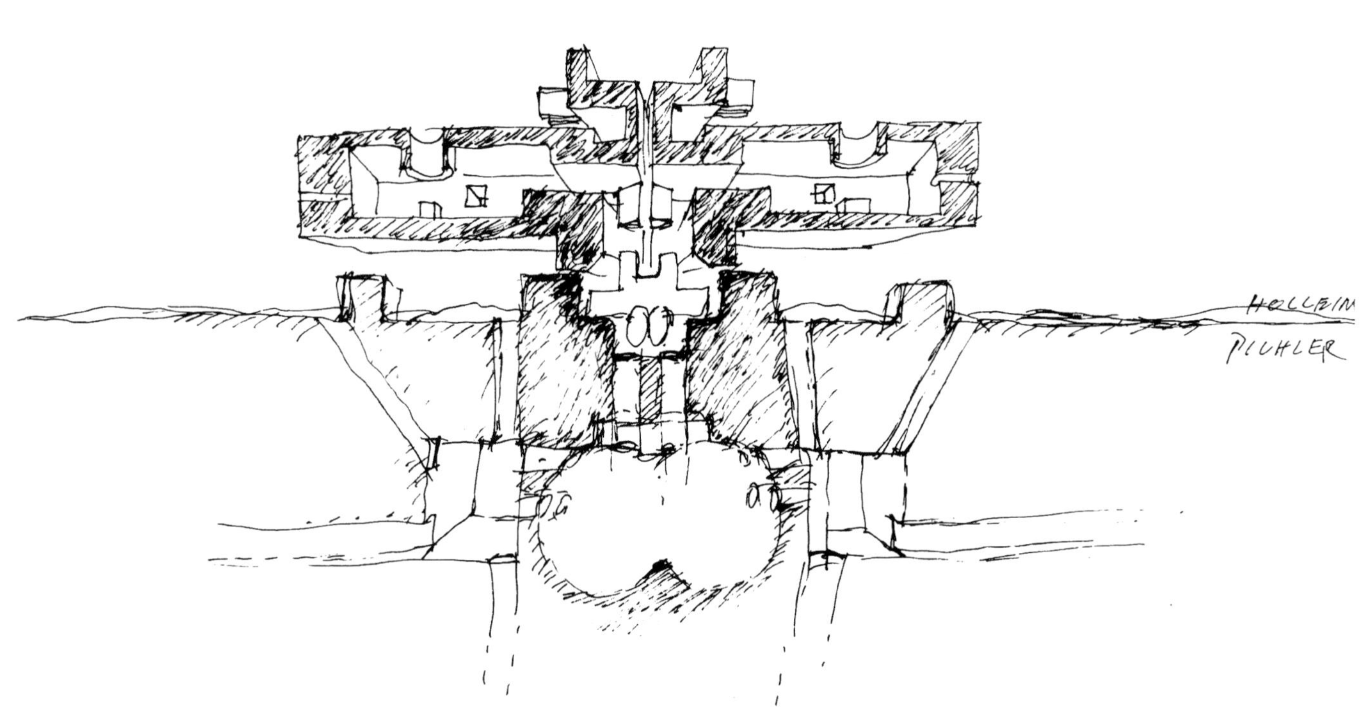

HOLLEIN
PICHLER

Inspection Medical Hermeneutics (Pavel Pepperstein, Sergej Anufriew)
PARAMEN, 1994

The series *PARAMEN*, which Pavel Pepperstein has developed in collaboration with Sergei Anufriev, consists of 22 works in which text and image coequally require and enrich one another. Contrary to our accustomed reading and viewing habits, the images serve neither the illustration of text—in this case fragments of Russian poetry and prose—nor does the text offer additional information about the images—there are no clear references or connections between the image and text, giving rise to the emergence of more room for free association.

The term *PARAMEN*, which was developed by Pepperstein and Anufriev denotes, "an entity of phenomena,"[1] and is the concept for this piece, which deals with the complexity of subjective perception and the interrelation and overlapping of sensations on a meta level. "Although we delegate our perceptions to the various sensory organs, we don't perceive any object just visually, aurally or tactilely. All sensory organs cooperate, and together with each perceived object, we also consume the circumstances of its cognition, which engages all sense organs. The result is an entirely random composition of impressions which formally accord a synaesthetic complex."[2] Moreover, the artists describe how the additional factors of physical and mental state, intellect and the memories of an individual form this unity. VA

1 On the etymology of the term cf. Sergei Anufriev: "The term 'Paramen' was composed (in the traditional method) by combining two Greek words. It indicates an entity of phenomena wherein the phenomenon is a concrete and the noumenon an abstract sensation. The Paramen includes the phenomenon and the noumenon as well as the sum of the sensations, which our perception of anything accompanies with our sensory organs. If we imagine perceiving an object, the Paramen is the sum of these factors, which composes an impression of the object, i.e. the sum, which is memorized. Our memory only recipient such 'bouquets,' as it cannot scan EVERYTHING." (Sergej Anufriev and Pavel Pepperstein in an interview on February 20, 1994, in Aachen. First published in: *Pastor 6*, Cologne 1997.)
2 Sergej Anufriev in ibid.

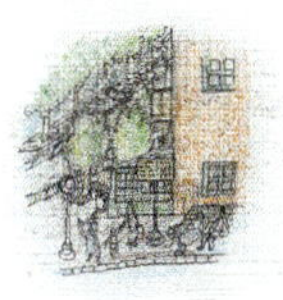

ВЕТЕР, ВЕТЕР,
- ТЫ МОГУЧ,
ТЫ ГОНЯЕШЬ
СТАИ ТУЧ !

<u>Hermann Nitsch</u>
Orgien-Mysterien-Theater,
since 1960

"In 1997 I held the 40th action painting performance in the Museum of the 20th Century. I poured blood and black oil paint on white canvas, some smocks were attached on some paintings. I redesigned the museum as a mausoleum for my deceased mother." (Hermann Nitsch)

Hermann Nitsch's painting originates from a complex analysis of topics ranging from cult and theatre to mental constitution of humans as well as a religion-like preoccupation with human existence. Against this background, Nitsch has been working on his idea of the *Orgien Mysterien Theater* since the 1960s, the concept of a performative art he devised in Prinzendorf and has since performed there regularly. A complex symbol language of organic materials and religious elements like the sacrifice shall transform the metaphors of our lives as well as our existence in reality, and serve a gestus of relief like Antonin Artaud or the theatre reformation movement of the turn of the century have already proclaimed. Within the meaning of gestures of relief and strategies of ego-dissolution in the 1960s also dealing with depth psychology plays a key role in Nitsch's opus. The artist has intensively grappled with Richard Wagner's ideas and his term Gesamtkunstwerk. It would be wrong to reduce the term Gesamtkunstwerk to the concept of the *Orgien Mysterien Theater* only. Particularly the transformation of a conceptual notation through the theatrical act in a poetic dimension of painting, the merging of victim gestus and artistic action is the artistic breeding ground, which Nitsch—based on his *Orgien Mysterien Theater*—has unfolded in painting. Theatrical illusion is transformed onto the stage of the real, concrete venue; the barrier between stage and spectator is dispersed and serves the realisation of these endeavours in theatre history, which have reached from Wagner and Piscator to the happenings in the 1960s influencing art in crucial areas. Nitsch seamlessly links his painting of free gestus and that of transforming this realm of experience to this cleansing process, which is achieved by excessive experiencing. **HK**

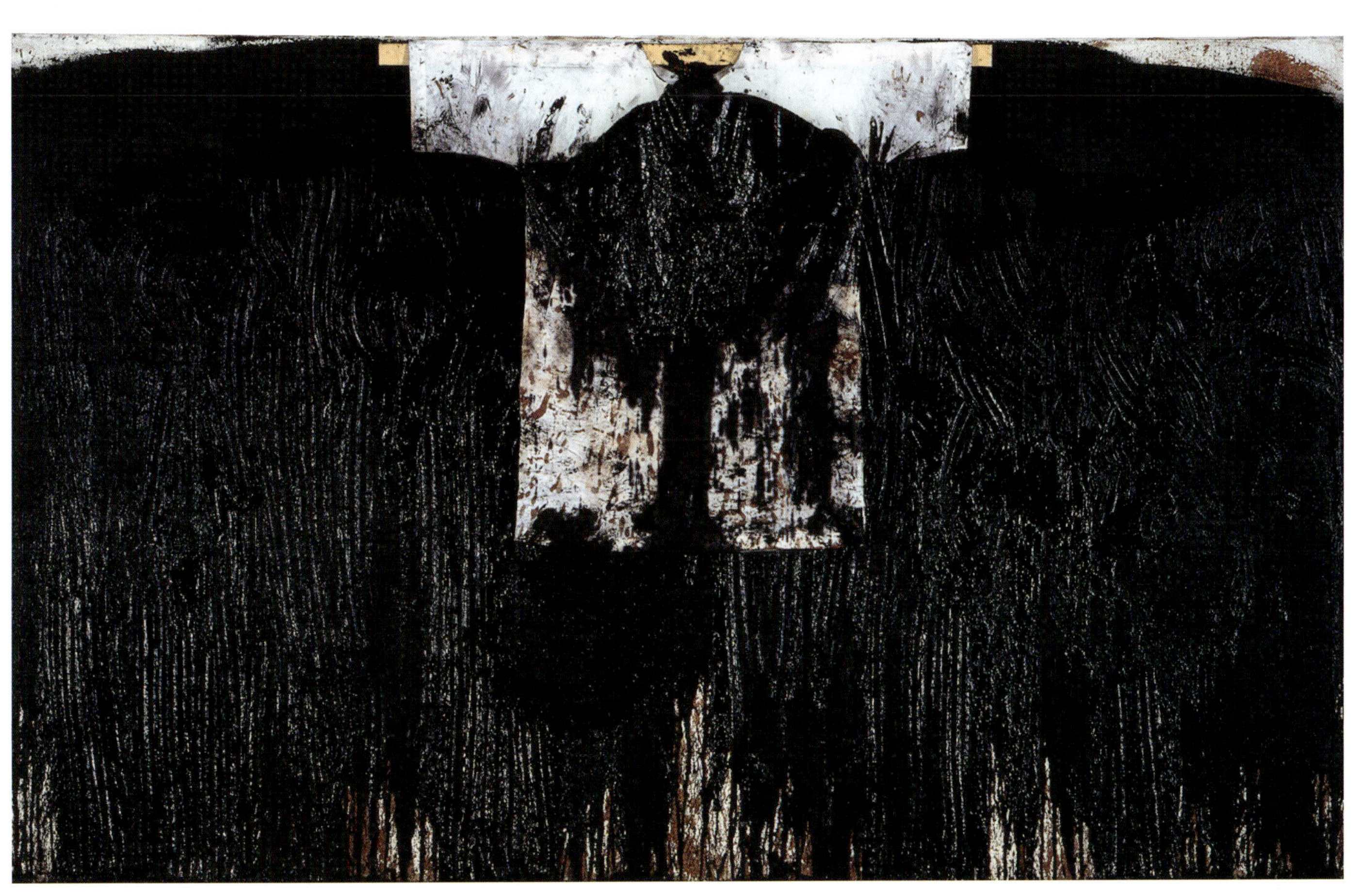

Oswald Oberhuber
Kunst ohne Künstler, 1969/2011

If you want to name the core motives in Oswald Oberhuber's artistic work, the figure of thought of permanent change is certainly one of them. Oberhuber has elaborated his work by incorporating complex relational spheres, which he believed to only make art possible. Oberhuber scrutinised the meaning of original and fake, the subjectivity of the artist, but mostly the traditional idea of the art object. The questioning culminated in the 1960s in the group exhibition *Künstler ohne Kunst – Kunst ohne Künstler. Surrealisten ohne Surrealismus*, in which Oberhuber presented various partly fictional artists. In the exhibition, he focused on the self-conception of the artist and art analysis. "Everything you put down, thrust aside, or conserve, can be art." (Oberhuber 1969) In his object *Kunst ohne Künstler* the artist agglomerates various everyday items, pledges and waste into stacked glass cubes. Randomness is predominant for the observer, although the artist expresses his individual mythology by selecting particular items. On the other hand, the transparency of the object conglomerate reflects a spatial condition, hinting architecture. In this context the connection to the architecture discourse of these days is interesting, that Oberhuber followed closely, and in which another Austrian, the architect Bernard Rudofsky, carried out a similar scrutiny of the creative act. In *Architecture Without Architects* (1964) Rudofsky emphasises that it is social and cultural parameters that change our architecture, and not the ingenious ideas of the architects. On another level this resembles a line of thought, which may be compared to that Oberhuber proclaimed for his artistic concept. The opus of the *Wiener Schule* was the philosophical point of reference Oberhuber had demanded so often, which had crucially influenced his thinking. **HK**

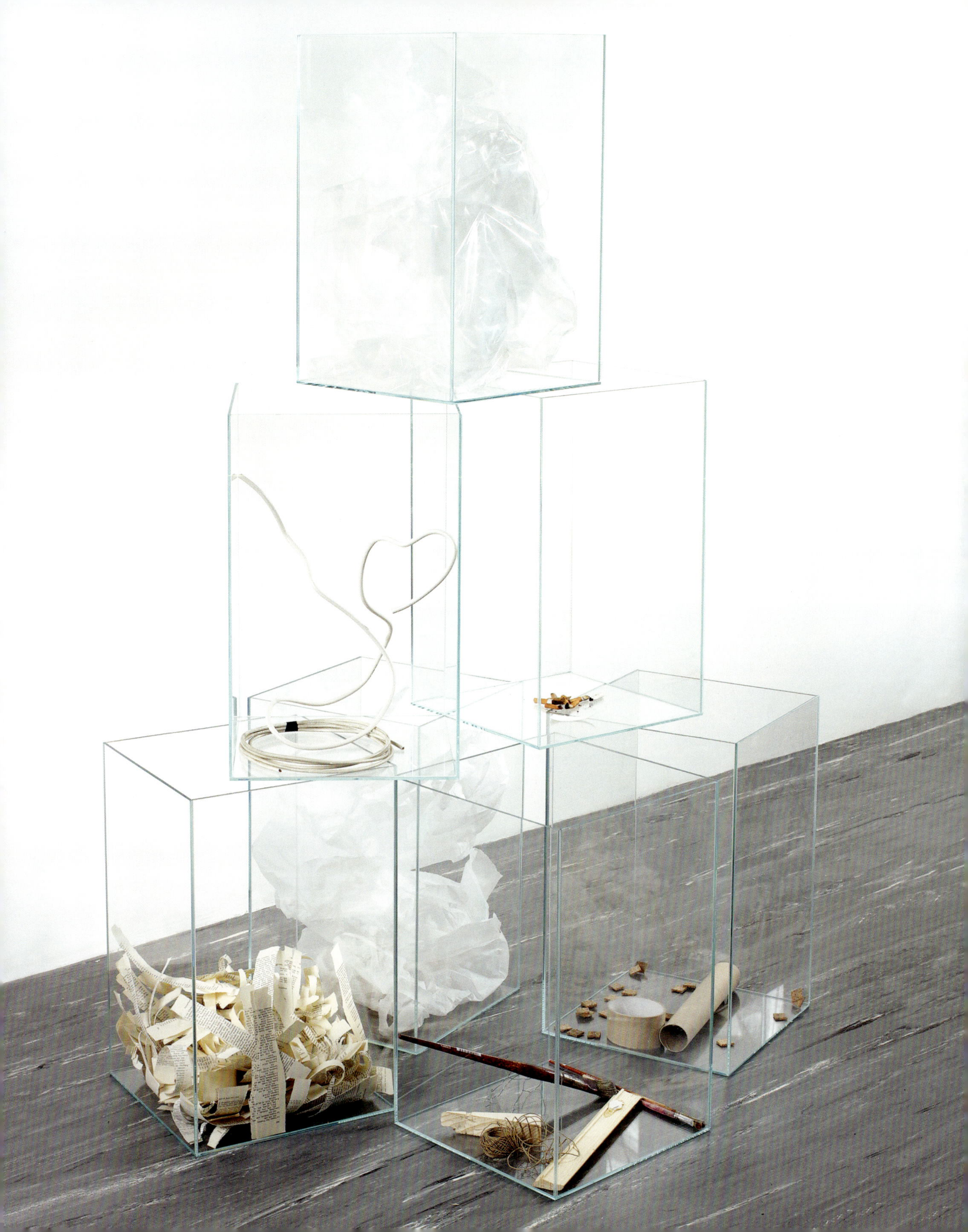

<u>Marjetica Potrč</u>
Monumental and Personal Modernism, 2002

Visual artist and architect Marjetica Potrč examines structures, mechanisms and processes in the field of contemporary architecture and urbanism. She places special emphasis on developments in the areas of safety, energy and fresh water supply, and the respective living standards of residents. In her so called "case studies"—examinations of city models of different social classes in various geographical regions, for example gated communities in the first world or ghettos in the third world—she comes to the conclusion that privately organized initiatives and small-scale projects often produce better results than officially sanctioned municipal programs. Potrč transfers these privately initiated concepts and projects into the artistic context, documenting them through models and sketches. She does not restrict herself to mere reflection in her artistic practice however, but also actively intervenes by developing and supporting projects that truly improve living conditions.[1] Through Potrč's method she reconfigures the social subject as her object, and her art appears not only conceptual, but actually takes on an active social role in which art and life form a unity. In her piece *Monumental and Personal Modernism*, Potrč counterposes a modernism guided by monumental, antiquated architectonic and urban planning measures with a more personal form of modernism that is shaped by and for the individual. VA

1 In her project *Dry Toilet, La Vega barrio, Caracas* (2003) Marjetica Potrč and architect Liyat Esakov designed and erected a waterless toilet facility for a ghetto in Venezuela's capital city, which was not connected to the municipal water system. Cf. Lívia Páldi (ed.), *Marjetica Potrč. Next Stop, Kiosk.* (exh. Moderna Galerija Ljubljana) Frankfurt/Main, Revolver, 2003.

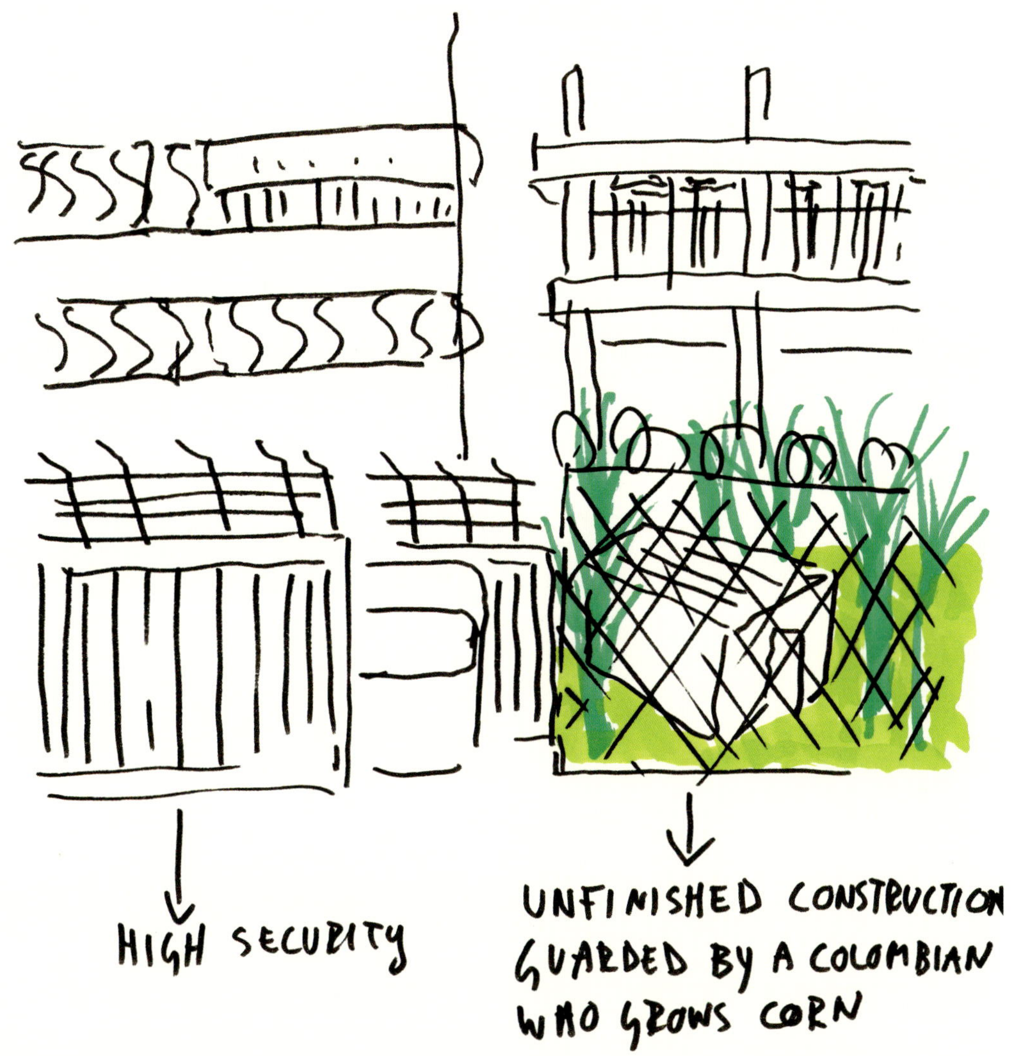

SEE WHAT HAS BECOME OF THE HOPES
OF MONUMENTAL MODERNISM
AS IT APPEARS IN DOWNTOWN CARACAS.

Christoph Schlingensief
Hase Fett, 2008
from: *Eine Kirche der Angst vor dem Fremden in mir*, 2008

The works displayed are part of Christoph Schlingensief's *Fluxus-Oratorium—Eine Kirche der Angst vor dem Fremden in mir* whose initial point is his analysis of developing terminal cancer. The oratory was first performed in 2008 on the occasion of the RuhrTriennale festival, for which the blower house in Duisburg was converted into a gritty, nightmarish church: Wooden benches served as seats for the spectators; monstrances contained x-rays of his infected lung. In his characteristically rich, Dadaistic language Schlingensief has developed a deeply shocking production of his battle against the disease, his struggle to stay alive as well as the fear of oncoming death. The confrontations are harsh: Super 8 mm films of a merry childhood collide with images of the tumour, mixed with gospel and children's choir music. References to venerated artists are embedded in the flood of images and sounds in *Kirche der Angst*: A *Cello TV* is a reference to Fluxus artist Nam June Paik, a *Fat Corner* with a dead rabbit—a subject, which also often recurs in Schlingensief's work—refers to Joseph Beuys. Beuys' quote "Who is showing his wound, will be healed" is printed onto the exhibition booklet and must be seen as the motif of the oratory. Alongside religion also art is analysed regarding its relieving effect and becomes an art-as-religion. VA

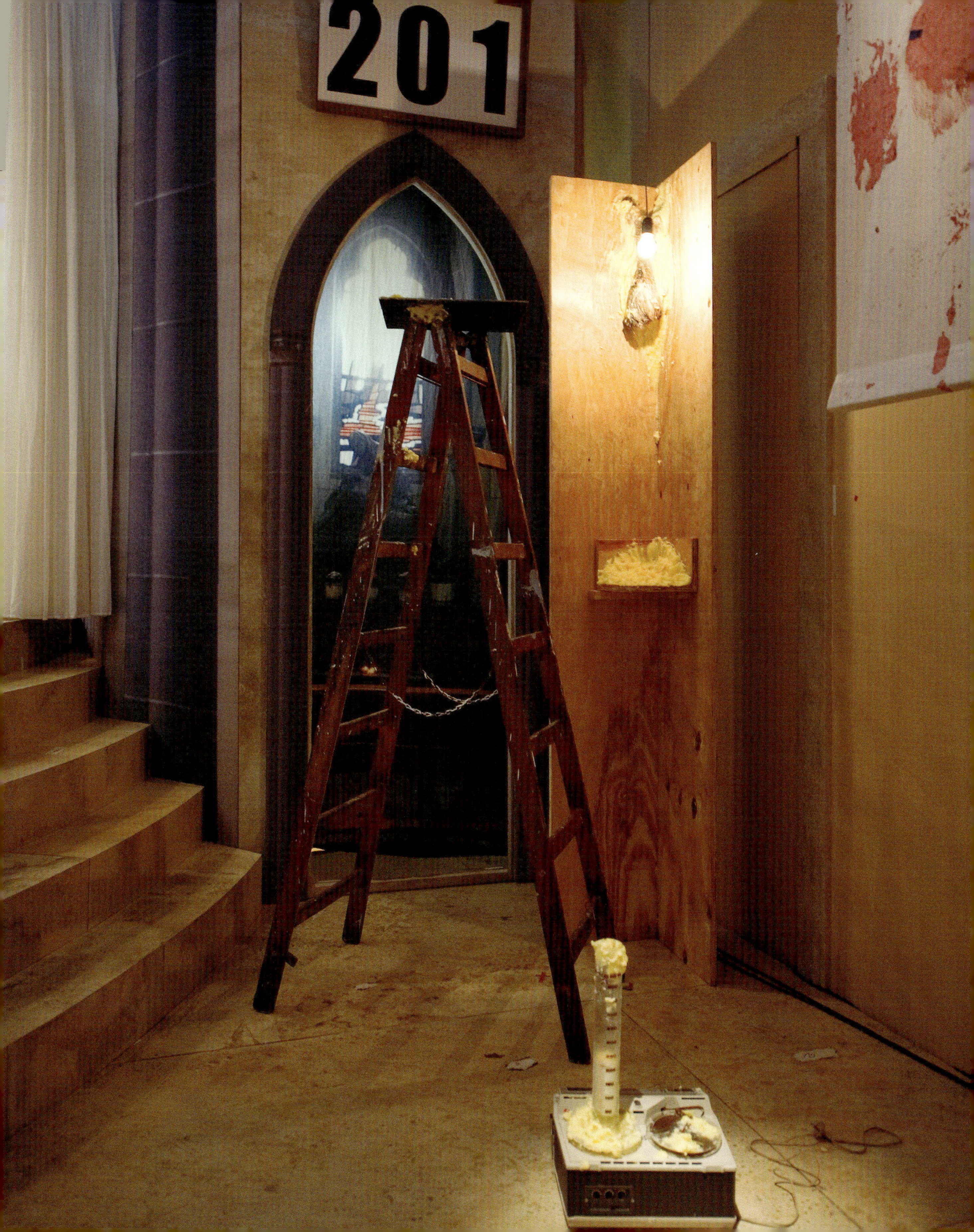
201

Una Szeemann
Montewood Hollyverità, 2003

In the video *Montewood Hollyverità*, Monte Verità and Hollywood, two places of desire that were founded at nearly the same time, merge. Beginning in 1900, utopians of all kinds began gathering on top of Monte Verità—the mountain of truth—in Ascona, to found a community in which life reformers, vegetarians, poets, musicians, dancers, revolutionists, feminists, architects, theosophists and anarchists could search for a third pathway, one between capitalism and communism. The Hollywood film empire emerged in 1911. Both scenarios have retained their charisma until today and are absolutely divergent,—while Monte Verità stands for authenticity, Hollywood is home to the world of illusion. What they both share however, is the intent to alter one's sense of life. Una Szeemann transfers the life reformers of Monte Verità to Hollywood, and makes them gain glamour, impersonating them by West Coast art world shooting stars. It gradually becomes apparent that the differences separating the "old" Monte Verità from the "new" Hollywood are perhaps not that big after all. Monte Verità founders Ida Hofmann and Henri Oedenkoven are impersonated by Olympic body building champions Pauliina Talus and Tommi Thorvildsen; body-conscious revolutionary dancer Rudolf von Laban by Jason Rhoades; Paul McCarthy is Elisar von Kupffer the homosexual poet, painter, philosopher, and creator of an androgyne paradise; anarchist and bohemian Erich Mühsam is played by Udo Kier, and Lawrence Weiner becomes the rich Baron Emden, proprietor of the Brissago Islands. **BS**

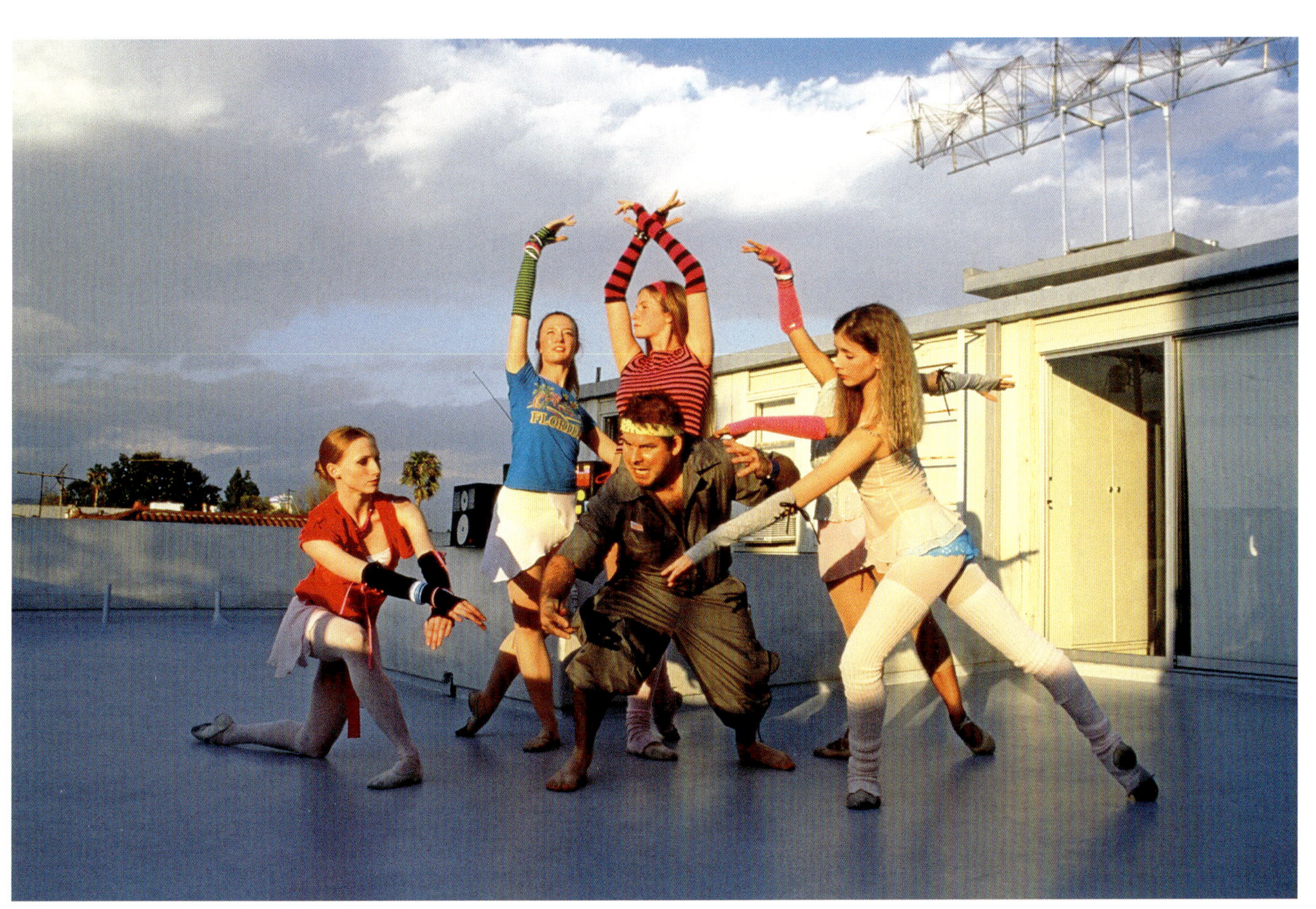

WochenKlausur
Medizinische Versorgung Obdachloser, Vienna 1993

In their projects, exhibitions, lectures and presentations the artist group WochenKlausur deals with socio-critical problems, aiming to elaborate and realise concrete suggestions for an improvement of social injustices. The name "WochenKlausur" (weekly conclave) was determined during the exhibition *11 Wochen in Klausur* (Vienna Secession, 1993), to which Wolfgang Zinggl had invited eight artists (Martina Chmelarz, Marion Holy, Christoph Kaltenbrunner, Friederike Klotz, Alexander Popper, Anne Schneider, Erich Steurer, and Gudrun Wagner). The artists decided against the concept of a standard exhibition, on the contrary developed the model of a mobile ambulance, offering unbureaucratic and free medical first aid to the homeless. The project has survived until today—at present under the direction of Caritas—and has become an indispensable social institution in Vienna. The artistic self-conception is carried by the thought of social responsibility of the artist who positions himself as an active member of society. A deliberate rejection of any "L'art pour l'art" tendency is manifested: "The formal-aesthetic dispute is exhausted, the self-referential somersaults have become inflationary, and the admiration of the ingenious has been replaced by other qualities." (www.wochenklausur.at) Art is understood as an instrument, which can and should intervene in the sense of a positive development of everybody's lived-in world. The term shifts from an art work to a permanent social intervention. **VA**

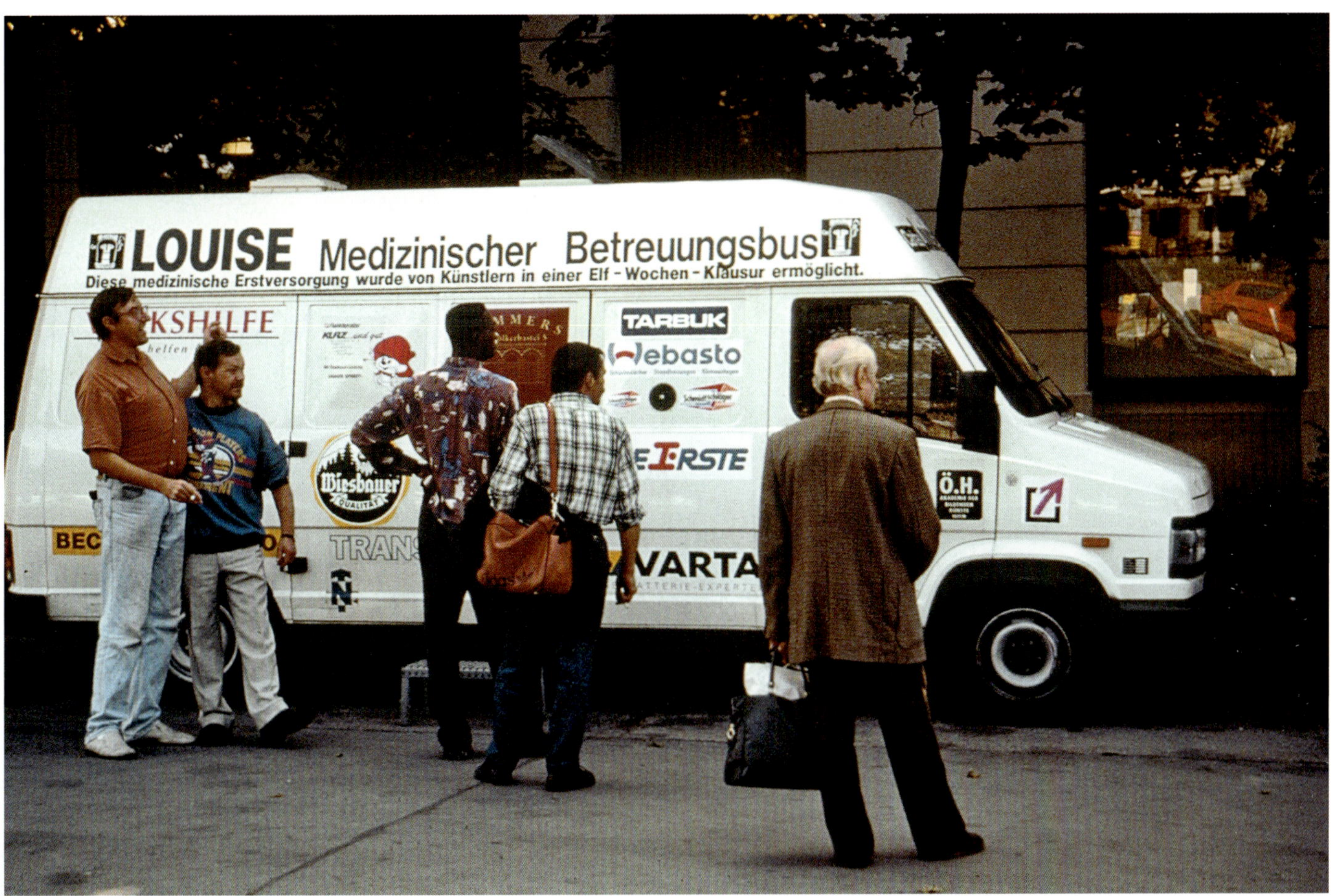

LOUISE Medizinischer Betreuungsbus
Diese medizinische Erstversorgung wurde von Künstlern in einer Elf - Wochen - Klausur ermöglicht.
KSHILFE
MMERS
TARBUK
Webasto
Wiesbauer
QUALITÄT
E RSTE
BEC
TRANS
VARTA
ÖH

Deconstru

ction

Utopia in Fragments:
Art, Politics, and the Total Work of Art

João Ribas

The *Gesamtkunstwerk*, or "total work of art," seems like an anachronism or an aberration, a utopian vestige of the romantic era. This aesthetic project for a unification of the arts, that dates back to the origins of modern culture, is one whose relevance or purpose has become undone by the horrors of totalitarian spectacle and the resulting contemporary rejection of such artistic totality or unity.[1] The very idea of a total artwork—combining poetry, dance, music and drama—has been stained by the political totalities of the 20th century.[2] The agency of such a radical synthesis is, in contemporary terms, also undermined by its apparent banality: it is precisely the kind of production readily afforded by consumer-grade digital technology. With its evocation of both monumentality and politicization, the concept has been relegated, along with many other post-romantic ideals to, in the words of architect Lebbeus Woods,the "trash-heap of history."[3]

Yet, with its origins in radical politics and historical crises, the utopian aspirations of the Gesamtkunstwerk may yet prove relevant to today's artistic practices.[4] The cultural roots of the total work of art lie in Romanticism—in Schlegel's call for a fusion of poetic genres, and the writings of Schelling and Schiller[5]—as well as in the burgeoning mass culture of the mid-nineteenth century.[6] The term is most commonly associated, however, with the unification of the arts in musical drama proposed by Richard Wagner in his essays *Die Kunst und die Revolution* and *Das Kunstwerk* der Zukunft, both written in 1849. As two texts central to the conception of the total work of art, along with his *Oper* und Drama (1851), it is here that Romantic influences and revolutionary politics combine to engender a theorization of the Gesamtkunstwerk in its fullest extent.[7] Wagner's political involvement in the May Uprising in Dresden in 1849, part of the so-called "Spring of Nations," led to a renewal of the conception of the social role of art inflected with politicized notions for utopian communities.[8] As Wagner writes in his autobiography, his ideas "on the subject of modern art in its relation to society" were arrived at through, "private and artistic experiences, as well as through the influence of the political unrest of the day."[9] By unit-

ing the so-called "tragic" and "social-radical tendencies" of Feuerbach with his own "conceptions of an all-embracing work of art," the *Gesamtkunstwerk* is proposed as being linked to social transformation.[10] Wagner historicizes this relationship between political and aesthetic revolution in the coeval decline of Greek drama and the Athenian state. Rehearsing the Hegelian trope of the 'holism' of the Hellenic ideal in *Die Kunst und die Revolution*, Wagner proclaims that the art of ancient Greece was the, "expression of a world attuned to harmony."[11] Furthermore, he writes that, "Hand-in-hand with the dissolution of the Athenian State, marched the downfall of Tragedy," which was replaced by "hypocrisy" and art "selling her soul and body" as the "mistress" of commerce:[12]

With the subsequent downfall of Tragedy, Art became less and less the expression of the public conscience. The Drama separated into its component parts; rhetoric, sculpture, painting, music, &c., forsook the ranks in which they had moved in unison before; each one to take its own way, and in lonely self-sufficiency to pursue its own development. And thus it was that at the Renaissance of Art we lit first upon these isolated Grecian arts, which had sprung from the wreck of Tragedy. The great unitarian Artwork of Greece could not at once reveal itself to our bewildered, wandering, piecemeal minds in all its fullness; for how could we have understood it?[13]

The unification, or reintegration of the arts in the *Gesamtkunstwerk* would thus be the reclamation of a supposed unity found in antiquity.[14] As with Schiller's "narrative of redemption by means of art," the total work of art suggests not merely the combination of artistic forms, but the attempt to 'recover' lost political and social unities.[15] Such a total work of art, Wagner as writes, can only arise "in fullest harmony with the conditions of our whole life."[16] The *Gesamtkunsterk* is thus also tied to the social role of art, and to a conception of totality that is inseparable from social unity. As a decidedly political project, it is part of what Matthew Wilson Smith calls, "the history of un-reconciled dialectical struggles performed under the sign of aesthetic totality."[17] As Smith writes, the *Gesamtkunstwerk* represents an, "uncompromising wish for a joyful community to be realized in this life, in this world [....] a longing for unity amidst fragmentation, for collectivity amidst alienation."[18] Though "total work of art" is in fact the most common translation of this term, "communal work of art," "collective work of art," and "unified work of art," are among other possible translations.[19] Smith suggests therefore, that the term connotes aspects of community as well as unity and totality.[20]

Wagner's utopian "mutual art work of the future" is in fact one born of "free artistic fellowship," whose "free communions" would stand as an alternative, "against the stiff political union of our time, upheld by outward force alone."[21] Here Schiller's utopian potential of the aesthetic is given a further Kantian basis, beyond the harmonious play of the faculties achieved by aesthetic play. While Kant similarly suggested a "combination of the fine arts in one and the same product,"[22] the potential of such a synthesis is extended to the realm of freedom and universal ascent by his conception of the *sensus communis*. In Kant's account of aesthetic judgment, judgments of taste are not reduced to an objective concept, as there is, "no rule in accordance with which someone could be compelled to acknowledge something as beautiful."[23] As Kant suggests, there would otherwise be no dispute about matters of taste. To claim that something is beautiful however, is to assert that this claim has "validity for everyone."[24] Even if it appears to be subjective, the judgment contains an appeal comparable to a demand based on an objective principle.[25] In fact, the subject makes the judgment "as if" it were objective, though there are no rules or concepts by which someone ought to be compelled to acknowledge such a claim or by which it can be proven.[26] The intersubjective character of aesthetic judgment lies in its implication of universal assent: based on a subjective principle of 'taste,' aesthetic judgment rests on the sense that others ought to agree. This

universality grounds taste in what Kant called the *sensus communis*, or "a critical faculty which in its reflective act takes account of the mode of representation of everyone else."[27] In Kant's epistemology, the act of judging itself is an inherently social relation, a fulfillment of what he places as the highest end of human, "sociability."[28]

It is Schiller who radicalizes Kantian aesthetics into an overtly political project:[29]

The aesthetic state alone can make [society] real, because it carries out the will of all through the nature of the individual ... All other forms of communication divide society, because they apply exclusively either to the receptivity or to the private activity of its members, and therefore to what distinguishes men from one another. The aesthetic communication alone unites society because it applies to what is common to all its members.[30]

Wagner's version of such an "aesthetic state" is the communitarian social dream of the "mutual art-work of the future," in which, "all will participate actively in genius, genius will be communal."[31] For Wagner, only revolution can generate the basis for the creation of this total artwork of the future: "art as social product" and a civic expression of community.[32] Such communality, in the wake of the revolutionary social projects of the last century, readily suggests stupefying proto-fascist spectacle or utopian socialism. Contemporary cultural practices seem more in line with Brecht's *Verfremdungseffekt*, or "estrangement effects" than with the Wagnerian *Gesamtkunstwerk*.[33] The total work of art conceived as an organic whole seems less relevant to contemporary culture than what Brecht—whose epic theatre stands in contrast to Wagnerian drama—terms a, "radical separation of the elements."[34]

This separation finds its clearest articulation in the autonomous work of art commonly associated with modernism. The autonomist conception of the arts proposed by Lessing's Laocoon, Kant's *Critique of Judgment*, and Greenberg's (Kantian) theorization of medium-specificity privilege a version of the individual artwork that seems diametrically opposed to the total work of art.[35] The relevance of the concept to contemporary artistic production is, as Juliet Koss suggests, thus questioned by a, "lingering presumption within the discipline of art history that such a model of artistic interrelation falls beyond the parameters of modernism," in particular in the "refinement and purification" of each medium towards their intrinsic and essential criteria, such as flatness or opacity.[36] In rejecting a synthesis of various artistic forms, the modernist artwork trades aesthetic *totality* for an emphasis on political *unity*. Political agency was in fact joined to formal autonomy in such conceptions of modernism,[37] eliding the political or social function of art as, in the words of Leon Trotsky, "historically utilitarian."[38] Political concerns were deemed to undermine autonomy, and thus art's critical or radical potential.[39] Such oppositional distinctions between politics and aesthetics run throughout the cultural programs of the last century; they find an attempted reconciliation, as Peter Burger, David Hopkins, Hal Foster have argued, in the historical and neo-avant-garde sublation of art into life.[40] What modernism ceded of the total work of art by rejecting aesthetic totality therefore, it arguably maintained in its overtly political dimension of overcoming divisions between art and life in the name of social transformation.[41] While numerous examples of contemporary *Gesamtkunstwerk* can be given—the productions of Christoph Schlingensief and Karlheinz Stockhausen's opera cycle *Licht* are oft cited examples[42]—the concept may have its truest contemporary form in a continued striving for such dialectical unity. Perhaps the contemporary total work of art is one that maintains the productive impulse—an extension of the historical avant-garde—which is the legacy of postwar leftist politics: uniting politics with the imagination.[43] It is such unity that speaks to the contradictory states—or the "fragmentation" alluded to by this volume—of

today's artistic practices in the wake of the collapse of the Eastern bloc and the anti-regime uprisings of the so-called "Arab Spring."

This supposed condition of fragmentation—drawing on yet another Romantic notion—is best encapsulated by Carolyn Christov-Bakargiev's suggestion that, "intellectuals, including artists, find themselves in the situation of linking together the following conditions: being under siege; being in a position of hope; being on retreat; being on stage."[44] Do contemporary artistic practices have a similar, "longing for unity amidst fragmentation," that have defined the total work of art as a result?How is the relevance of the Gesamtkunstwerk implicated in a prevalent, "desire for a society worth living in, and the question as to what models of living today are still once again possible" that seems central to the focus on community and collectivity in recent art?If contemporary artistic practices do face a condition of fragmentation, then this itself should form the work's position, in particular, the realization that culture can no longer sustain the illusion of a vantage point apart "from the street and from the control room."[45] Rather than a belief in what Miwon Kown describes as the, "self-conscious desire to resist the forces of the capitalist market economy,"[46] much of contemporary artistic production maintains a fragmentary position that is, as Johanna Drucker explains, simultaneously both, "complicit *with* and an alternative to hegemony and capital,".[47] The forms of radical critique that structure cultural ideals such as the *Gesamtkunstwerk* have also been subjected to re-appropriation by contemporary forms of "iconoclasm and fundamentalist spectacle."[48] The recent rise of censorship and iconoclasm itself suggests that the global circulation of culture has made contemporary art a realm of contention in the current political climate, with art both on stage *and* under siege, spectacularized as well as censored.[49] What distinctions can artists, critics, or curators then make between what is taking place "on the ground," in terms of political agitation, and within the symbolic, on today's geopolitical stage? Is it not the nature of power to regulate, repress, or appropriate both as political commodities?

As a result, in order to affirm their engagement as both political and aesthetic practices—in essence, a kind of *unity*—contemporary artistic forms need to formulate new relations between the political and the aesthetic, between autonomy, imagination, and political agency. In its social, political, and aesthetic dimensions, the *Gesamtkunstwerk* is a potent historical example of such a generative relationship between the political and aesthetic. A new "total" unity of the political and aesthetic suggested by the utopian trope of the total work of art that entails the ongoing affirmation of the role of culture in a politics of freedom and plurality. That is to say, what can we do with Wagner's "beauty of a noble Universalism" today?[50]

1 Danielle Follett and Anke Finger, "Dynamiting the Gesamtkunstwerk," in: Anke Finger and Danielle Follett (ed.), *The Aesthetics of the Total Artwork*. Baltimore: Johns Hopkins University Press, 2011, pp. 1, 7.
2 Ibid, pp. 14-15; and Jurgen Soring, "The Completed Work is a Rejection of Disintegration and Destruction," in: Anke Finger and Danielle Follett (ed.), *The Aesthetics of the Total Artwork*. Baltimore: Johns Hopkins University Press, 2011, p. 75. For a chronological and thematic discussion of the term, see Danielle Follett and Anke Finger, "Dynamiting the Gesamtkunstwerk," p. 10.
3 Danielle Follett and Anke Finger, "Dynamiting the Gesamtkunstwerk," p. 7 and Lebbeus Woods, *Gesamtkunstwerk*, September 7, 2010, http://lebbeuswoods.wordpress.com/2010/09/07/gesamtkunstwerk-2/ (accessed September 6, 2011).
4 Juliet Koss, *Modernism After Wagner*. Minneapolis: University of Minnesota Press, 2010, p. 11; and Danielle Follett and Anke Finger, "Dynamiting the Gesamtkunstwerk," pp.1-2.
5 Matthew Wilson Smith, *The Total Work of Art: From Bayreuth to Cyberspace*. Routledge, 2007, p. 14; Olivier Schefer, "Variations on Totality," in: Anke Finger and Danielle Follett (ed.), The Aesthetics of the Total Artwork. Baltimore: Johns Hopkins University Press, 2011, pp. 29-51; and Juliet Koss, *Modernism After Wagner*, p. 11. For my analysis of the political relevance of the total work of art today, I am indebted to the discussions of the aesthetic and political dimensions of the concept in the historical and cultural studies by Smith and Koss cited throughout.
6 Smith, *The Total Work of Art: From Bayreuth to Cyberspace*, pp. 3, 11-14.
7 Ibid. pp. 3, 8; and Koss, *Modernism After Wagner*. p. 27.
8 Smith, *The Total Work of Art: From Bayreuth to Cyberspace*, p. 1-8; Koss, *Modernism After Wagner*, p. 13; and Olivier Schefer, *Variations on Totality*, p. 37. On Wagner's role in the Dresden uprisings see Richard Wagner, *My Life*. Cambridge: Cambridge University Press, pp. 217-448; Curt von Westernhagen, *Wagner: a Biography*. Cambridge University Press, 1981, pp. 137-141; and Koss, pp. 1-9.
9 Richard Wagner, *My Life*, vol. 1. New York: Dodd, Mead and Company, 1911, pp. 515-516 and Smith, *The Total Work of Art: From Bayreuth to Cyberspace*, p. 8.
10 Wagner, *My Life*, vol. 1. p. 522.
11 Richard Wagner, "Art and Revolution," in: *Richard Wagner's Prose Works*. trans. William Ashton Ellis, London: Kegan Paul, Trench, Trübner & Co., 1892, p. 39; and Koss, *Modernism After Wagner*, pp. 14-15.
12 Richard Wagner, "Art and Revolution," p. 35.
13 Ibid, p. 52.
14 Koss, *Modernism After Wagner*, p. 13.
15 Smith, *The Total Work of Art: From Bayreuth to Cyberspace*, pp. 3, 11. As Smith explains, Schillers writings suggest that, "the total work of art implies not only an intermingling of art-forms but also an attempt to create an organic synthesis of arts that recovers supposedly original, lost, organic unities: unity of the individual subject, unity of the social body, unity of life and art."
16 Ibid, p. 9.
17 Ibid, p. 3.
18 Ibid, p. 8.
19 Ibid. pp. 8-9; and Danielle Follett and Anke Finger, "Dynamiting the Gesamtkunstwerk," in: Anke Finger and Danielle Follett (ed.), *The Aesthetics of the Total Artwork*. Baltimore: Johns Hopkins University Press, 2011, p. 5.
20 Ibid.
21 Wagner, "The Art-work of the Future," in: Richard Wagner's Prose Works. trans. William Ashton Ellis, London: Kegan Paul, Trench, Trübner & Co., 1892, pp. 201-203.
22 Kant, cited in Olivier Schefer, "Variations on Totality." p. 31.
23 Immanuel Kant, *Critique of the Power of Judgment*. Paul Guyer (ed.), trans. Paul Guyer and Eric Matthews, New York: Cambridge University Press, 2000, pp. 5:216, 101.
24 Ibid. pp. 5:215, 101.
25 Ibid. pp. 5:240, 124; and Henry E. Allison, *Kant's Theory of Taste*. Cambridge: Cambridge University Press, 2001, p. 156.
26 James Kirwan, *The Aesthetic in Kant: A Critique*. London: Continuum, 2004, p. 16; and Tamar Japaridze, "The Kantian Subject: Sensus Communis, Mimesis, Work of Mourning." (Albany: State University of New York Press, 2000), 72.
27 Kant, *Critique of the Power of Judgment*, 5:238 and Tamar Japaridze, "The Kantian Subject: sensus communis, mimesis, work of mourning." p. 89. See also Hannah Arendt, *Between Past and Future*. New York: Pengiun Books, 1993, p. 222; and Harald Pilot, "Kant's Theory of the Autonomy of Reflective Judgment as an Ethics of Experiential Thinking." Nous 24, no. 1, March 1990, p. 111-135.
28 Kant, p. 176; and Ronald Beiner, "Interpretive Essay," in: Hannah Arendt, *Lectures on Kant's Political Philosophy*. Ronald Beiner (ed.), Chicago: University of Chicago Press, 1992, p. 120.
29 Smith, *The Total Work of Art: From Bayreuth to Cyberspace*. p. 12.
30 Friedrich Schiller, *Aesthetical and Philosophical Essays*, vol. 1. Nathan Dole (ed.), Boston: Francis A. Niccolis & Company, 1902, pp. 108-109. See also Smith, *The Total Work of Art: From Bayreuth to Cyberspace*, p. 13-14.
31 Smith, *The Total Work of Art: From Bayreuth to Cyberspace*, p. 9.
32 Danielle Follett and Anke Finger, "Dynamiting the Gesamtkunstwerk," in: Anke Finger and Danielle Follett (ed.), *The Aesthetics of the Total Artwork*. Baltimore: Johns Hopkins University Press, 2011, p. 11.
33 Smith, p. 72; and Robert Kaufman, "Singin' in the Marxist Rain," in: Anke Finger and Danielle Follett (ed.), *The Aesthetics of the Total Artwork*. Baltimore: Johns Hopkins University Press, 2011, p. 341. As Smith writes, "Brecht has long been understood as Wagner's foil, his *Verfremdungseffekt* ("estragement effect") the very antithesis of the *Gesamtkunstwerk*."
34 Smith, *The Total Work of Art: From Bayreuth to Cyberspace*. pp. 4, 75. Smith argues Brecht's "openly divided and critical mixture of the arts" could still be deemed "a Gesamkunstwerk."
35 Koss, *Modernism After Wagner*. p. 12 and Danielle Follett and Anke Finger, "Dynamiting the Gesamtkunstwerk," pp. 2; 8-10; 13. Koss dis-

cusses the relevance of the Gesamtkunstwerk to modernism, and argues that, "notions of artistic purity, autonomy, and medium specificity were central to Wagner's initial formulation of the Gesamtkunstwerk in 1849." Follet and Finger argue that the total work of art, "forms one pole of the recurring debates on the autonomy of media and on the relation of art to life."

36 Koss, *Modernism After Wagner*. p. 22.

37 Johanna Drucker, *Sweet Dreams: Contemporary Art and Complicity*. Chicago, IL: University of Chicago, 2005, p. 62.

38 Leon Trotsky, *Literature and Revolution*. William Keach (ed.), Chicago: Haymarket Books, 2005, p. 142.

39 David Hopkins, *Neo Avant-Garde*. Amsterdam: Editions Rodopi B. V., 2006, pp. 4–5. See also Boris Groys, "Critical Reflections," in: Art Power. Cambridge: MIT Press, 2008, pp. 111–113.

40 Peter Bürger, *Theory of the Avant-Garde*. Micheal Shaw (trans.), Minneapolis: University of Minneapolis Press, 1984; David Hopkins, *Neo Avant-Garde*; and Hal Foster, *The Return of the Real: The Avant-garde at the End of the Century*. Cambridge: MIT Press, 1996, p. 56.

41 See the discussion of the, "transgression of the borders between art and life" proposed by the *Gesamtkunstwerk* in Danielle Follett and Anke Finger, "Dynamiting the Gesamtkunstwerk," p. 4. Follet and Finger write of the three aspects of the total work of art: the aesthetic, political, and metaphysical.

42 See Danielle Follett and Anke Finger, "Dynamiting the Gesamt-kunstwerk," p. 12-15; and Ivanka Stoianova, "*Gesamtkunstwerk* and *Formelkomposition*: The Formal Principles of the Multiple Work-Totality in Karlheinz Stockhausen's *Light*" in: Anke Finger and Danielle Follett (ed.), *The Aesthetics of the Total Artwork*. Baltimore: Johns Hopkins University Press, 2011, p. 346-369.

43 Lionel Trilling, *The Liberal Imagination*. New York, NY: New York Review of Books, 2008, p. 103.

44 Carolyn Christov-Bakargiev with Daniel Baumann, Barbara Casavec-chia, Anselm Franke, Anthony Huberman, Raimundas Malašauskas, and João Ribas. "Entangled Positions." Mousse 29. Summer 2011, pp. 114-120.

45 Here I am borrowing the phrase from Reinhold Martin in, "Financial Imaginaries: Toward a Philosophy of the City," in: *Grey Room* 42. Winter 2011, p. 62.

46 Miwon Kwon *One Place After Another: Site-Specific Art and Locational Identity*. Cambridge: MIT Press, 2004, p. 12.

47 Drucker, *Sweet Dreams: Contemporary Art and Complicity*, p. 21

48 Sven Lutticken, *Idols of the Market: Modern Iconoclasm and Fundamentalist Spectacle*. Berlin: Sternberg Press, 2009.

49 Some of the better-known examples include the dismissal of Jack Persekian, Artistic Director of the Sharjah Biennial, the removal of David Wojnarowicz's work from an American exhibition on sexual difference, the defacement of a photograph by Andres Serrano in France, and the detention of Ai Weiwei in China.

50 Richard Wagner, "Art and Revolution," p. 53.

<u>Klaus Auderer</u>
Groundzerosystems: Baghdad 2003, Phnom Penh 2005

In his artistic research Klaus Auderer uses photography in order to acquire the specific "culture of images" in connection with political, religious and social conflict situations. The result is less a photo atlas-like documentation of the topographically concrete conflicts, but rather an attempt of a higher-level search of traces to figure out why global intercultural life forms seem impossible. Part of his artistic work is dedicated to the visual rhetoric of war documentation, which his photographic works reflect. He probes the images conveyed in the media with a certain directness using concrete war events, which he enforces in *Reisen in Krisengebiete in Europa, Afrika und Asien* by his own physical presence and contradicts with broadcast images. When he correlates Ground Zero and Baghdad, Auderer rather aims at examining how Western and Arabic media have interpreted the respective political systems. With his photographic encyclopaedia of terror, Auderer harbours the utopian desire for the establishment of thinking processes in favour of global life forms without any abuse by cultural or political identities. **HK**

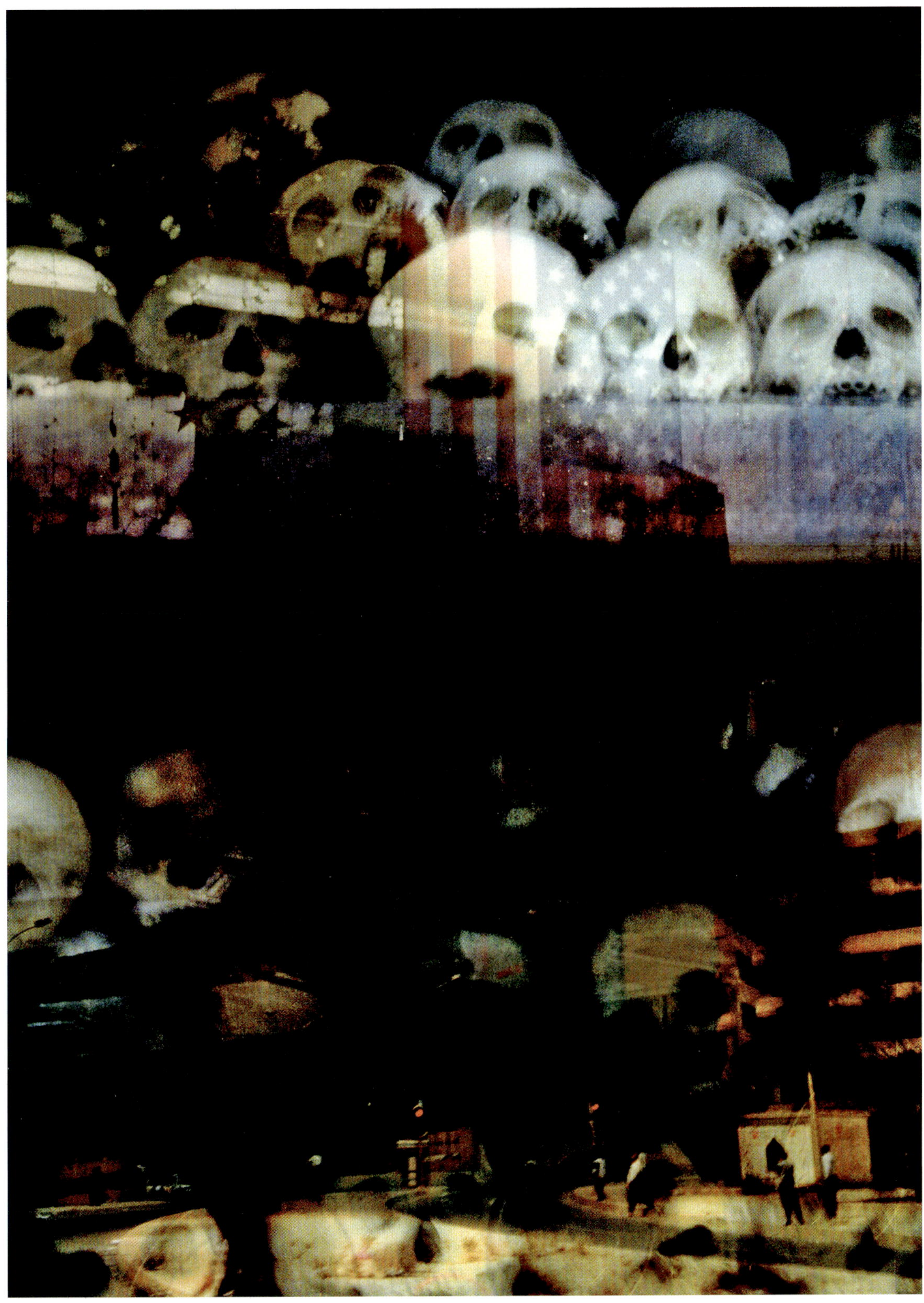

<u>Joseph Beuys</u>
7000 Eichen, 1982–1987
Documentation

"I wanted to go public and make a symbolic start for a project regenerating people's lives inside the body of human society, and in this context preparing a positive future." (Joseph Beuys)

On the occasion of documenta 7 in Kassel in 1982 Joseph Beuys, supported by the Dia Art Foundation, placed 7,000 basalt blocks in a gigantic wedge-shaped triangle on Friedrichsplatz in front of the Museum Fridericianum with the motto, *7000 Eichen – Stadt-verwaldung statt Stadt-verwaltung.* Anyone who donated 500 Deutschmarks could remove one basalt block and plant an oak tree in its place, which was then accompanied by the corresponding boulder. The project was coordinated by the Free International University (FIU) whose tasks included financing the project, gaining approval for the trees, and planning and realizing their planting.

Afterwards, the "Verein 7000 Eichen" was founded, which has maintained responsibility for the project. The art work, which was categorized as a "social sculpture," not only permanently effected the topographic and social structure of the city, but also obliges the spectator to actively participate, and has remained operative until today. Ecologic, economic, philosophical and aesthetic aspects have merged and necessitate a permanent theoretical discourse around this artwork. Beuys regarded his project as a healing process for the urgent problems of his day. Furthermore, the process that culminated in this "social sculpture" was a test of the expanded term of art he had long been preaching. **BS**

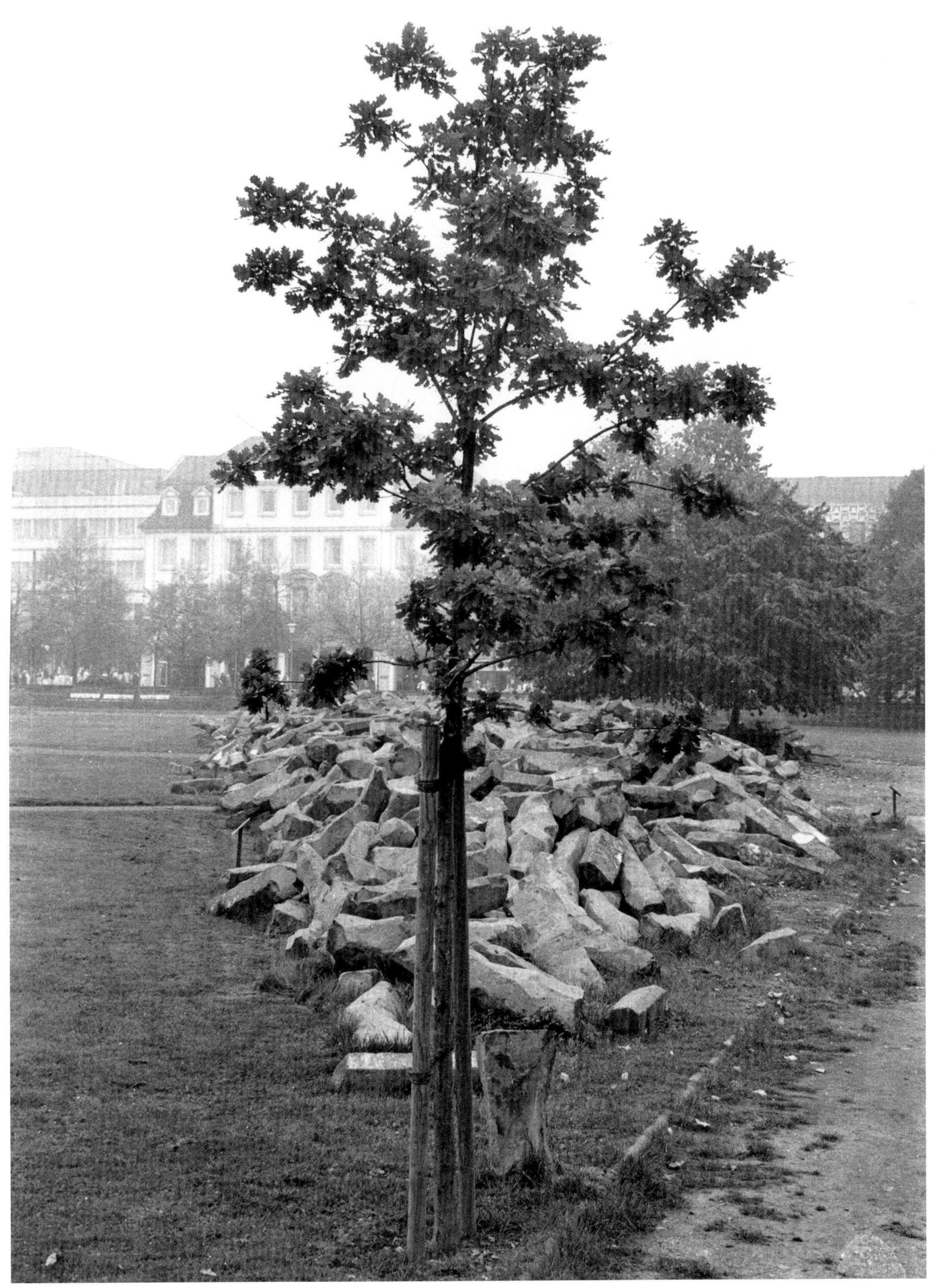

Monica Bonvicini
We Finally Built Walls, 2010

The installation *We Finally Built Walls* was first shown in 2010 at the Museum Fridericianum in Kassel. Bonvicini referred explicitly to the history of the building: The Museum Fridericianum has always been an important exhibition space for the documenta. Regarding documenta 7 (1982) its artistic director Rudi Fuchs, who focused the show on painting, stated as follows: "I feel that the time one can show contemporary art in makeshift spaces, converted factories and so on, is over. Art is a noble achievement and it should be handled with dignity and respect. Therefore we have finally built real walls."[1] The safety glass panels used for *We Finally Built Walls* were taken from the built-in skylight of the Vienna Secession. The Museum Fridericianum is considered to be the first building in Europe that was planned as a public (art) museum, while the Secession building in Vienna is regarded as the first "White Cube." Thus, *We Finally Built Walls* refers to the architecture and vision of two milestones in European art history. It also refers to the *Gesamtkunstwerk* that is closely connected to the Secession in Vienna. On the glass panels Bonvicini painted quotes of well-known architects, artists and poets like Anthony Vidler, Louise Nevelson, Anne Sexton and Ayn Rand which related to a discontent with spaces at large. **BS**

1 **Douglas Crimp, "The Art of Exhibition" in: *On the Museum's Ruins.* Cambridge, 1993, p. 240.**

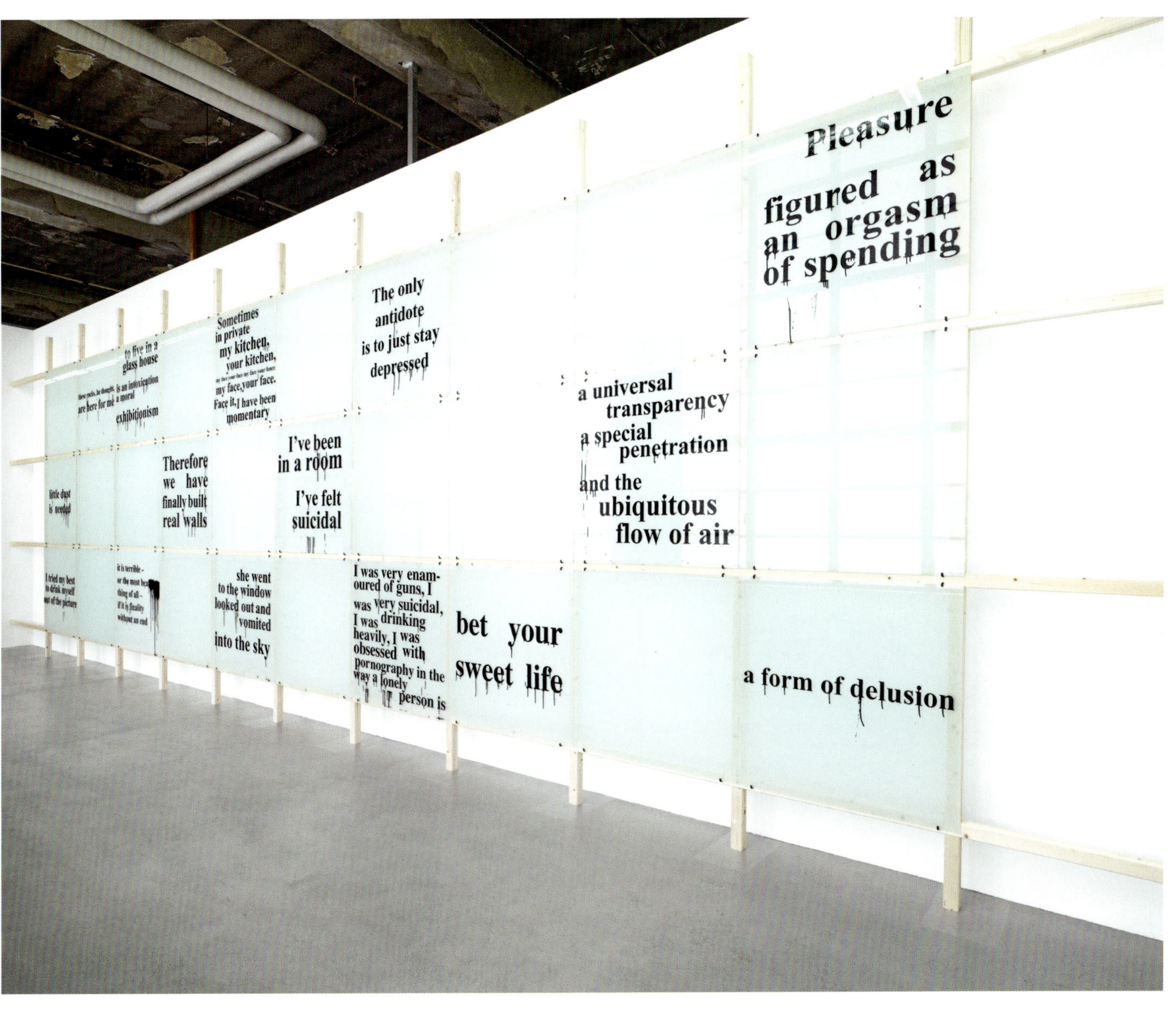

to live in a
glass house

Sometimes
in private
my kitchen,
your kitchen,
my face, your face.
Face it, I have been
momentary

The only
antidote
is to just stay
depressed

Pleasure
figured as
an orgasm
of spending

these rocks, he thought, is an intoxication
are here for me a moral

exhibitionism

a universal
transparency
a special
penetration

and the
ubiquitous
flow of air

little dust
is needed

Therefore
we have
finally built
real walls

I've been
in a room

I've felt
suicidal

I tried my best
to drink myself
out of the picture

it is terrible –
or the most beautiful
thing of all –
it is a finality
without an end

she went
to the window
looked out and
vomited

into the sky

I was very enam-
oured of guns, I
was very suicidal,
I was drinking
heavily, I was
obsessed with
pornography in the
way a lonely
person is

bet your
sweet life

a form of delusion

<u>Marcel Broodthaers</u>
Musée d'art Moderne, Départment des Aigles, 1969

Marcel Broodthaers' *Musée d'art Moderne, Section XIXième Siècle* was a fictional museum from September 17, 1968 until September 27, 1969. It was situated at the ground floor of Broodthaers' home at Rue de la Pépinière in Brussels, in the room, which used to be his art studio, where Broodthaers named himself the director.

The room displayed empty art transport crates with signs saying "Fragile" and "Keep Dry" as well as artistic postcards with 19th century covers, lamps and a ladder. At the opening a hauler truck was parked in front of the house. Projecting slides onto a white wall as well as onto a crate rounded off the exhibition. *Musée* was written on the facade of the house, *Departement des Aigles* on the garden wall and *Section XIXième Siècle* on the gate. The exhibition appeared like an empty hull of what is displayed in large museums—the content was only a given reference, e.g. the "Fragile" sign.

Broodthaers questioned the fictionality of his museum without giving an answer though. The reason for founding the museum was the art revolution of 1968, in the course of which also the Palais des Beaux-Arts in Brussels was occupied and the occupying artists could hardly wait to exhibit their works in it. Broodthaers, however, preferred to open his own museum. The fact that Broodthaers continued to live in his house together with his family, moved the social field closer to the artistic field. This scrutiny of the ideology of the museum and its establishment as a venue of discourse was an important extension of the museum space. **NH**

MUSEE D'ART MODERNE
Département des Aigles

Marcel Broodthaers prie

....

de bien vouloir assister à la cérémonie de clôture de la Section XIXe S. du
Département des Aigles, le samedi 27 septembre à 18 h.
Un service d'autocar est prévu pour emmener les invités à Anvers dans les
locaux de A 37 90 89, Beeldhouwersstraat 46, où aura lieu l'inauguration
de la Section XVIIe S. par

Monsieur P. K. VAN DAALEN, Dr. Hist. Art.
Directeur du Zeeuws Museum Middelbourg

R. S. V. P.
30, rue de la Pépinière
Bruxelles 1 - Tél. 02 / 12 09 54

<u>Claire Fontaine</u>
I, 2009

"The destructive character knows only one slogan: Making room; only one activity: clearing. Its thirst for fresh air and open space is stronger than any hatred." (Walter Benjamin)

In their artistic practice the two members of Claire Fontaine examine the condition of political powerlessness, and pose questions regarding the crisis of singularity that seem to shape contemporary life. They experiment with forms of collective production, détournement and the production of various technical devices, that allow for the division of mental and private property. In the piece I, which is placed on a flatscreen on the floor of the exhibition space, one of them experiences the demolition of an iPhone. In this case the work is not about division, but about the destruction of a cultural item that is more than a just a simple technical device.

In his essay *Der destruktive Charakter* Walter Benjamin claims that every revolution needs a certain structure of feeling and affect, because it is only possible to achieve change through passion, which includes aggression. Thus contextualized, destruction becomes an emancipatory act, a positive barbarism that may stress Apple fans, but that also points to the lack of democracy in our methods of communication and one's corresponding involvement. The destruction is almost physically perceptible and shows the relation between the human body and the possibility of a sensible life as manifested within our biopolitical regime. **BS**

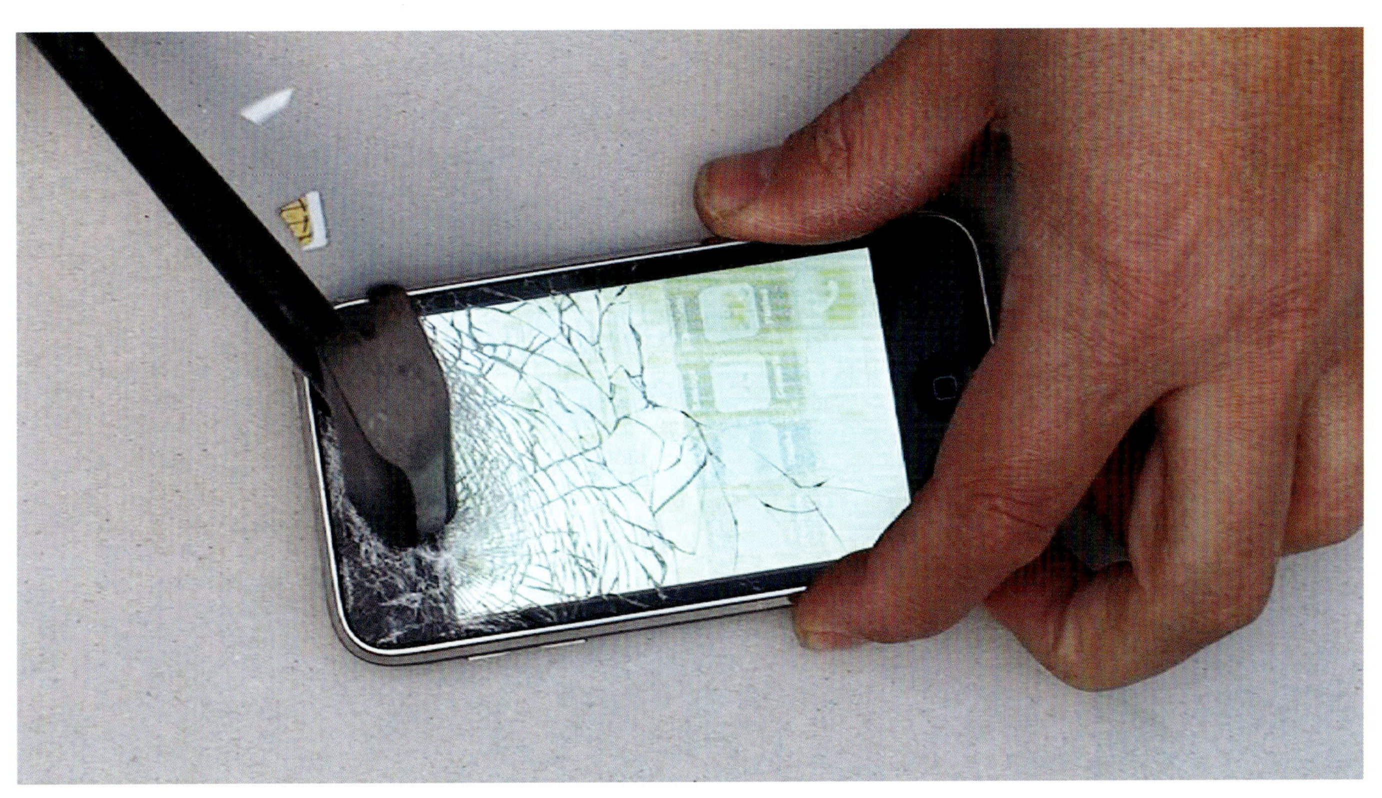

<u>gelatin</u>
***B-Thing**, (from the series: **World Trade Center**), 2000*

On March 19, 2000 between 6:15 and 6:30 a.m., gelatin exited their studio on the 91st floor of the World Trade Center (WTC) in New York onto a self-constructed and self-installed balcony. The structure was made of wood and just large enough to hold one person. After this inspection the balcony was dismantled and the facade replaced. Unnoticed by the public, gelatin realized this project that could only be planned and carried out in top secret. First, the building materials had to be smuggled past security and into the building. Their activities had to go undetected, not least of all by co-scholars in other ateliers. With their carpentered makeshift balcony, gelatin countered the perfectionism and powerful architecture of the WTC, affirming provisional, simplicity and risk-taking. Previous research conducted by the artists had shown that the public sculptures on the grounds of the WTC not only served as aesthetic superelevators of public space, but also as disguised roadblocks that could fight off attacks by terrorist groups. Thus, in the course of an art project based on distraction and deceit, it became apparent that the art at the WTC building already served this purpose of deception and camouflage. Stopping terrorist access to the building by disguised art found a disarming counter-image in gelatin's approach that was only reinforced by the terrible events of 9/11. **BS**

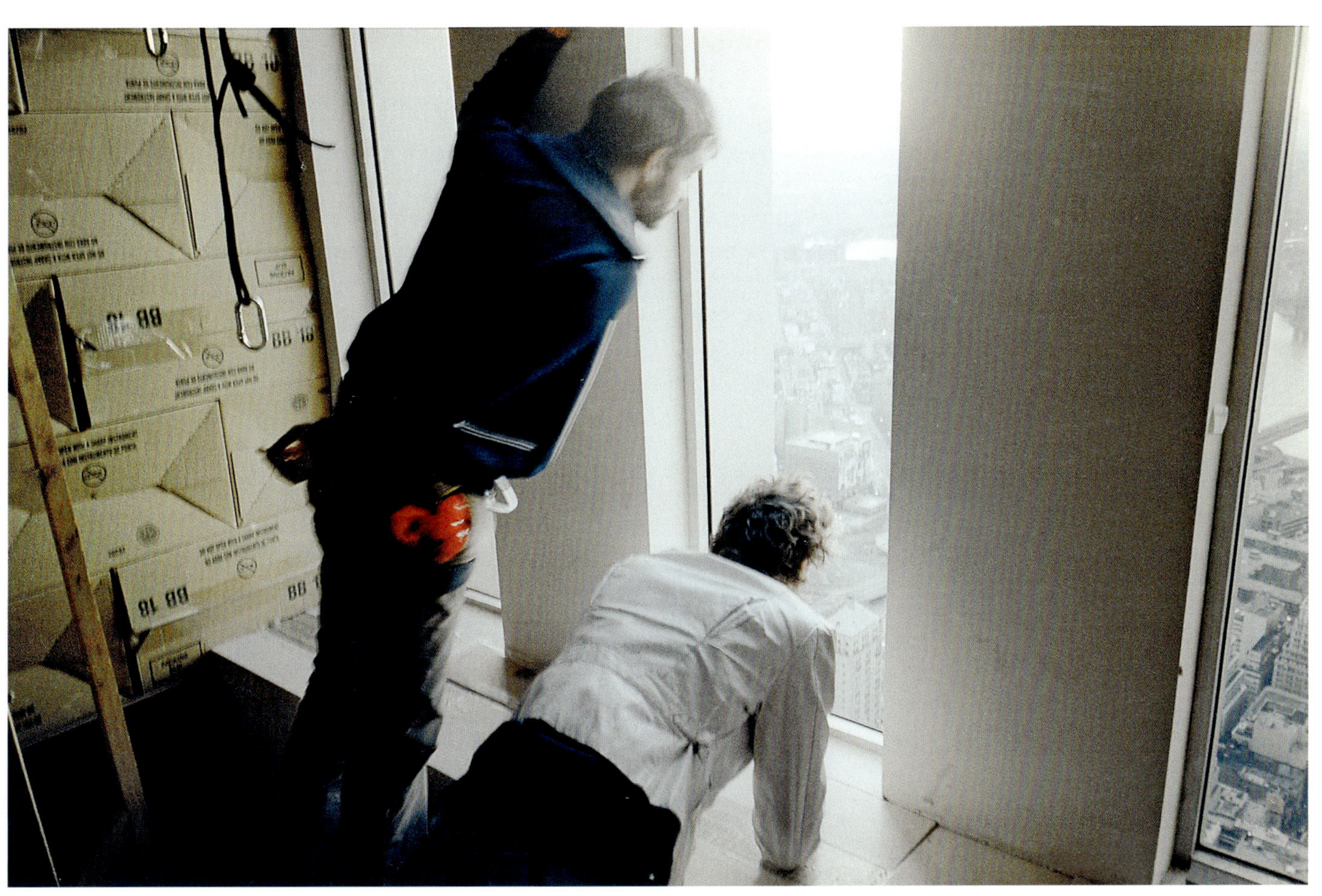

Isa Genzken
empire vampire III, 19, 2004

empire vampire III, 19 is part of Isa Genzken's *empire vampire* series that she created after 09/11. It is a narrative of the complexity of those events as well as of an apocalyptic scenario and its media presentation: *empire* stands for the Empire State Building and *vampire* for the Chrysler Building, both in New York, which are now once again numbers one and three in the ranking of the city's tallest buildings.

The many different perspectives from which her piece can be looked at are reflected in the mutability and diversity of the materials utilized and are further enhanced by the repeated use of components within the series: toy figures, plastic objects, and industrially manufactured goods. The combination of a.o. valuable glass products, plastic fantasy figures and white paint abstracts from the context to create a new one, which unites everything on the level of a waste heap. The bucket of the world as a treasure chest and as a place of shifting perspectives: Isa Genzken regards this series—as she does her film productions—as a forum to examine critically from various angles and create new scenes from combinations of different "shots".

Similar to B-movie production, Isa Genzken's *empire vampire* sticks everything together thus thematizing mass consumption, war as a media spectacle and the end of conceptualism. The cinematic scene-likeness of her objects summons the ghost of the very moment in which the shots were taken, and point to either their fore or thereafter: glancing at moment of a certain perspective in the film when it becomes a sculpture again, "THE WORKS SHOULD FUNCTION AS MOTION PICTURES RATHER THAN SCULPTURES." (Isa Genzken) NH

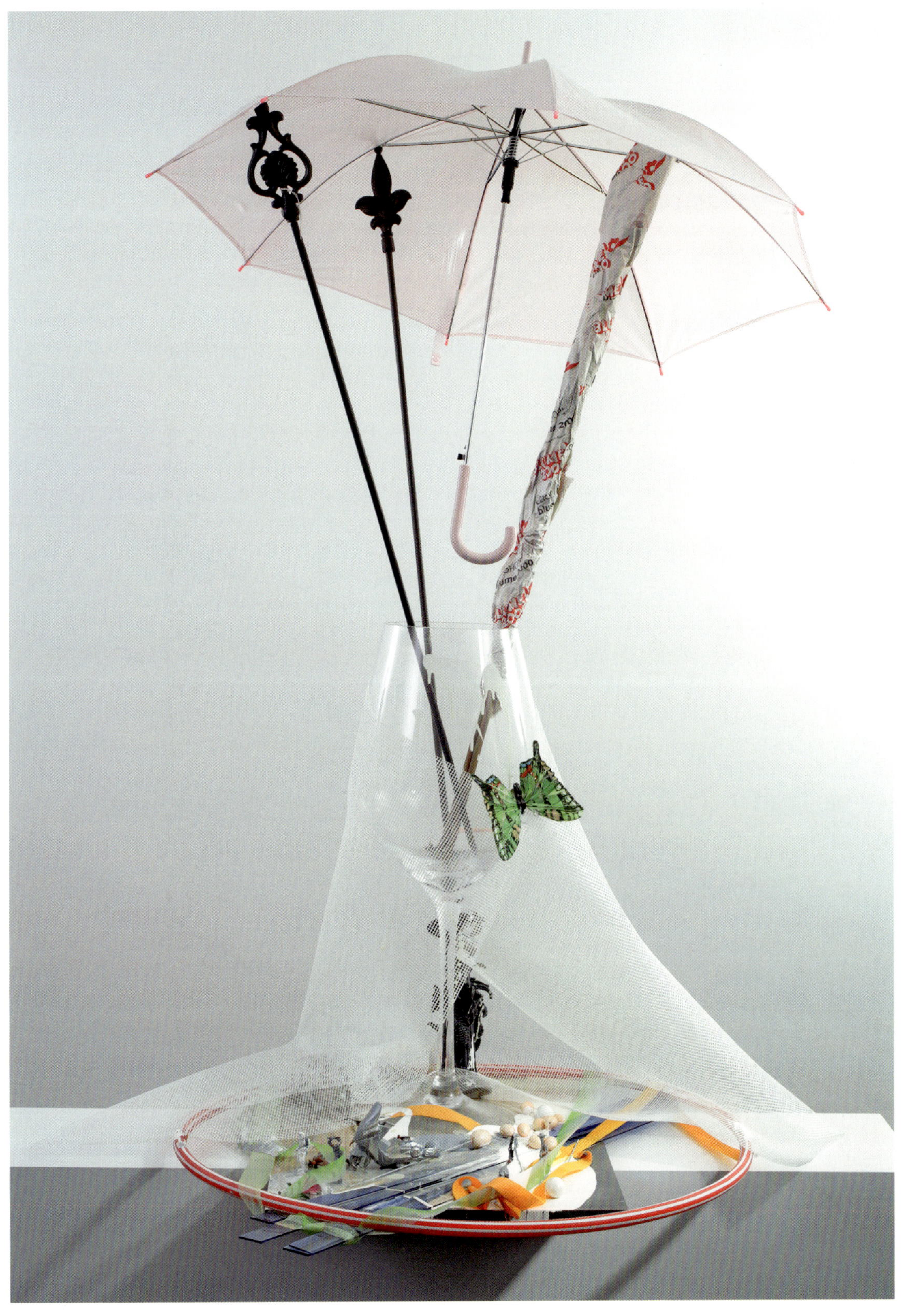

Tillman Kaiser
Innenblick Kirche, 2011

Tillman Kaiser's artwork is characterized by the reassembly of formal and contextual elements and objects in order to create new levels of meaning. For his piece *Innenblick Kirche* the artist placed a model of a church on a fish trap. Instead of windows the building has eye-shaped holes that allow for different views of the interior. The fish trap serves as the building's foundation. The use of the term "fishing" alludes to the apostles who, as the first representatives of Christianity, are referred to in the gospel of Matthew as "fishers of men." The church is a massive building founded on human belief. Due to recent negative developments including sexual assault, and a blimpish attitude that has severely damaged the church's image, this beautiful metaphor becomes embittered, and the fish trap's function as a "trap" becomes accentuated.

In this context Tillman Kaiser's piece takes on a highly critical position, and in connection to the concept of *Gesamtkunstwerk* a new approach with other interpretations is possible. The church itself as a building may be understood as a *Gesamtkunstwerk*, as it unites architecture, sculpture, painting and craftwork to form a unit in which they coequally affect and enrich one another—during Mass this unit is expanded by music, and the liturgical actions fill this space with content.

It is interesting that Christianity, and essentially every religion, follows the deep human desire for the unity of a vast, universal whole, an element that is also essential for the *Gesamtkunstwerk*. This is especially true in times of crisis when art confronts the search for unity and the question of how to create new meaning. **VA**

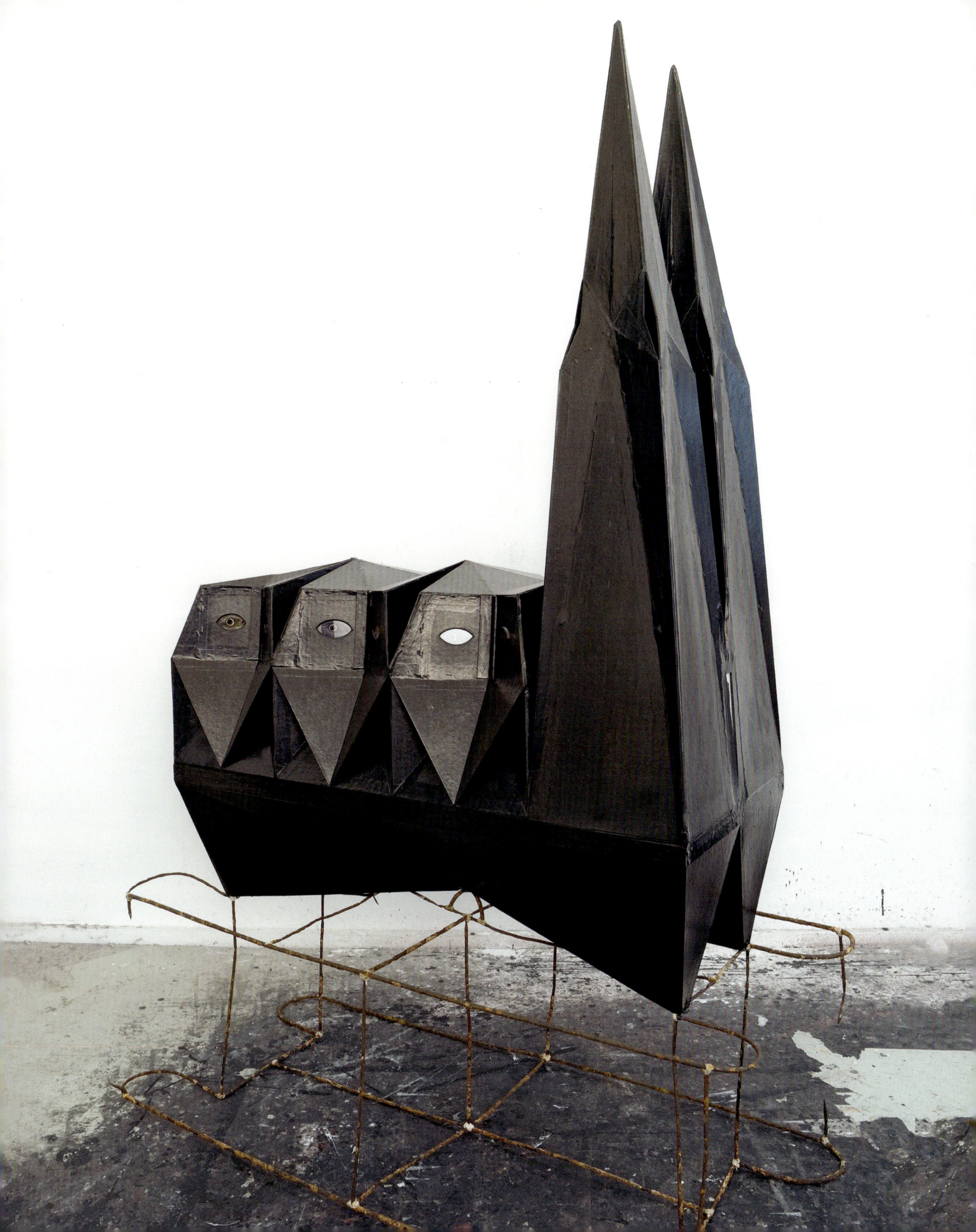

<u>Ian Kiaer</u>
Grey Cloth Project, 2005

London-based artist Ian Kiaer has dealt intensely with topics of architectural modernism in the 1990s. His works are characterised by an artistic interpretation of historic texts and projects, which have essentially shaped the theoretical discourse. Thus, in times of a predominance of the Young British Artists, Kiaer elaborated a subtle and complex reference system, which grants his multi-part installative pieces an approximate character. Starting point of the *Grey Cloth Project* is the novel *Das graue Tuch und 10 Prozent Weiß* by Paul Scheerbart and its interpretation. Based on his protagonist, Scheerbart problematises successful greenhouse architect Edgar Krug—a paraphrase on expressionist architect Bruno Taut—as well as the theoretical problems between architecture and applied arts. Kiaer paraphrases the dispute and translates it using a small hand-crafted architectural model, which again refers to a greenhouse by Bruno Taut. Apart from German expressionist architecture, Kiaer had already dedicated himself to theories of Austro-American architect Friedrich Kiesler in the 1990s. Kiaer was interested in his project *Endless Theater* and the corresponding theory of correalism. **HK**

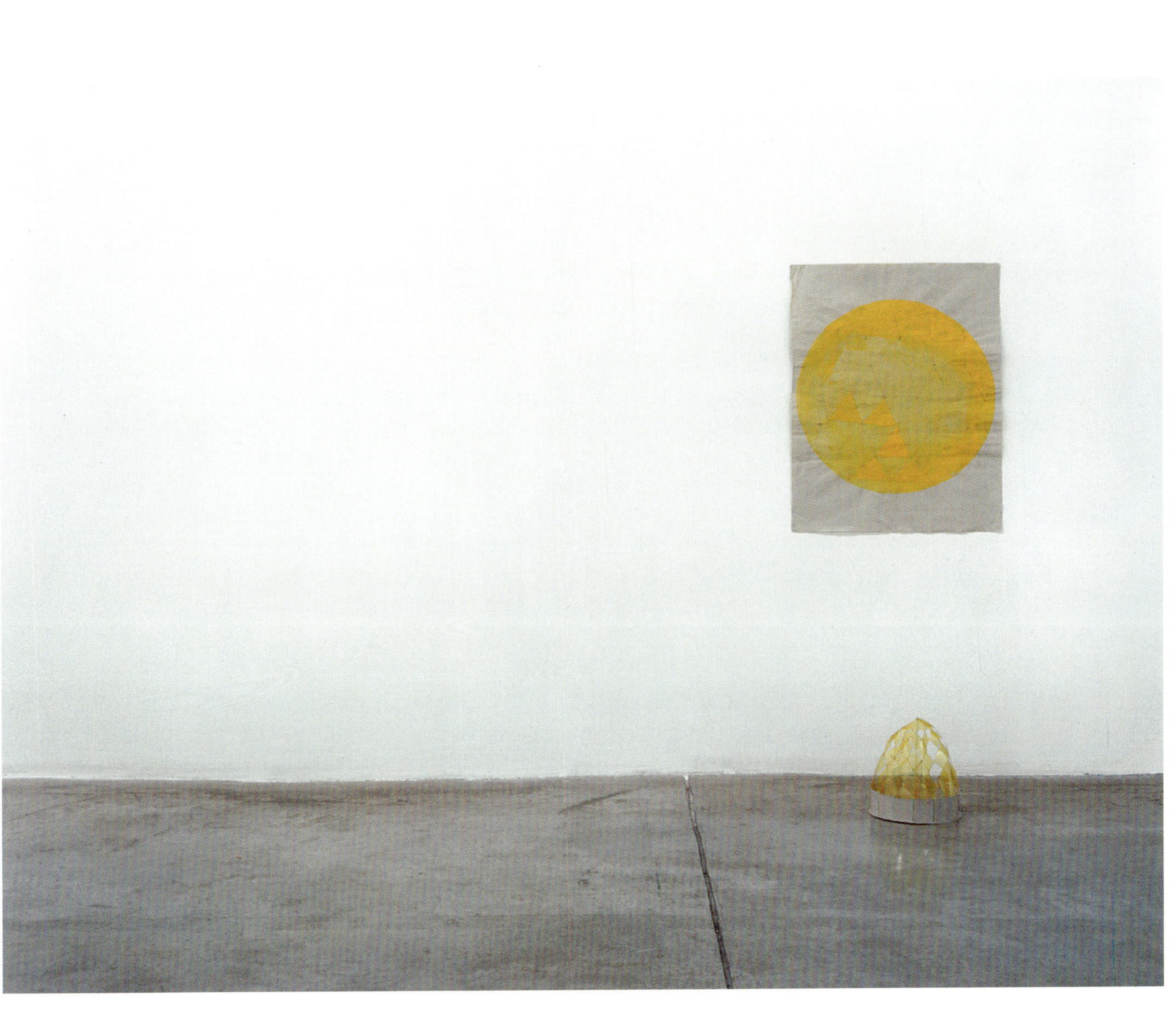

<u>Friedrich Kiesler</u>
***Manifeste du Corréalisme*, 1949**

Friedrich Kiesler's *Manifeste du Corréalisme* from 1949 summarises the studies on architecture, stagecraft and exhibition design he wrote in New York. The exhibition *Le Surréalisme* at the Maeght Gallery in Paris in 1947 released the pulse for this paper. Kiesler was asked by André Breton and Marcel Duchamp to realise their concept of a comprehensively laid out surrealist exhibition as chief designer. Kiesler created the display of the *Salle de Superstition* (Room of Superstition), which he also referred to as "magic architecture". Kiesler staged works by Joan Miró, Marcel Duchamp, David Hare and Max Ernst, produced and erected in Paris under his guidance. Retrospectively, he described his ideas writing: "I am bidding defiance to the mystery of hygiene, which is the superstition of functional architecture, with the reality of magic architecture, which has its roots in the totality of a human being and not in the blessed or cursed aspects of being [...] The new reality of plastic arts manifests itself as an interrelation of facts, which are not based on the perception of the five senses, but also accommodate the mental requirements. 'Modern functionalism' in architecture is dead. As far as 'function' has remained as a remnant—even without an examination of the physical world, which it was based on—it has failed and amounted to nothing more than the mysticism of hygiene and aestheticism."

The term "correalism" is interesting for several reasons. It is an "ism" invented to explain an art theory, which insists on the relation between psychological studies of perception and real-theatrical space and exhibition concepts. It describes a theory based on scientific parameters to gain new spatial-architectonic views. Kiesler has developed this constructive worldview by dealing with function in architecture and the incredible space of thought of the surrealists in the 1920s. In his organic architecture and his surrealist art pieces he worked on the abolition of the contrast between "functional" and "sensory".
Especially concerning the role of exhibition architecture in connection with the surrealist exhibition in Paris it becomes apparent in the catalogue of 1947 that he was focusing on a unity of space, art and display, which was supposed to merge in architecture. That he played an active role in the conciliation of the Gesamtkunstwerk *Ausstellung* (exhibition) as the artistic curator is more than just worth mentioning. **HK**

1 **Friedrich Kiesler, „L'Architecture magique de la Salle de Superstition", in: André Breton/Marcel Duchamp (Hg.),** *Le Surrealisme en 1947,* **Paris 1947, p. 13. Translations from: Dieter Bogner,** *Inside the Endless House,* **1996.**

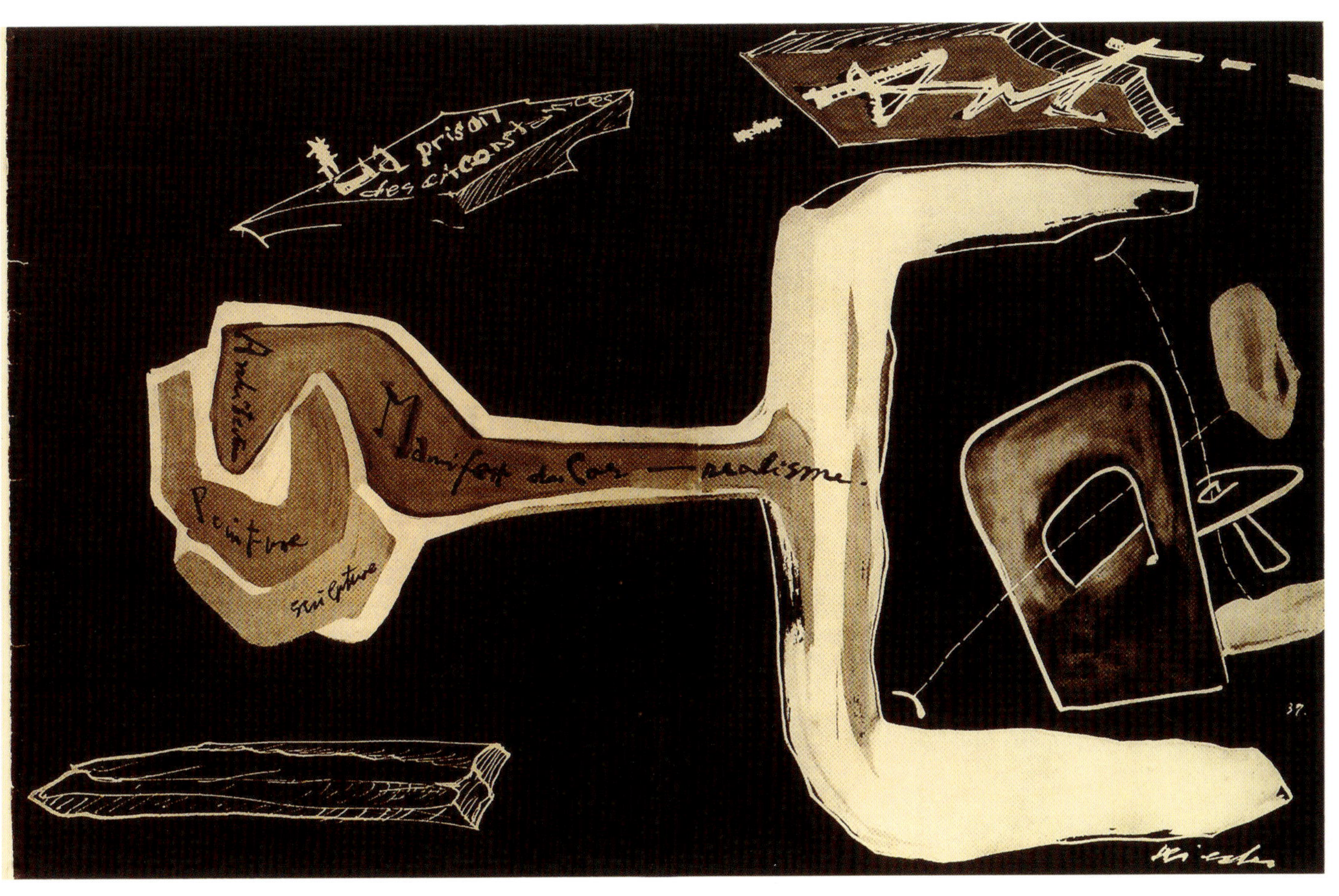
La prison des circonstances
Architecte
Peinture
Sculpture
Manifest du Cor — realisme.
37.

<u>Gordon Matta-Clark</u>
Bronx Floors: Floor Above, Ceiling Below, 1972

In affinity to the works of Robert Smithson, to the concepts of artists like Dan Graham, the theories of the Situationists like Guy Debord and Deconstructivism characterised by Jacques Derrida, Gordon Matta-Clark chose an artistic approach for his work, which radically treats cultural and socio-psychological aspects at the example of, and particularly in the way it deals with architecture. In well-considered formal steps Matta-Clark dissects houses and buildings, unveiling their interior and entering new, sculptural forms. In *Bronx Floors: Floor Above, Ceiling Below* he saws holes into walls and floors of a dilapidated building in the South Bronx, which allow views into the adjacent rooms and the below floor. Matta-Clark pursues culture-critical and socio-historic approaches, mixed with metaphysical ideas. "The gesture of destruction is not the demolition of the given structure, but is derived from the Latin word *de-struere* meaning *grinding off, ablating*. It is thus about a [...] violent, but actually careful removal of surface layers to change the existing structure and thus allow different perspectives [...] Matta-Clark's phenomenally described destructive gestus of cutting in, out and through, however, he also points to the interior mental process, which is not represented in the piece, but can be conveyed—using psychology of perception—as a self-destruction, i.e. an ablating of one's self."[1] BS

1 Matthias Korn, „Ein bescheidener Vorschlag zum Kennenlernen von Architektur: Destruieren. Gordon Matta-Clarks *Building Cuts*", in: *Wolkenkuckucksheim*, Vol. 13, issue 1, May 2009, http://www.tu-cottbus.de/theoriederarchitektur/Wolke/wolke_neu/inhalt/de/heft/ausgaben/108/Korn/korn.php (last called up on Dec 9, 2011).

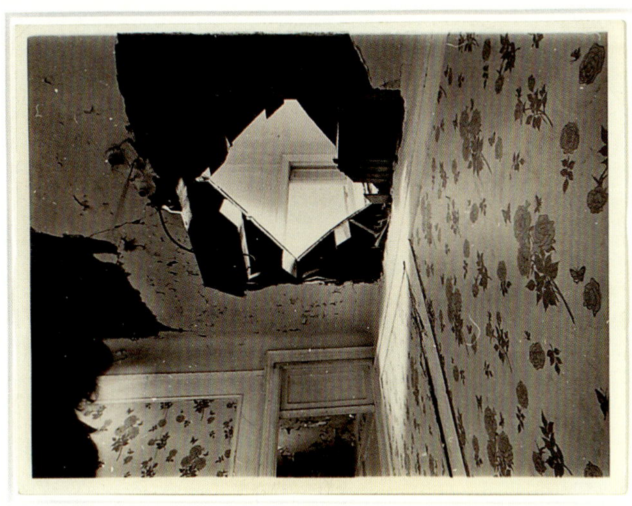

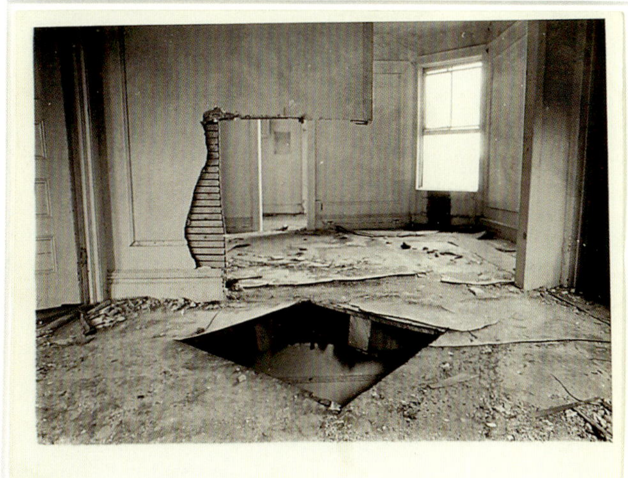

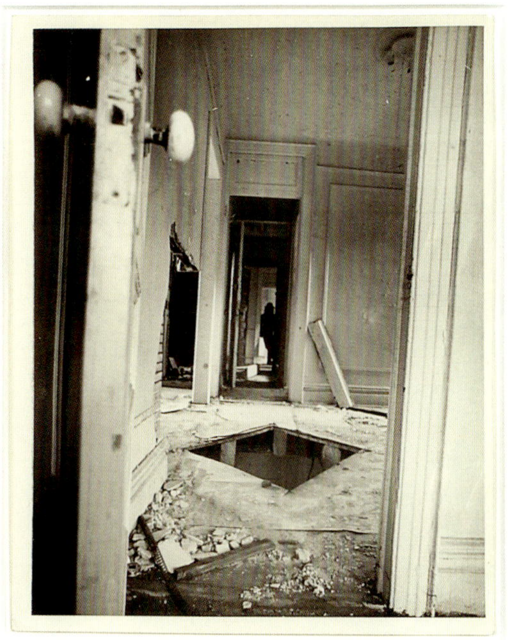

Hermann Painitz
Planierung der Alpen, 1969

In an interview with Rosemarie Schwarzwälder on the occasion of his exhibition in the Vienna Secession in 1975 Hermann Painitz named crucial influencing variables on his art: "My work has, as strange as it may seem to the casual observer, also got Austrian roots. I would like to mention Otto Neurath and his isotypes, and the Vienna method of pictography, which was derived from the language criticism of the Wiener Kreis, into the visual, the coloured." This clear methodological reaction of his art to the fields of linguistics, semiotics and philosophical aesthetics is applied in the concept *Planierung der Alpen*, which deals with the legibility of his paintings as a language and as a temporally linked activity. What Painitz suggests is an act of transformation. But how are nature and culture related to each other? In his work Painitz problematises the artificial interference of man in nature as an act of exemption. Therefore, his definition of resistance against nature incorporates something relieving. "Any form of freedom is a freedom of nature", Painitz writes in his text *Planierung der Alpen* in 1971, also arguing why the separation of technology and art in modern times has rendered this interpretation of the role of art in our society wrongly. According to Painitz art is the basis of any technology. Thus, his project *Planierung der Alpen* is a political work, which attempts to obtain a reunion of technology and art, or in other words, the restoration of the unity of man and society. **HK**

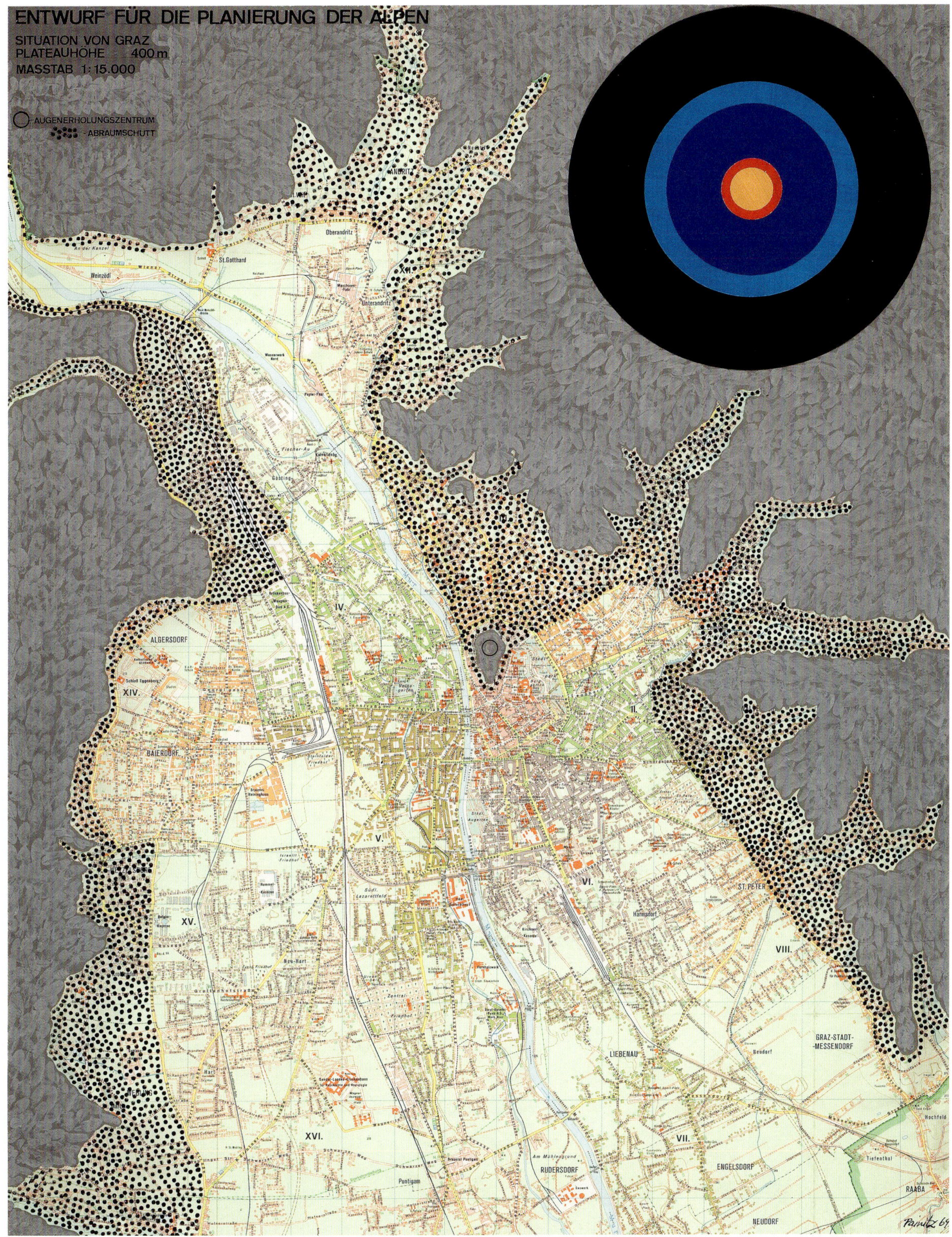

ENTWURF FÜR DIE PLANIERUNG DER ALPEN
SITUATION VON GRAZ
PLATEAUHÖHE   400 m
MASSTAB 1:15.000
-AUGENERHOLUNGSZENTRUM
-ABRAUMSCHUTT

<u>Thiago Rocha Pitta</u>
Heritage, 2007

During the turn of the 19th century German and English Romanticism lent passion and fear to the concept of nature that science had previously restricted to an object of study. The *Heritage* series of films stills shows two trees planted in soil sailing across the ocean on a boat. By "planting" trees in the ocean instead of on land, Thiago Rocha Pitta creates a playful, puzzling scene. He lets the trees drift away on a rolling sea, turning the elements upsidedown, and reminding us that nature is full of mysteries and forces that are at times unimaginable. In our contemporary age of rigid pragmatism and scientific certainty nature has lost all of the mysterious, wild attributes of the sublime that the Romanticists once lionized. Rocha Pitta suggests the sea-faring experience as an early foundation of modernity, and as dependent for its development on natural forces as it is on scientific knowledge. While testing the limits and function of nature this piece develops an inverse logic. It is an organic process and the boat—which usually represents shelter—is a reminder that we are part of nature, of its power, and of the occasional need to protect ourselves from its forces. In Rocha Pitta's work nature and time obtain greater powers, and once the artist has initiated the processes, they continue unobstructed, eventually gliding out of even his control. There is no justifiable center, no possible hierarchy. Thiago Rocha Pitta's work is closely connected to the writings of the novelist and sailor Joseph Conrad. Witnessing the forces of the sea, Conrad developed a deterministic view of the world which he expressed in an 1897 letter, "What makes mankind tragic is not that they are the victims of nature, it is that they are conscious of it […] There is no morality, no knowledge and no hope; there is only the consciousness of ourselves which drives us about a world that […] is always but a vain and floating appearance." **BS**

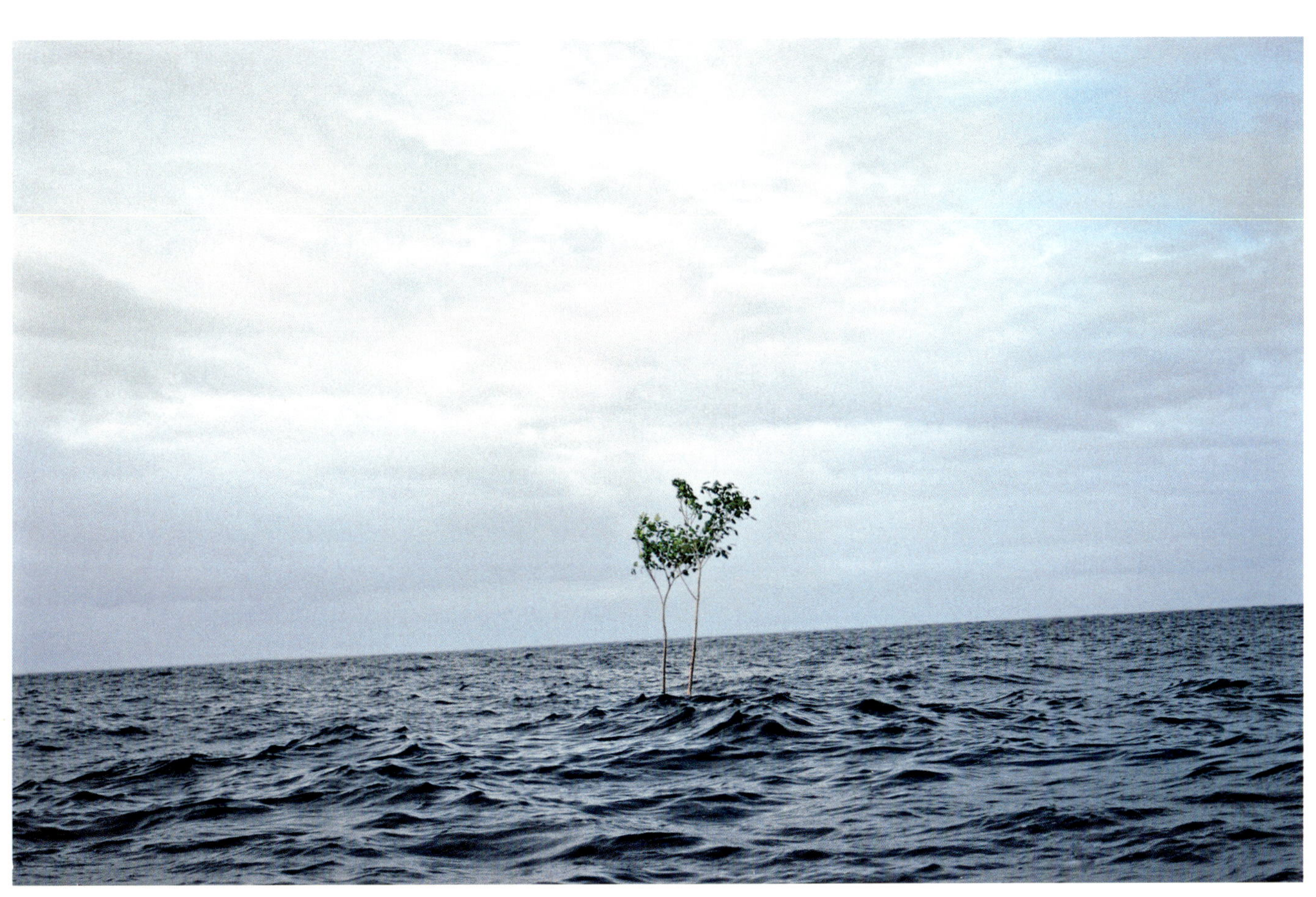

<u>Gerwald Rockenschaub</u>
2002

The work of Gerwald Rockenschaub is the result of an analytical process, which at first was expressed in a cinematic work. Computer-generated cubes topple and fall into a two-dimensional image, slide into the picture and create a contemplative scene, whose effect is enhanced by constant repetition. The formal realisation using the colours black and white can be seen as a reference to the cinematic avantgarde of constructivism and also reminds of Hans Richter's abstract movies. In the piece shown in the exhibition Rockenschaub converts three constellations of the cubes into a room-filling wall surface. The transformation strategy is visible only in the specific exhibition space. Rockenschaub is certainly also interested in a beautiful effect, but his main concern is the analysis of the cultural context. His movie productions undergo certain transformation processes, permanently recording pictorial worlds of different subcultures to evoke an aesthetic of the here and now. Thereby, Rockenschaub integrates elements of mass culture like e.g. the Techno movement of the 1990s, which are crucial impulses to the artist. If the Techno movement is interpreted as a form of Gesamtkunstwerk in the sense of "total" enactment, Rockenschaub's references to club culture represent the same critical reflections as they had been discussed in avantgarde film or minimal art. It also provokes to question the own artistic self-conception once again. **HK**

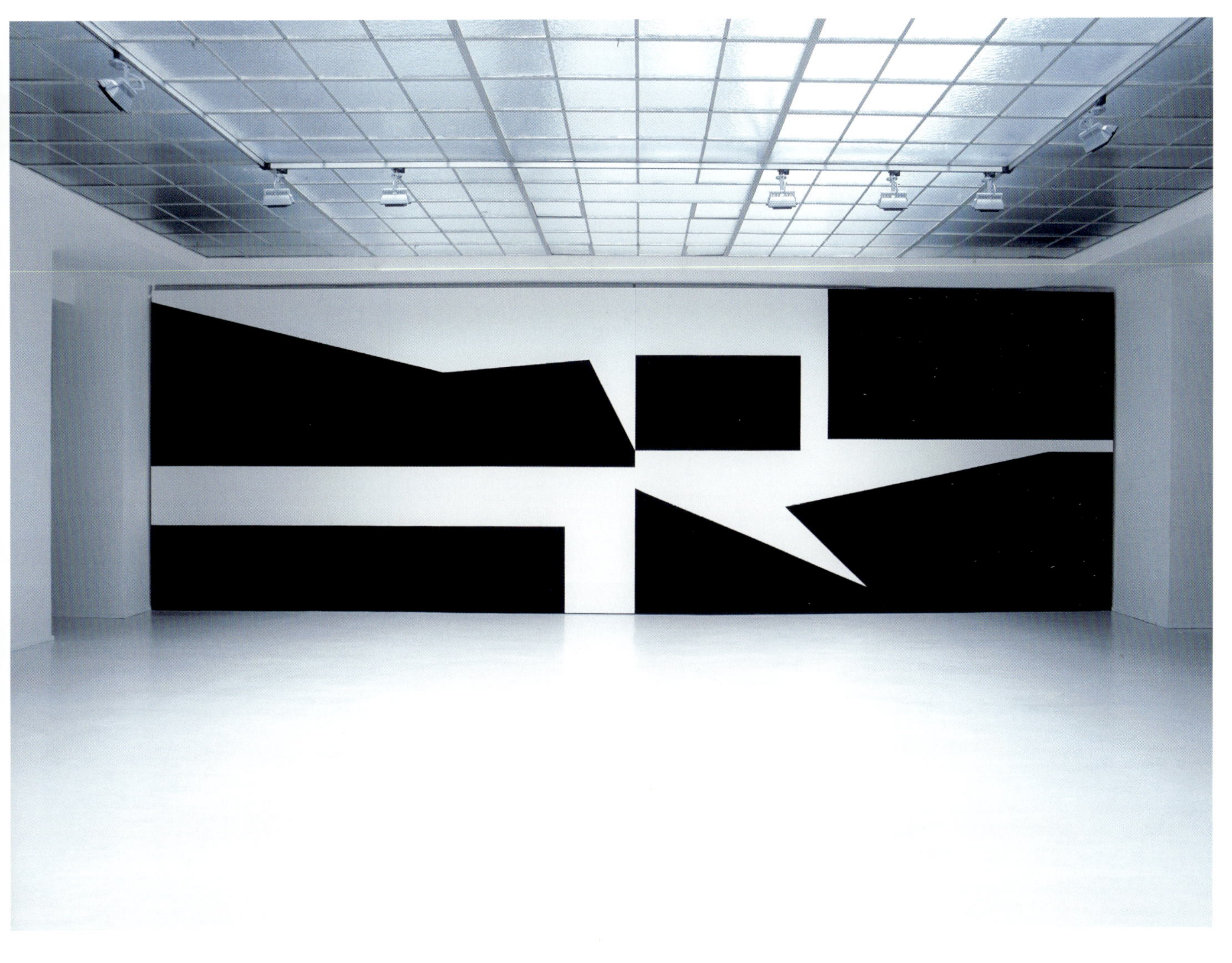

Peter Weibel
Das gequälte Quadrat, 1976

The installation *Das gequälte Quadrat* by Peter Weibel supplied the title for the 4th Buchberger Kunstgespräch (1989), at which the quarrel of the "geometries" in theory and practice, and the terms "constructive, deconstructive and conceptual" were reviewed. Weibel's work fans out the contextual and methodical dimensions of geometrical art and examines the content, ideas, ideals, visions and fears that are related to and illustrated by the simple square form. The design principle of his piece deals with the reality problem of visual perception in the change from two to three dimensions, and thus expresses a constructive artistic concept. The title, which is connoted negatively, a contradiction to the positive world of ideas of the traditional concrete-constructive art—which attaches a positive contextual meaning to all geometrical shapes, and the square in particular—is to be found. To Weibel the contorted square shape symbolizes a breach of the "sacred icon of geometrical design," and at the same time is set against the backdrop of a discussion on the current state of post-constructive art and its various theories. In this piece moreover, Weibel shows that polar opposites need not be resolved, but rather that "debating contradictory situations resp. conditions in a productive interaction characterized by a relativizing scepticism"[1] can prove interesting. **BS**

1 Dieter Bogner, „Das gequälte Quadrat", in: *Kunstforum International*, Vol. 105, January/February 1990, p. 80.

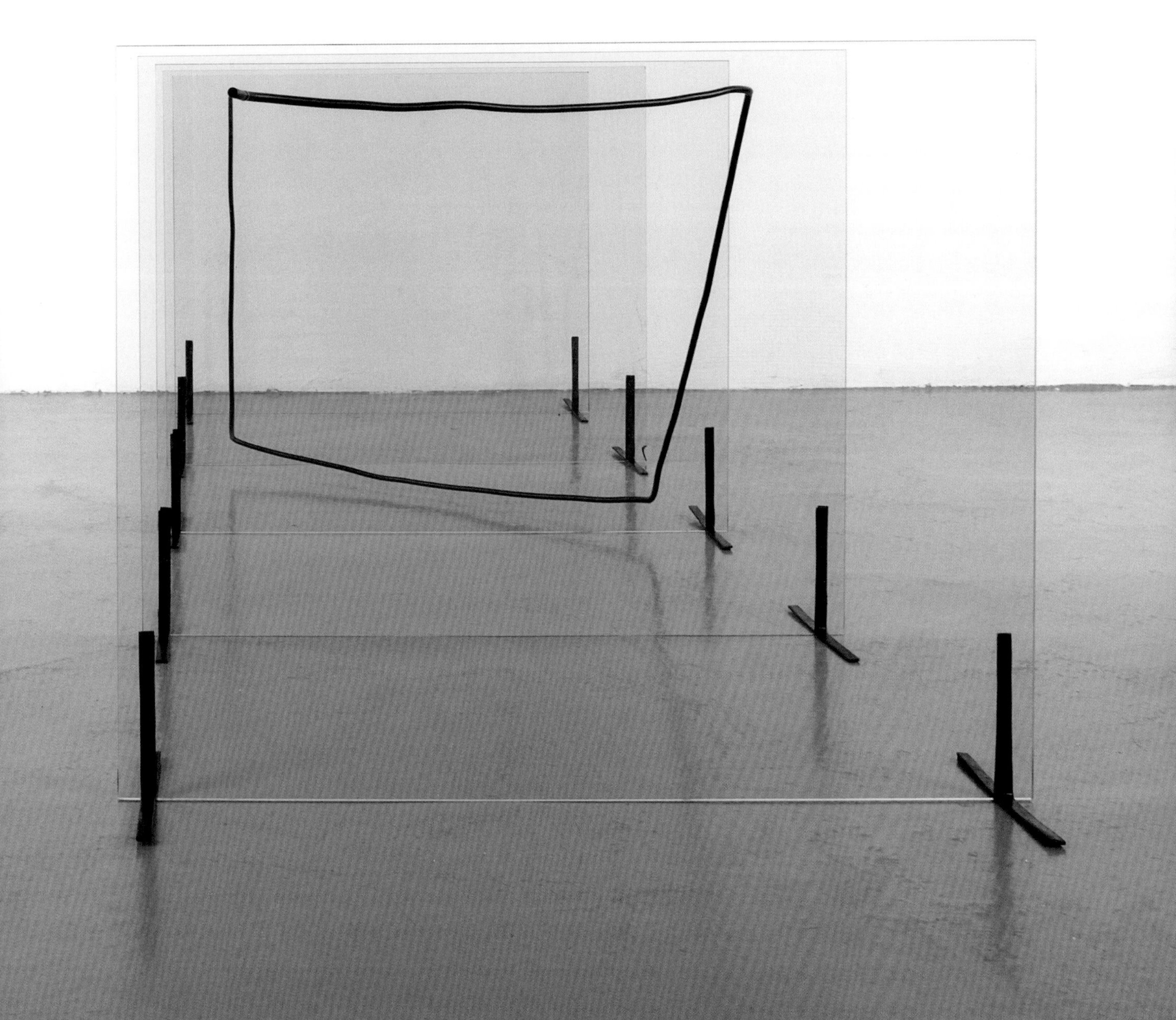

Heimo Zobernig
ohne Titel, 1993

Heimo Zobernig's work is based on the critical analysis of Unité d'Habitation[1] as developed by Le Corbusier. This public housing project, geared toward effectiveness, profitability and functionality, was intended to offer its residents comforts and interiors that facilitated everyday life, thereby perfectly meeting their various demands. The envisioned residence however, proved to be an elusive utopia. The Unité d'Habitation stands at the beginning of an architectural development that has resulted in the barely humane residential and living conditions of prefabricated construction, a form of architecture that conjures the immediate associations with the isolation of its residents and which fuels rather than quells social conflict.

In 1993, during the course of a project on problems in social and cultural coexistence, Zobernig and a number of other artists were housed in Unité d'Habitation apartments in Firminy. Zobernig turned his apartment into a café that served as a social meeting point. The entrance of the two-floor apartment was connected to the lower living area by a set of stairs. By using the original size of these for his replica, Zobernig quotes this spatial situation, but has reduced the residential unit to its individual elements, and only conceptually outlines its functionality.

Offering his café as a small working nucleus of communicative processes as a reply to the failure of modernism and socially orientated architectural design, he infiltrates the prestigious object of this eventually utopian architectural concept while undermining belief in the progress of modernity with an ironic subversity. VA

1 The Unité d'Habitation (housing unit) is a modern residential housing type that was designed by Le Corbusier as the ideal architectural form to ameliorate the lack of accommodation in post WWII France. The first of five realized blocks of apartments was erected in Marseille between 1947 and 1952. The incorporation of shops, a kindergarten, playground, hotel, theatre, gym and running track into these structures embodied Le Corbusier's ideal of a vertical city.

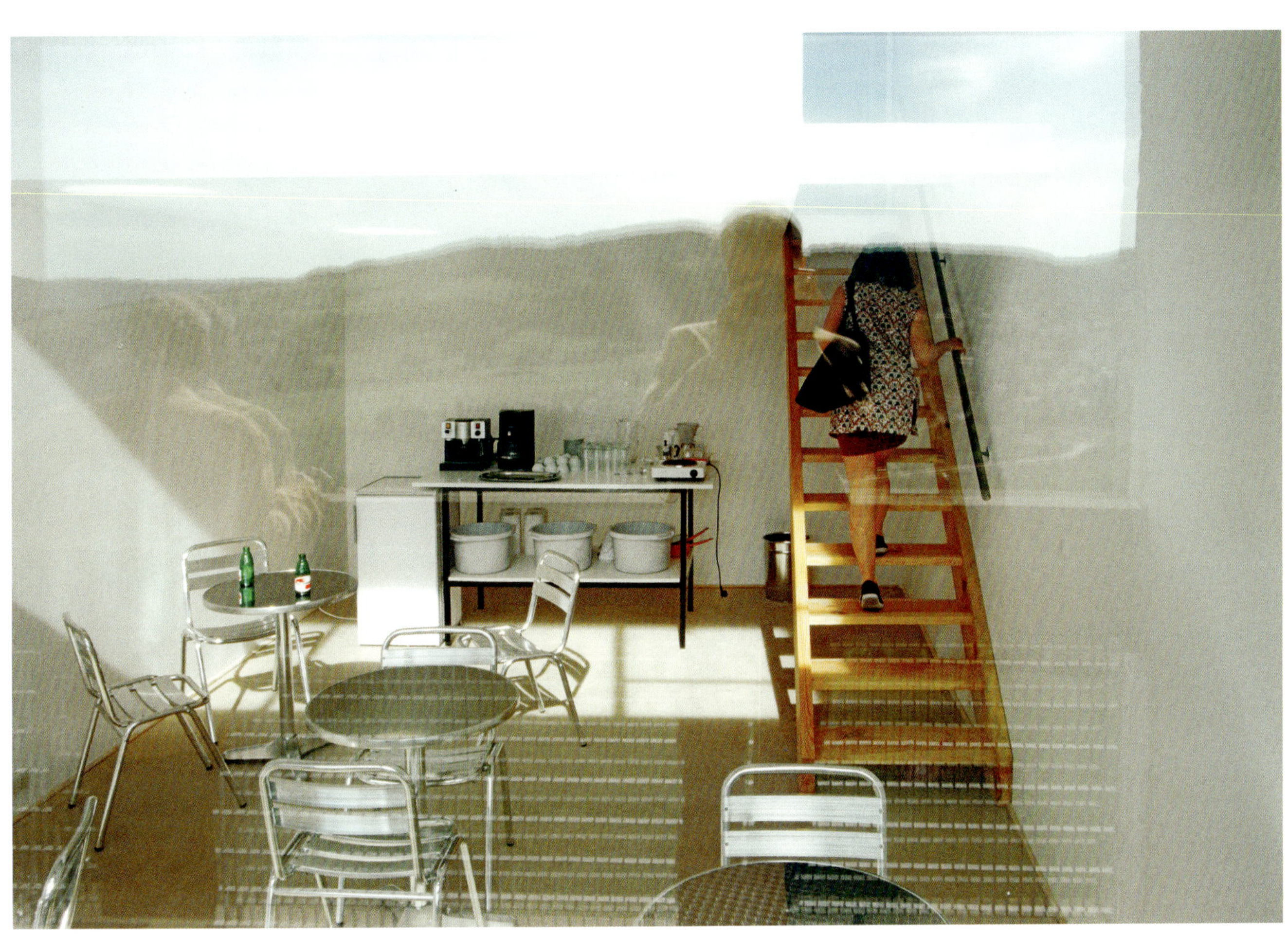

Technology of the Unconsci

ies

us

The Battlefield of Immanence: Psyche and Staginess

Anselm Franke

If there is an obvious clustering of "theatrical forms and strategies" in contemporary art today, it is not about theatre or acting as an art form, which has earned the respect from visual arts. That is by no means the case. What is allegedly currently so interesting about theatrical forms to visual arts are rather the model scenes of the Theatre of the Psyche and the problem of expressed immanence. This immanence really touched the nerve of times, it questions the media constitution of social collectives and it resembles a contemporary experience concerning the performative construction of the self.

Within contemporary visual art, however, every "theatrical situation" is always a quote, a model, an example, or a situation "as such". It is automatically put in brackets and exhibited. The space of visual art has since its radical extension, since the dissolution of the canonical, static forms become a systemic model space, which essentially depends on this bracket function. The effect of this bracket is not always clear, although the production of a utopian universal immanence is a historic constant of its function. This is the quasi-theological horizon of secular modern project "art", the idea of art as a universal language. Earlier versions of this utopia of immanence, as they found expression in the aesthetic autonomy and the demanded overcoming of alienation were now replaced by the steering towards immanent social relations with the "theatrical form" as their medium.

Universal immanence as a utopia of art spaces is a horizon, the attainment of which would be the self conquest of art, like in the hotly discussed fusion of art and life. At the moment of its realisation it would stop just being a model. It is thus this state of art as an art (which is only manifested within the bracket function today), which guarantees that the experience remains unfinished, rather possible than real, and therefore structurally open. In Adorno's work this resembles the formula of art-as-mimesis-without-imperative-for-identification. The aesthetic experience in its framework is thus always characterised by a double movement: becoming immanent in this concrete situation (in the classical sense of the confrontation with a piece) and an abstraction of this situation as a model or a possible scenario. From this abstraction its claim for universality is derived.

The trade cycle of theatrical forms in contemporary art is not least also a consequence of the dematerialisation of an art work. And it reflects, on a broader scale, the shift of a focus on the object to one on the subject. Not the status of the work as an object, but the performative production of subjectivity, its embodiment and its affectual economy are at the centre of attention. The theatrical situation, independent of its particular form, is transformed in art space, which may be called a "subject sculpture"—an interleaving of exhibited and exhibiting subjectivity. It is the tendency to mere performance and pure dialogic process in statues. In this so-called subject sculpture guise and essence concur like in Charcot's scene. Its form is the immanent mediumship of the gesture, because the gesture only consists during its transition from illustration and perception, figure and base, "inside" and "outside", at zero, as a pure possibility or model.

Contemporary art space occupies this zero strategically by superimposing the utopia of immanence in art and the social immanence of subject performance. One may speculate, whether the popularisation of contemporary art in the past few years has been generated from this dissolves of art brackets and subject productions. The art space would then turn into a factory of subject designs and their abstraction. The formula "the more abstract, the more mobile" would generate a hierarchy.

Therefore, the intensive correspondence between contemporary constitution of the subject and of art space was expressed in the trade cycle of theatrical forms. Both can be reduced to the mere bracket function, to an enclosing frame or an encircling, to zero, which expresses its potential as a pure function within a field without boundaries. The bracket "art" corresponds with that of the "self" both are framing and systemic functions. The bracket "art" is enforced by the dialectics of negation and affirmation. Within its systemic coordinates thus any successful negation becomes an affirmation on the next level. Modern art has gone through this process paradigmatically in painting, on the art object and the subject as an author. Its meaning for the extended field, which is only structured by the performance of the bracket functions anymore, has yet to be measured. The same rings true for the subject. The more "universal", the more it becomes a possibility and a medial bracket at zero, presented as a pure possibility. Andy Warhol has epitomised and presented this development exemplarily. Warhol's Factory can be seen as a paradigmatic "scene" to which transformation of art space as well as the self has become a pure "function", at the zero point of affirmation and negation, under "neutral" application of the art bracket. It is a scene of the rediscovery of immanence and its medial function. But it is also a new scene of subject production at the "Factory", showing how the subject bracket is filled or occupied by the performance of a "self".

"Immanence" is a battlefield, in which the fronts are much vaguer than in the transcendences of standard metaphysics. As long as a disciplinary society of confinements was based on standard metaphysics with its categorical subject/object distinction, their rigid categories and exclusions could be attacked with the perspective of immanence, and with this criticism of the dynamic transformative dialogical principle of "living" that everything and above all has always seemingly contained desire. Thus a large part of the intellectual inheritance of modernism, especially if close to aesthetics, can be read like a search for "lost" immanence or an accusation of the existing order, attempting to hinder or to scar it by such exclusions. In the course of the 20th century the worm has turned.

The "discovery" of the unconscious was a decisive step in the claim for immanence. It usually follows two steps: At first constitutive exclusion must be identified and claimed as the missing half of reality, as the negative, which helped positive reality emerge, as its precondition. Complemented by this missing half, reality is converted into a diagramme of dynamic relations. Within the relational diagramme things stop having stable, ultimate identities and instead appear "constructed", as effects and reciprocities. Reality is then not simply "given" anymore, but a dynamic field of powers—and with this change of perspectives understandably vast historic hopes were connected. This dissolution of discrete existences and separations paved the way for the magic words of the 20th century: communication and media.

The terms "media" and "communication" are contemporary heirs of anger with the soul. With these terms the ancient trench warfare could be pacified and the parts of reality, which had been excluded in the name of disciplinary order, were reclaimed. This was made possible by the powerful idea of self-regulated systems, as cybernetics or ecology propagated. A new concept of social immanence under the primacy of communication was born and was expressible in advertisements! Transformed into systems the idea of immanence looses its anarchic terror and opens up unforeseen possibilities for control and production of reality.

This is the story of an ontologic upheaval in which representation, substance, categorical and transcendental thinking of western modernism were replaced by the paradigm of communication and a new systemic immanence claiming that nothing exists outside the relations and processes, in which it is embedded and which form its reality. Performative, relational reciprocity is the new imagination of reality, and the soul automatically looses its status as a sole inner world, it is much more an in between, also in its new radical reductions to a communication code. Intersubjectivity is a typical catchphrase. A large part of the second half of the 20th century is the story of the "discovery" of the prefix *"inter"*, previously excluded middle (*medium*) and their technological disclosure, containment and modulation. If we speak of a crisis of criticism today, it is not least the case, because a large part of the critical theory tends to charge open doors rebelling against old categorical borders by addressing the transcendental subject, the tyranny of patriarchal significants, or essentialism, but by disregarding the reorganisation, the flexibilisation and the technological management of technologies of power under the consent of dissolution and mediumship.

The consent of dissolution, which has established itself in the past four decades, has developed a hegemonial presentation culture, in which the soul is in great demand again. It seems we are closer today to the times before the crucial theological debates, which had once banned the soul from the outside world into the human inside and transcendence, than in the 19th century. For this reason, media theoreticians like McLuhan symptomatically speak of a return of archaise. Its correspondence turns up in the hyper visibility of global immanence, the oceanic under water aesthetics of "Everything is possible" on flat screens, in which communication, movement and dialogue of universal positive are represented. It is aesthetics without the outside, which has replaced the ancient psychological theatre and its boundary staginess. "Soul" now universally serves the "appetite for fervour". In the rebellion against the identificatory disciplinary regime, trying to break free from confinements and institutions, it was the outside of the positive which negated life. The outside doesn't keep any promises anymore, if it is not entirely vanished, it has at least become clinical—because now is the old institutions like the psychiatry, which expect us should we e.g. fail to manage our own psyche. Thus, today nearly everybody wants to be "inside" rather than "outside": into networks, into institutions, into discourse, into life etc. Resistance, and thus also the resistance potential of art, has been deprived of its resources by the development. The phantom limb pains of this containment and acquisition still remain, but the alternatives were cut back: Should we now defend the formerly challenged boundaries and reactionary attitudes? And if so, why and how? By waiving the difference in favour of a performative affirmation?

The remnant in the vast process of becoming systemically immanent is the self, which must be realised by permanent positivisation. The contemporary form of the Theatre of the Psyche is a popularised therapy. This therapy is a process of claiming immanence, the translation of seemingly static, gridlocked reality (patterns of action) into relational diagrams and dialogical reciprocities. But it is also a process of inscribing oneself, the acquisition, the adaption, a new form of conformity, at which the entire responsibility for success is privatised. In this constellation exclusion cannot be sold or sued theatrically anymore. Within systemic immanence ideologically there is no exclusion, because everything is possible inside as long as a "self" is performatively demanded. The only actual exclusion thus concerns a subject in its totality. The pathological form, which resembles this constellation, is depression. Depression is unrealised, failed immanence, in which there is no way out into transcendence.

The historic experience of the last decades has brought a new figure into being: imposed immanence under the conditions of privatisation, which manages the remnants of transcendental subjectivity. The old psychological drama is pacified in the entrepreneurship of the psyche. The subject has a negative attitude towards capitalism: Profits are collectivised, losses privatised.

The vast turf wars are over since psyche was determined as the new inexhaustible resource for exploitation, by making it a legitimate territory of immanence, which is also bracketed by the self—a state which it actually is according to its connection to communication. The stability of this pacification, however, largely depends on the unveiling of its costs—the form of this silence is the contemporary self. The self guarantees indifference of immanence, the pillar of the peace treaty, the signing of which has enabled the new order. The self only exists in its performance, a performance of a framing. As this framing contains all and nothing at the same time, it goes shows that it is the inheritance of the old psychological theatre, which totters in between impotence and almightiness. The self creates its own world: Any self optimisation starts with this realisation. And each realisation in such a self optimisation is aware of its opposite.

Resistance against becoming immanent is lacking the resources today, because the ancient categories and boundary technology are not available anymore, even if one would try mobilising them. The question remains, whether the process of abstraction and excluding dissolution, countering immanence within the art bracket, cannot be turned into a political answer to the production of indifference—as an anti-systemic insistence of incompleteness. Maybe the utopian possibility lies therein to not only negate psychologisation, but even reverse it: Understanding "therapy" actually as a process of the genuine development of subjectivity and of the definition of immanent relations for discussing and constructing their qualitative dimension. An essential precondition for it is handing off the possibility to make implicit conditions subject of negotiation, or to develop a new, inauthentic language of the "self". This would be a language, which is mostly used in the passive voice, and which answers to the omnipresent interpellations and framings mimetically, but "without coercion for identification". Is art still the model space for this idea?

"To remain autonomous, art at some stage started imitating everything that was not autonomous. There was no lack in supply and demand, because power, as we know, can only be applied with the production of truth, otherwise it doesn't work."[1]

The consent of dissolution has since the historic moment of "conceptional reduction" (Jeff Wall) also dominated art history. The modernist paradigm of media specificity was succeeded by today ongoing extension and hybridisation of forms and reference frame. After the so-called immaterialisation of the work by conceptual art, the genre borders were systematically transgressed, which at first manifested itself in the introduction of time-based art genres, in happenings, film, performance, music and the hybrid form of the installation. Parallel another process was launched, in which art turned towards its own frame and background conditions, were these economic, institutional, social or political nature. Critics like Clement Greenberg and Michael Fried saw these dissolutions as something like pollution by mimetic adaptation, submission, or even prostitution, in the context of which Fried reproached "Theatrality", as the ultimate endangerment of autonomy in the canonical modernist media of record. His opponents made an involuntary submission for Fried helping him damage this understanding of autonomy effectively and irreversibly. Hence nothing stood in the way of the entry of theatrical forms anymore.

According to Peter Friedl's argumentation in his quote above, the systematic dissolution has saved autonomy in art in a wider sense. However, it does not lie in the autonomy of the medium, but in its ability to acquire and illustrate everything that does not exist, whilst keeping up the decisive difference, i.e. the bracket "art", the difference of possible model and topicality. Precisely this difference is increasingly in danger resp. is punished with disinterest, because it is a product of a too complex historical constellation and as such blocking the way for an immanent social "scene" on the artistic global stage. Contemporary art, one might argue, increasingly tends to use its mimetic power to acquire everything, free itself from all criticism and capitalise from its adoption ability. The difference produced by the bracket becomes a monster of an abstract, performative imperative for identification. In 2008, Friedl called the relation of art and theatre in a lecture the capitalism "the best contemporary artist", because its abilities of acquisition, adaptation and capitalisation were uncaught. Thus, at the end of dissolution stands mimetic identity, indifference as self-abandonment. If history repeated itself as a farce, Michael Fried would be right. But maybe it is the next transformation of capitalism that helps art out of this "identity crisis".

1 **Peter Friedl, *Der Fluch des Leguans*, Frankfurt/Main 2000.**

Marc Adrian
Großes Sylvesterbild, 1977

His interest in human perception processes and the dynamic procedures between seeing and thinking has led Marc Adrian to the "verre eglomise" montages, which he has started developing in the 1950s. As a scholar of Fritz Wotruba, Adrian dedicated himself to movement in art, creating first logans and mobiles. This early artistic research led to first film productions already in the 1950s, which he extended gradually. But Adrian did not remain formalistic: He expanded his artistic concept by adding language, a symbolic sign language, ethnographic film work and by using pornographic pictorial worlds. These different contextual levels reflect Adrian's criticism of the existing definition of culture and formulate a social criticism, which can only superficially be interpreted as scandalous. His montages of different levels of meaning are complex generators of new realities, which in a certain manner always want to be realistic.

Adrian's work in structural filming is linked to his studies on cognitive psychology. His early works—elaborated in cooperation with Ferry Radax—rank among the pioneering achievements in Austrian abstract film. In his film work, Adrian systematically acquired computer knowledge to generate random fonts as picture compositions. What distinguishes Adrian is his permanent socio-critical interpretation of artistic media, whose relation to each other is questioned by the use of broadcast images. Adrian's theory on methodical inventionism, the methodical idea of the automatization of text and consequently also film and image production, must be seen against the background of the literary opus of the Wiener Gruppe (Vienna group). Adrian thus continued the Viennese tradition of structural methods in artistic work, which had a major protagonist in music with Josef Matthias Hauer.[1]

Dealing with film Adrian also questioned the entire system of the film industry, i.e. cinema and television. He had the utopian idea of revolutionising both artistic film and TV with new, innovative programme formats. **HK**

1 Cf. Dieter Bogner, „Kunst ohne Bewegung ist überflüssig", in: Anna Artaker/Peter Weibel (ed.), *Marc Adrian*, Klagenfurt 2007, p. 30ff.

<u>Tom Burr</u>
Derailed 2, 2005

In his objects Tom Burr reorganizes different pieces, partly found, adapted, fragmented or even produced, and introduces them into new contexts of meaning. The game of re-combination does not end in merely formal references on art history, in particular on minimal art, it also incorporates the problematic of public space. In his work Burr integrates public space in order to analyze it on specific topics via his objects. Again, Burr not only focuses on the White Cube, more likely he is interested in socially problematic spaces regarding art and/or society. His artistic strategy reflects the socio-critical and politicising attitude of art in the 1990s, which repositioned itself in the course of the political and economic upheavals and discussed the frame of references of art. Burrs relational minimalist object conglomerates enrich the examination of public spaces hidden power structures in our society. The theatrical character of the pieces creates an irritating limbo of object, documentation, display, art, everyday life, installation and fragment. **HK**

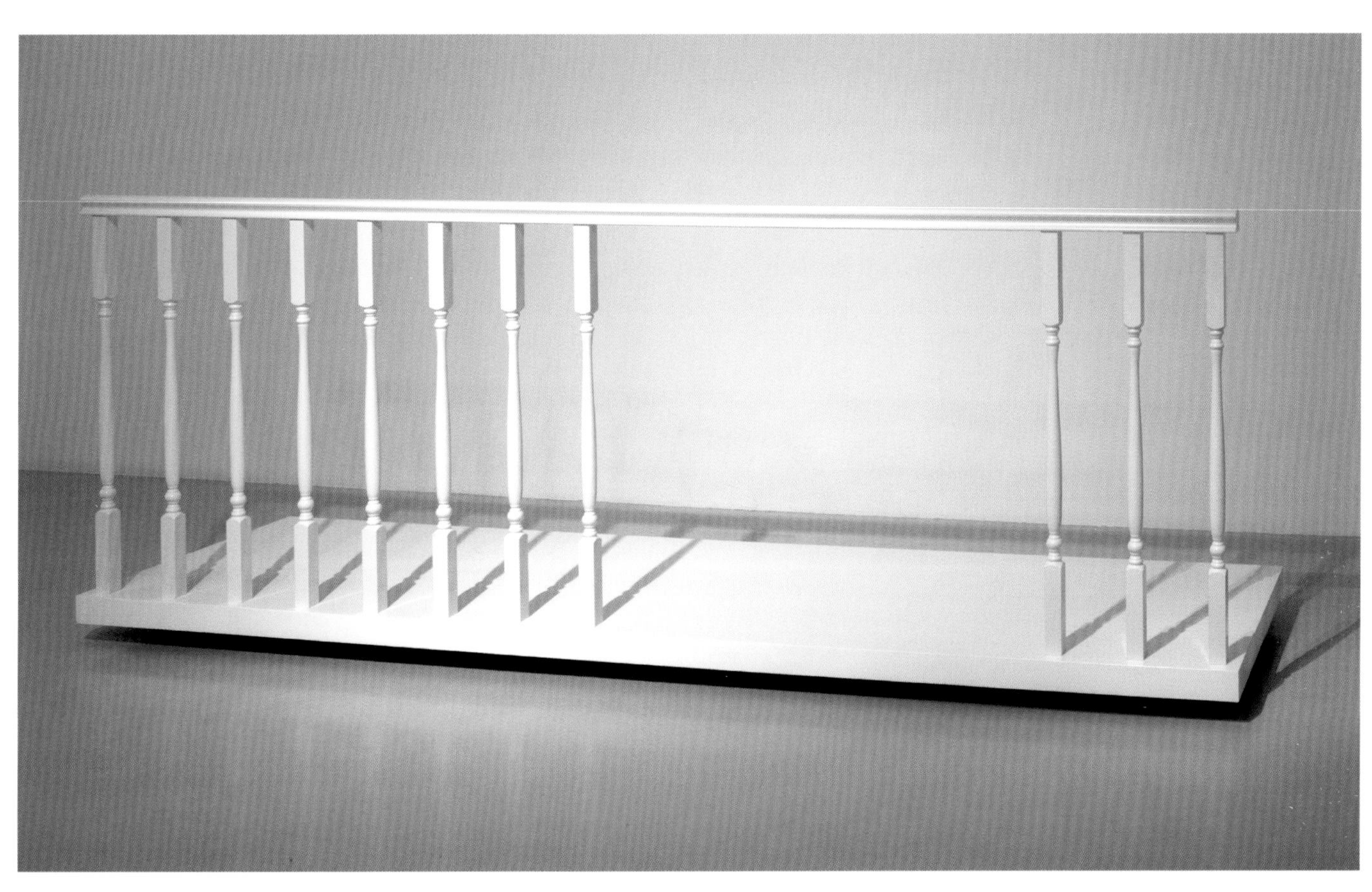

VALIE EXPORT
Restringierter Code, 1979

VALIE EXPORT's live video performance *Restringierter Code* (Munich, 1979) examines the social constraints that are created by one's social environment and which require and convey certain codes. The restricted code denotes a stereotypical and grammatically simple form of expression that opposes the elaborate code of the "educated class." The body becomes the symbol of the societal codes, exploding these limits and thereby repeatedly stretched its own. The attempt to get to the bottom of these restraints is also connected to the cultural field and a rejection of certain patterns of behaviour. During the performance VALIE EXPORT sits in a cage, dressed formally, secured by electric current and equipped with a table, a chair, cutlery, a glass, wine and food for man and beast. She starts eating, but her method of consuming becomes increasingly abnormal. Afterwards VALIE EXPORT imitates the animal behaviour of a bird, a dog and a hamster, all of which are kept beside her in isolated transparent glass cages. She similarly mimics the baby, which lies in a cot beside the cage. VALIE EXPORT exaggerates the movements to ecstasy. The action is filmed by two video cameras that point alternatingly at the animals and the baby, and is broadcast on six screens, which are also set up on the stage. Microphone and speakers serve to catch the sounds of panting and munching. The fragmentation in six videos interprets the everyday activities and behaviours of man and beast—as mimicked by VALIE EXPORT—for the media and in doing so points at their repetitive stereotypy. **NH**

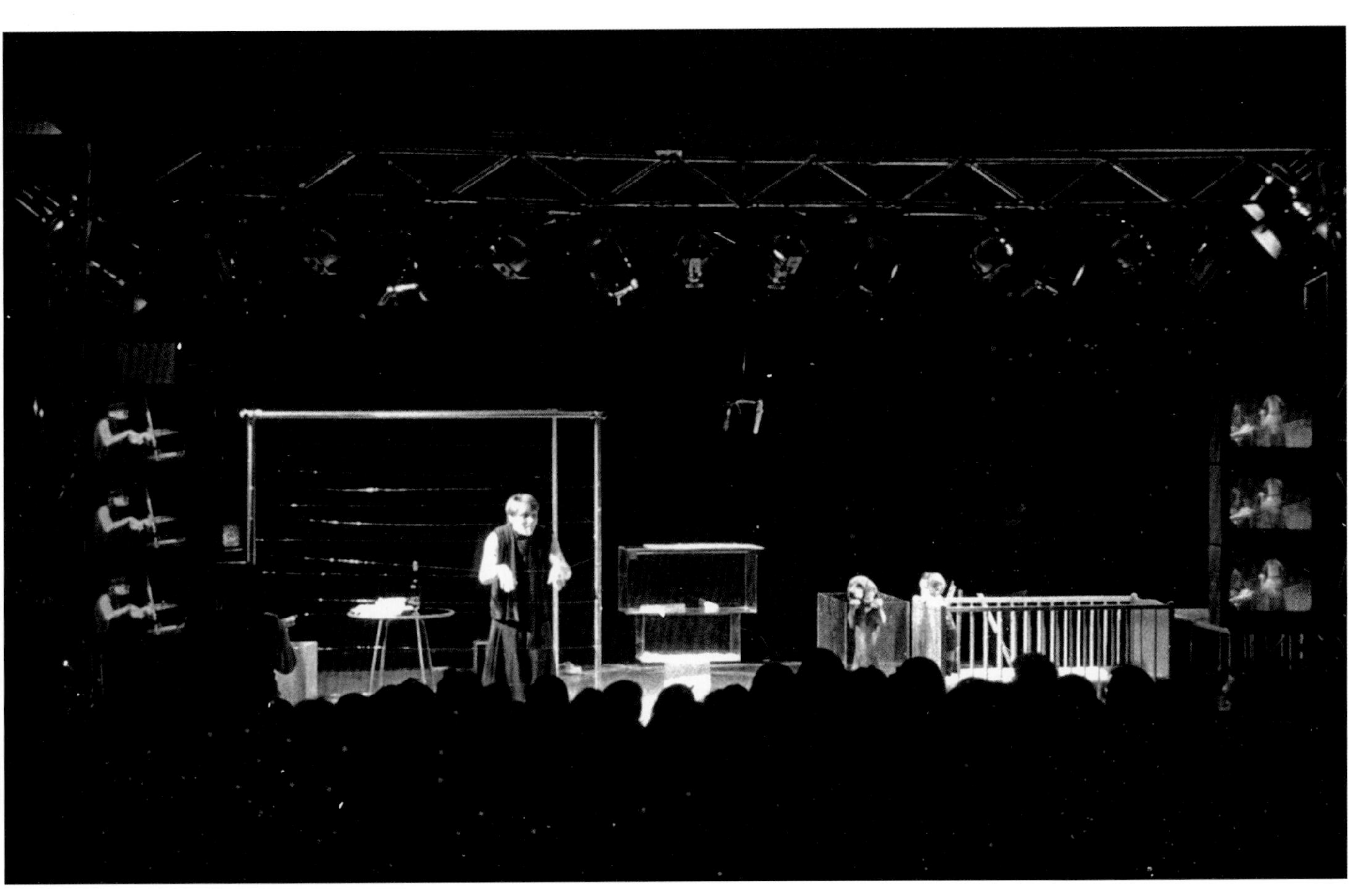

Peter Friedl
Bilbao Song, 2010

Peter Friedl examines political, artistic, biographic and aesthetic configurations of power, developing artistic strategies to disarm and exhibit them. The work *Bilbao Song* was filmed on the empty stage of the Serantes theatre in Santurtzi near Bilbao. Friedl captures the process of dream-like images in static tableaux vivants inspired by Basque history. The figures are professional actors and special guests like Julen Madariaga (lawyer, politician, co-founder of ETA) or the popular clown duo Pirritx and Porrotx. Jean-Auguste-Dominique Ingres' painting *Henry IV and the Spanish Ambassador* (1817) was the initial point for the work and we find references to *El paria castellano* by Juan de Echevarría (1917), *El orden* by Gustavo de Maeztu (1918/19), Aurelio Arteta (1937) *Tríptico de la guerra and Soldado con Mulata* by Bilbao born Patricio de Landaluze, who emigrated to Cuba in 1850. The only action taking place on stage is the live performance of the "Bilbao-Song" from the rather unsuccessful musical *Happy End* by Bertolt Brecht (resp. Elisabeth Hauptmann) and Kurt Weill, a performance without lyrics played by a pianist and an accordion player. *Bilbao Song* transfers Basque history into an imaginary world, being reincarnated as an allegory of tableaux vivants in order to avoid the reduction on one single image. **BS**

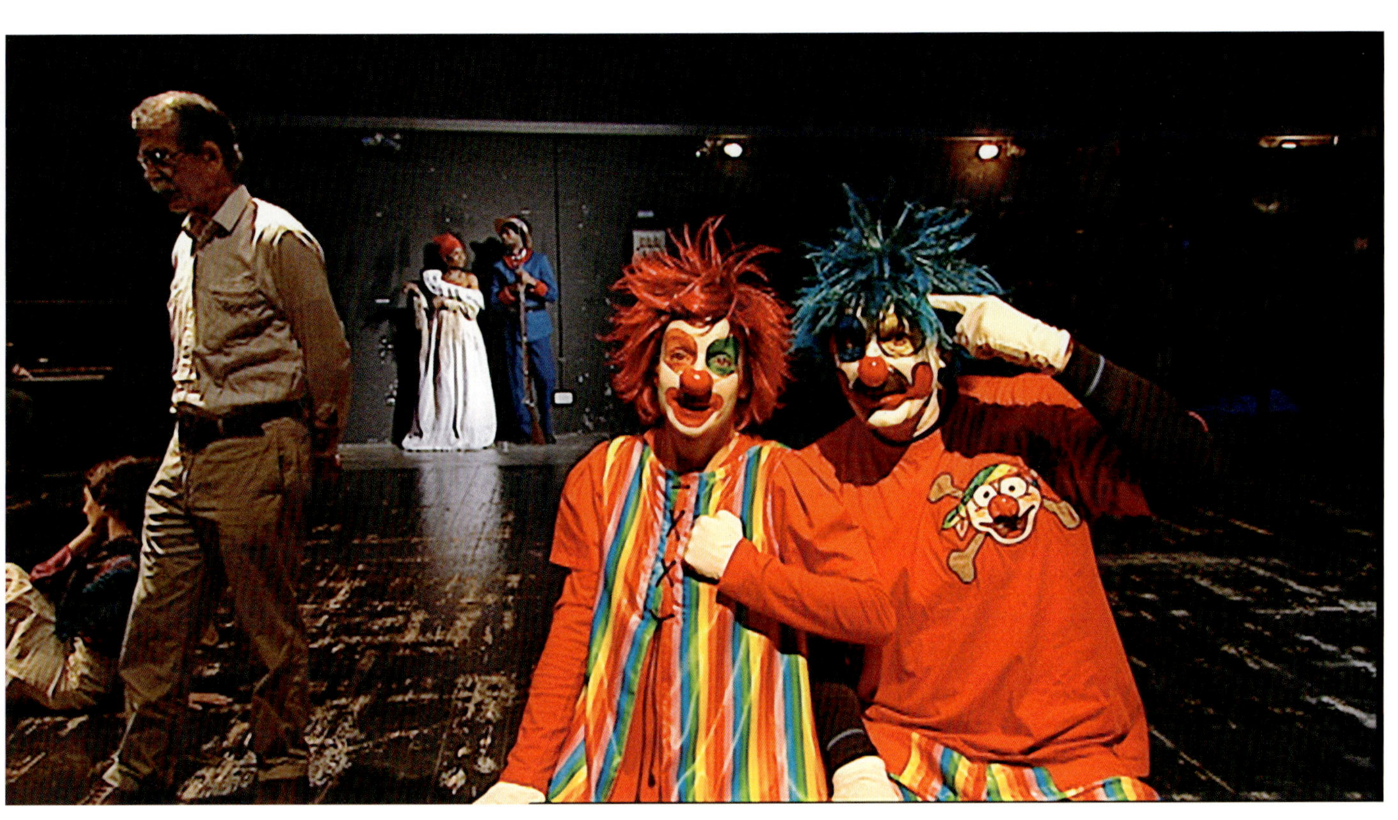

<u>Liam Gillick</u>
***Volvo Bar*, 2008**

A key aspect in Liam Gillick's artistic work is the negotiation of possible models of coexistence. He focuses on relevant questions of time, working relations, partnerships, and new forms of dialogue, cognitive processes and strategies, which don't sidestep crises and complex questions, but face and master them. The artistic thinker Gillick analyses precisely, structures politically and dares taking a visionary gander. With *Volvo Bar*, a project in which the phenomena of the postindustrial society are negotiated, during a solo exhibition, the artist has originally converted an exhibition room of the Kunstverein Munich into a production space, which served as the setting for a theatre production: *Mirrored Image: A Volvo Bar*. Gillick developed the play with a group of young Munich actors and acted it out during the exhibition. Several characters meet in a bar nearby a car factory: "Franck Stairs celebrating his birthday– a group of people, familiar but somehow seeming indistinct—a crisis at the director's office— a group, locked up in a discussion room. The collapse of identity and a corresponding use of a projected self-image. A precise structure, which will contain new declarations of intent." (Liam Gillick) Converting the exhibition room into a stage, Gillick sets up a physical room of thought and communication, in which models of communality can be tested or associated. **BS**

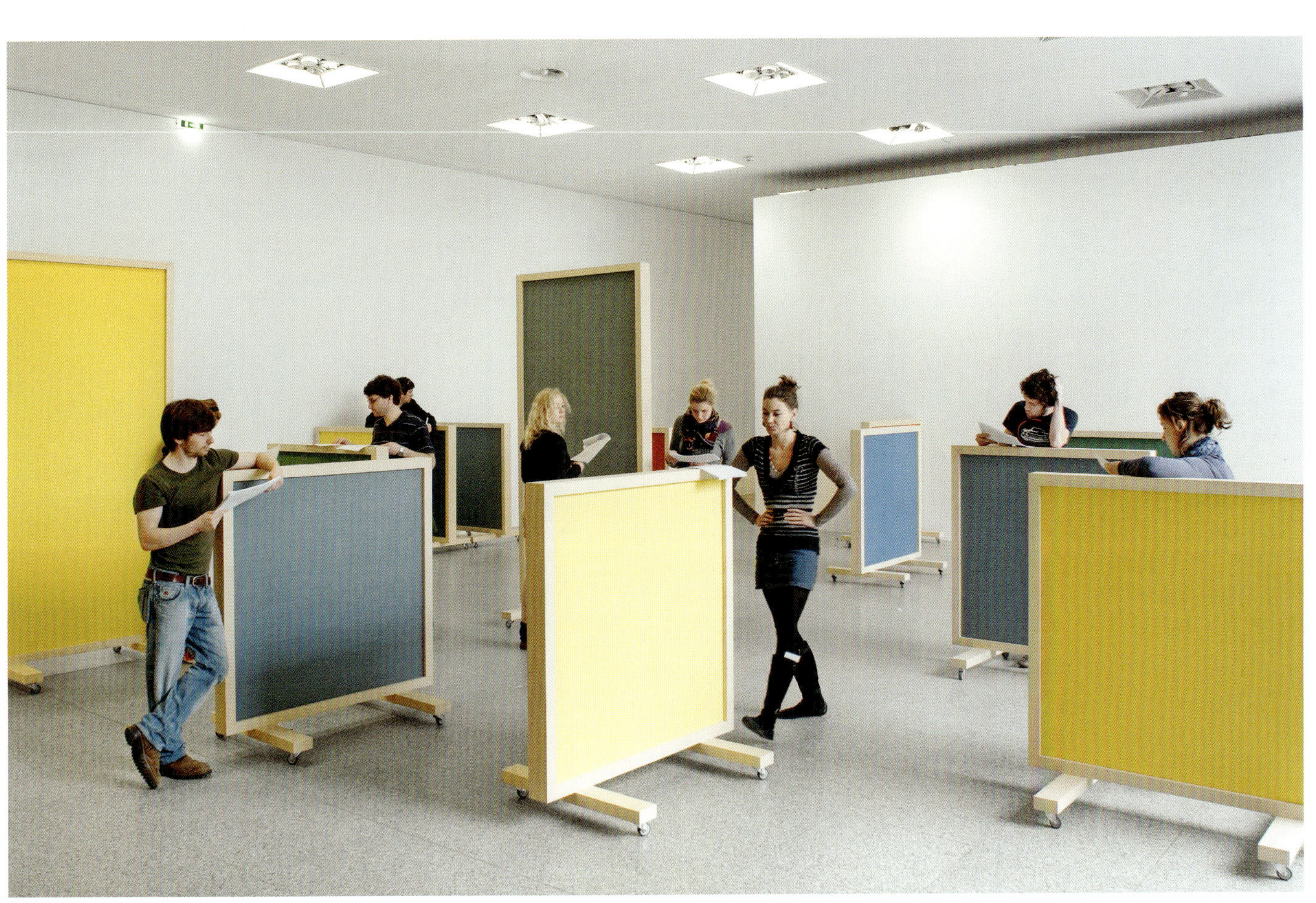

<u>Franz Graf</u>
DERR SCHRECKEN JEDOCH VERMEERTE MEIN INTERESSE, 2011

Franz Graf has elaborated and realised interconnected structures of thought, using them as a reaction to the ongoings on political, social and cultural level. With his system of networks, nexuses and overlappings of various elements, he overrides the borders between space and work to reformulate them in sketches, objects, installations, photographies, works in public space, neo-conceptual paintings as well as music.

Graf uses elements of bondage and the S&M scene like masks and ropes, which hang down from the ceiling to create a kind of magic artistic chamber. The reduction on black & white abstracts these everyday objects and refers to the loss of their original meaning. In *DERR SCHRECKEN JEDOCH VERMEERTE MEIN INTERESSE* the cabinet represents the reservoir for this hotchpotch: "Combinatorics of ludic drive, a ragbag of these articles of daily use, some of which were made fetish items, circle a personal, partly (auto) erotically charged mythology." (Brigitte Borchardt-Birbaumer) This mythologization of objects plays a key role in Franz Graf's opus. Text serves as open content and, on the other hand, obfuscates resp. transports connections and confusion. His poetic, sometimes fragmentary use of language and the deliberate involvement of typography emphasise and idealise, connect and deconstruct the fragments of this hotchpotch. **BS**

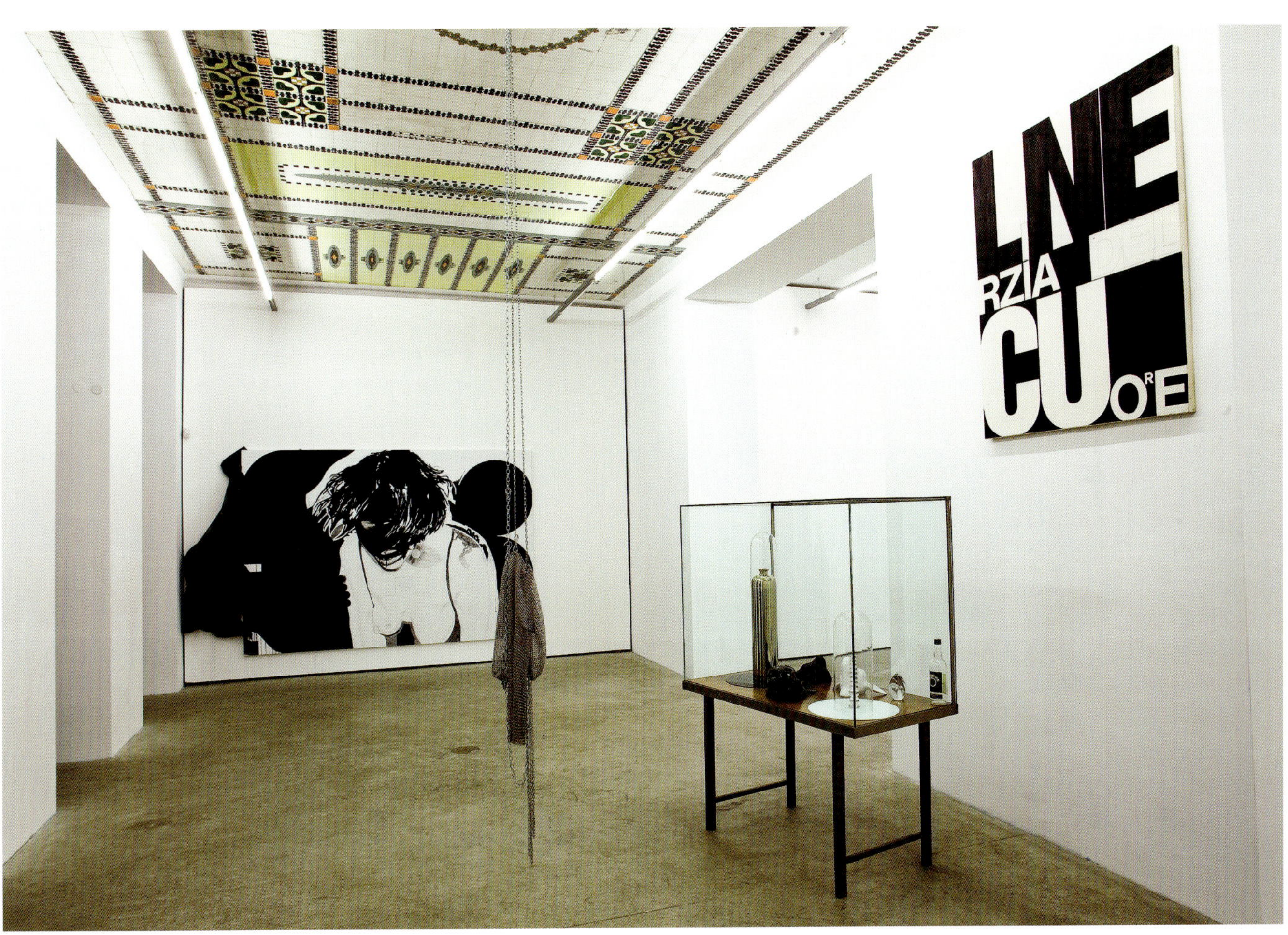

Christian Jankowski
Telemistica, 1999

Christian Jankowski ironically examines structures and mechanisms of media culture and the art and cultural sector, which is increasingly facing the demand for entertainment. Connections and inter-relations between artist, artwork and recipient play a central role.

For his piece *Telemistica* he created for the 48th Biennale di Venezia, Jankowski studied basic Italian to be able to interview fortune tellers about his personal future live on TV. Jankowski consulted a total of five tarot card readers and posed simple questions concerning his application for the Biennale, his respective piece of art as well as his future as an artist in general. "The result was a vast, poetic linguistic confusion—and in the end, the diviners were not only turned into pieces of art themselves, but were also proven right, as this very artwork made him famous."[1] In *Telemistica* Jankowski infiltrates the mass medium television, tackles it from an artist's viewpoint and incorporates it in his work.

In his artistic work Christian Jankowski generates and stages special situations in the entertainment and media industry. In doing so, Jankowski unites stage and audience, the individual (partly uninformed) protagonists and recipients become part of an interactive *Gesamtkunstwerk*; actually they become its precondition. "The fool not only describes his grotesque world. He also breaches the gap between stage and audience and addresses the spectators as active participants of his *Totaltheater*"[2] VA

1 Niklas Maak, "Frührentner in Horrormasken," in: *FAZ*, 24. 10. 2008.
2 Harald Falckenberg, "Danke, Gott. Danke. Christian Jankowskis Beitrag zur Pathologie des Kunstbetriebs," in: *Parkett* 81, 2008, p. 73.

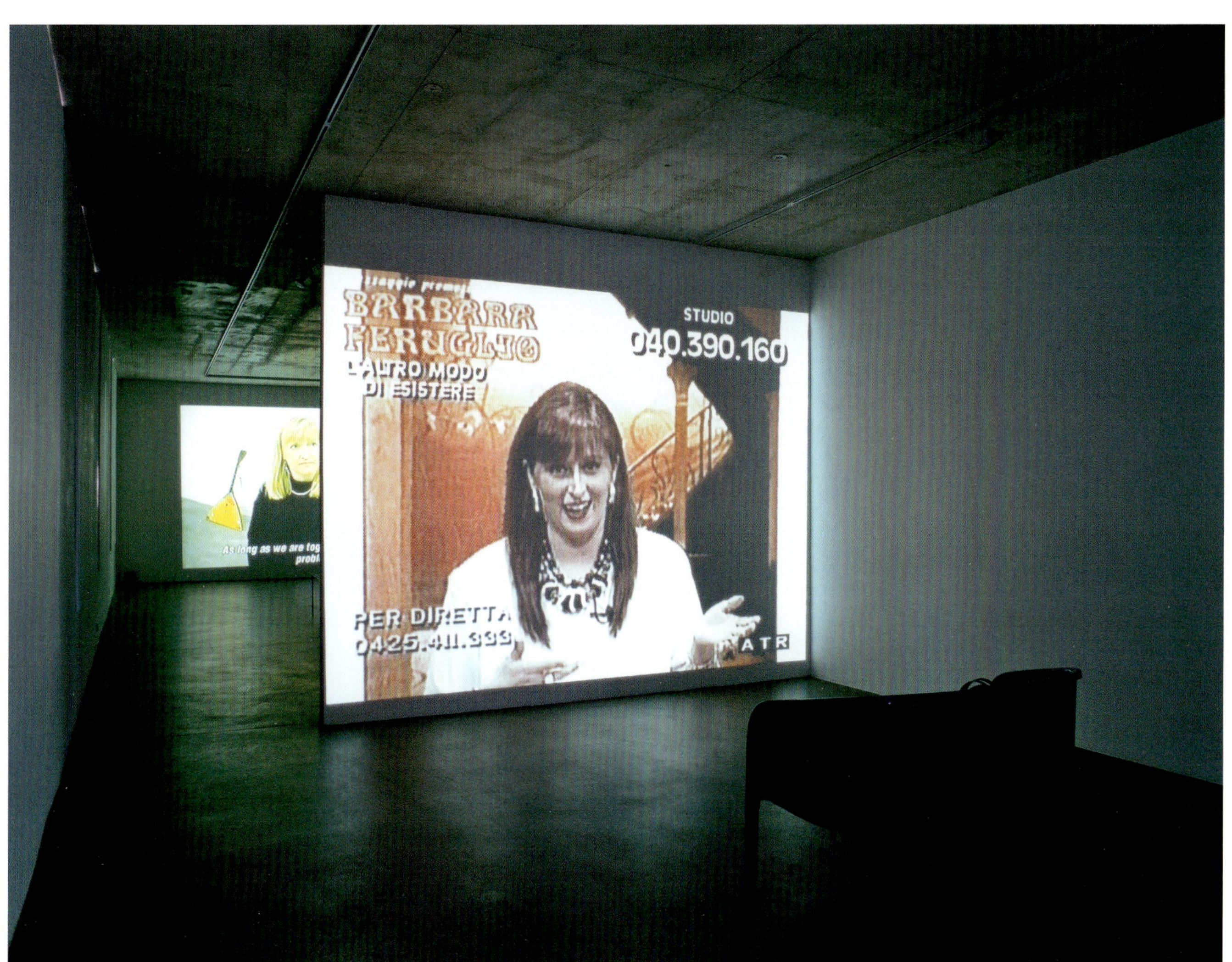
BARBARA
FERUGLIO
L'ALTRO MODO
DI ESISTERE
STUDIO
040.390.160
PER DIRETTA
0425.411.333
ATR
As long as we are tog
probl

<u>Paul McCarthy</u>
Basement Bunker, 2003

Paul McCarthy's Video *Bunker Basement* is an allegory on the economic crisis, on political intrigues and Disneyland as well as on the influence of popularity and financial means on politics and democracy. A President (George W. Bush), several Queen Mums and a terrorist (Osama bin Laden) seem like comic figures being issued from an animated series on the Iraq war with lots of blood and toys. The President and the terrorist are part of the massacre that the protagonists of the play perform: McCarthy's figures are uncompromising. They show the world as a worst-case scenario, which peters out in a conglomerate of liquids and colours.
Levels of reality overlap creating a new tier somewhere in between fiction and documentation.

The location of *Bunker Basement* is a labyrinth in McCarthy's studio in Los Angeles, whose construction is based on that of a TV studio. The narrow rooms, which gradually densify, remind of chambers in which victims are kept and which are hermetically sealed. The theatrical setting is changed repeatedly, objects are moved, walls drilled and passages created, until the room eventually becomes a studio. The exterior world can only access such locations through media like film or photography, just like in Michel Foucault's Paradigm of the Panopticon or in Big Brother, which allow the invisible to be accessed. **NH**

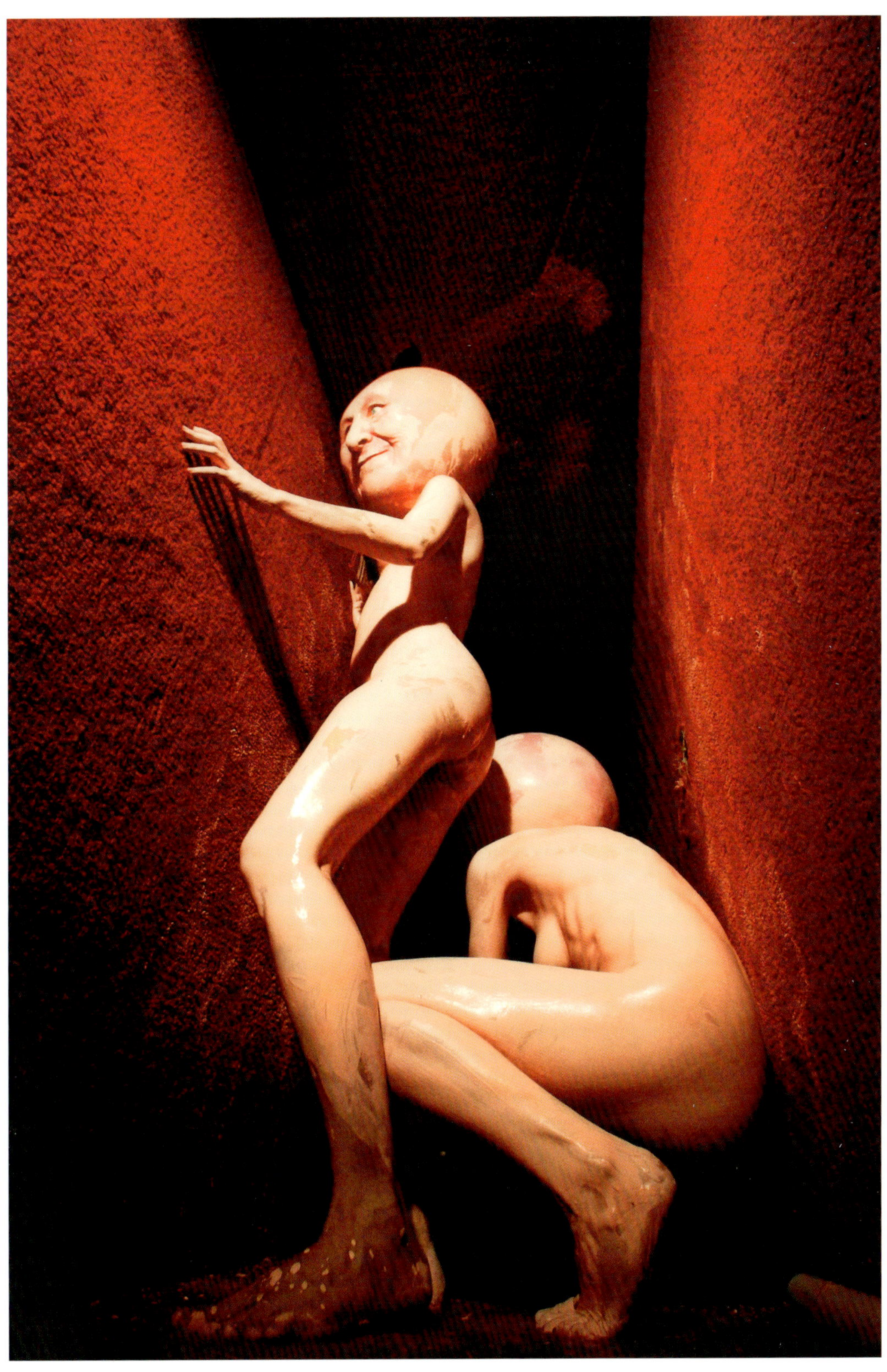

<u>Jonathan Meese</u>
***TOTALADLER, Baby-CHEF der Kunst
(das Ei des Columbussy), 2007***

The eagle is Germany's heraldic animal, but Jonathan Meese renders it—in the form of a Wagnerian *Gesamtkunstwerk*—as a zombie or muscleman who is too heavy to fly and therefore needs three legs. Using the square, circular and triangular shapes contained in this sculpture, as well as the symbol for infinity that remains hidden in the "Egg of Columbussy" in *Erzstaat Atlantisis*, Meese introduces his symbols for the dictatorship of art to the world, a dictatorship which is dedicated to total art and total revolution, and in which only *Erzstaat Atlantisis* can be a neutral playground for a total future. In a 2008 article on *artnet* Kathrin Luz wrote, "Meese acts extremely, even terroristically to investigate the acceptance limit of his art." She acknowledges Meese's specifically artistic achievement of deconstructing the "individual and collective creation of myths and their staging," praising him for his critical work at the precise interface where," the aura of power is formed." He depreciates the creation of the myths of former rulers by banalising them, and makes central historic figures (Hitler, Wagner) meet fictional characters (James Bond, Little Joe), exposing them to ridicule and thus regaining liberties. The sculpture *TOTALADLER, Baby-CHEF der Kunst (das Ei des Columbussy)* is an allusion to the total state, the "Baby boss" of art, who no longer has any simple solutions and thus faces the present helplessly. Here as in his performances, Meese stages a "theatre without drama and dramaturgy" (Gerrit Gohlke), proclaiming a form of art that, pseudo-religious and universalistic, connects to a supra-individual utopia. **BS**

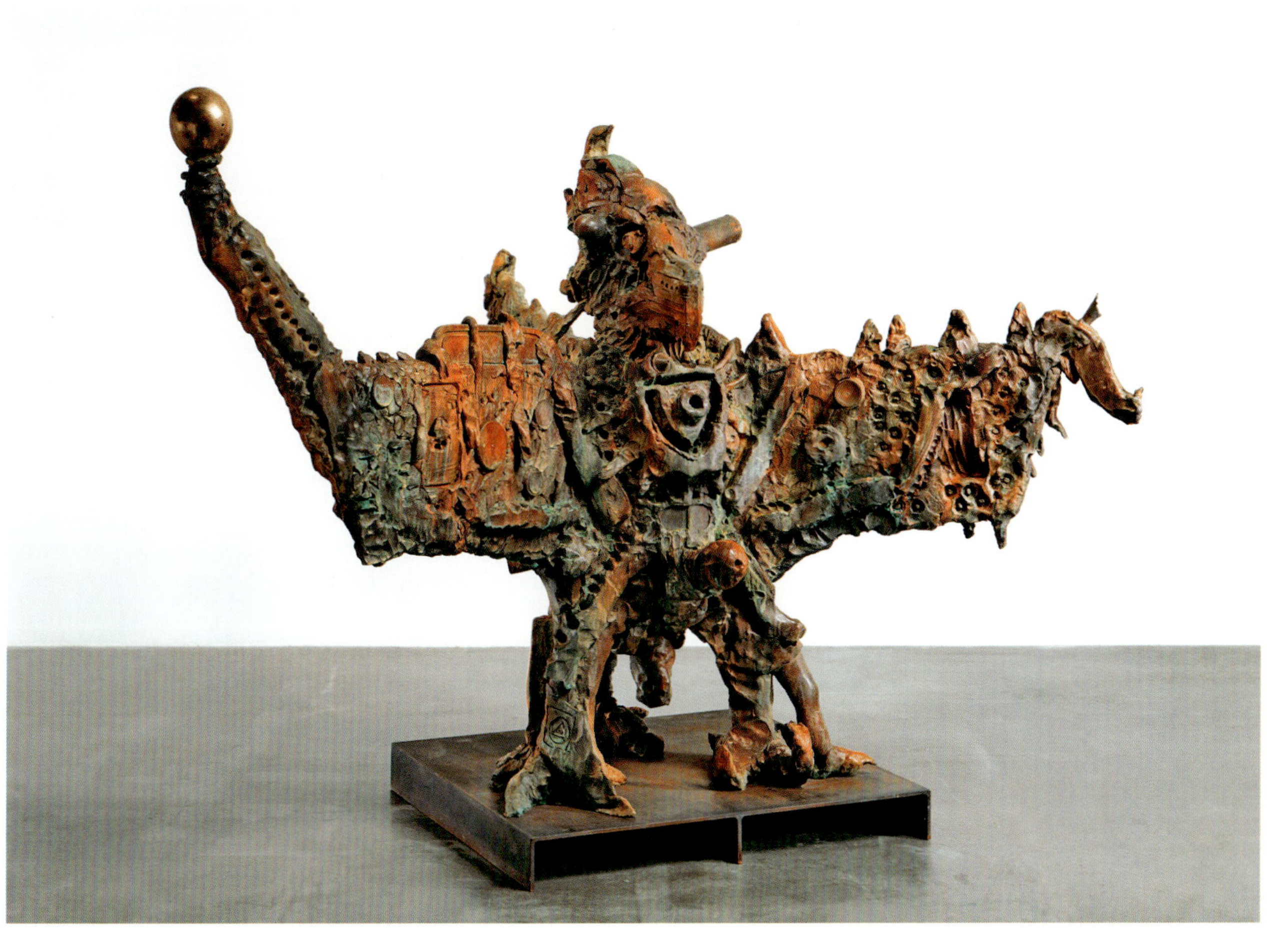

<u>Seb Patane</u>
Patrons Paper, 2011

The basic material elements of Seb Patane's practice are images, objects, and sound. The images are found—usually in newspapers or magazines—creating something that is continuously in motion: never settling on a fixed or final form. Patane's work shifts back and forth between the suggestion of narrative and its un-doing into fragmented shapes. There is a consistency of certain archetypal images, like the figures in *Patrons Paper* series, four large screenprints on found sewing patterns. These pieces depict costumed and shrouded figures sometimes obliterated by masks. They are related to one another by mirrored postures and by their curious uniforms, which are usually both anachronistic and unidentifiable, and therefore timeless. Patane is playing an intricate game of references, symbols and signs. The four patterns seem to open a stage, a stage which analyses group behavior by means of Brecht's "alienation effect." Patane himself says that, "Eventually, my interaction with those images becomes in fact an act of respect rather than subversion, but it feels as if, as a reaction to that psychological violence, the outcome ends up looking like a need for abstracted concealment of some sort, almost to balance out that sense of devotion towards the image. It's a game of contradictions." And then there is always the line, a repetitive element in Patane's work. The line gives structure in sewing patterns, which are the basis for his collages or lines appear covering faces in the collages. These can also be construed as the line of history that encompasses such events as Victorian living, wars as they are reflected in certain imagery, or in the writings of Dupuy or Kuntsman on the ways violence, sexuality and nationhood intertwine to create a sense of nationhood and how masculinities become representative of a nation. **BS**

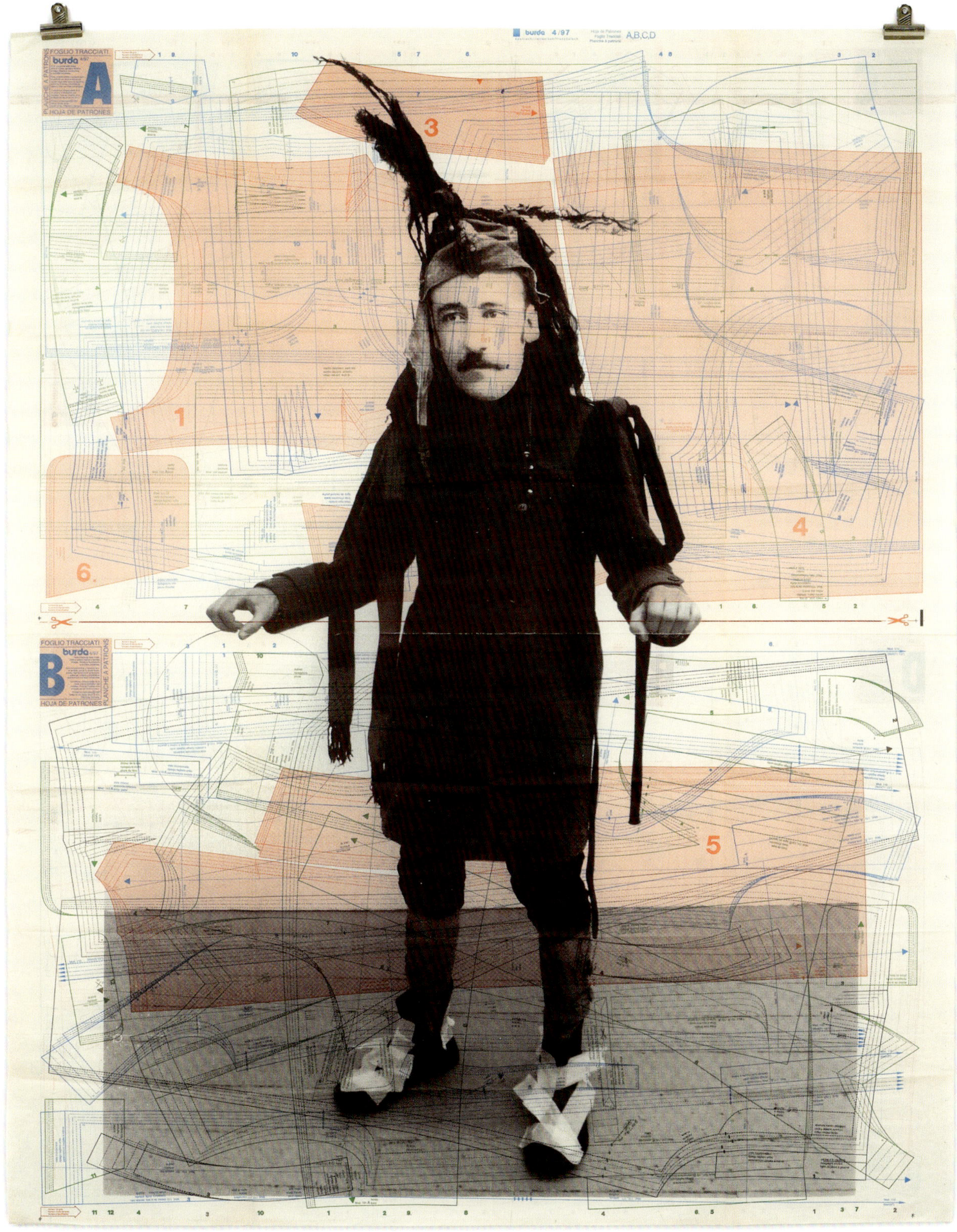
burda 4/97
A,B,C,D
FOGLIO TRACCIATI
A
HOJA DE PATRONES
3
1
6.
4
FOGLIO TRACCIATI
B
HOJA DE PATRONES
5

<u>Constalze Ruhm</u>
My_Never_Ending_Burial_Plot, 2010

"Hence the zombies sing a song, but it is that of life."
(Gilles Deleuze)

The photographs in this exhibition are taken at the set of Constanze Ruhm's film *Crash Site / My_Never_Ending_Burial_Plot*, the sixth part in the *X Characters* project, which attempts to update the identities of iconic female film characters in modern cinema as contemporary versions. The characters realized in the sequel are laid out interdisciplinarily and examine the representation of female identity in contemporary art practice, thereby relating to the history of cinematographic and theatrical forms as well as its role in the production of new media. In this context, a new version of Andrej Tarkowskij's Hari in *Solaris* meets two other zombies of film history: Godard's Nana of *Vivre sa vie* and Antonionis's Giuliana of *Il deserto rosso*, who underwent a sex change to become Julian. Lost in an abandoned forest glade, the three characters are revenants of other fictional worlds who attempt to come to terms with their past, "perish," "leave the past behind," kill themselves, or beat each other to death. The narration revolves around a funeral that never ends, thus becoming an infinite loop. The three protagonists are stuck in the present, which repeats itself in variations. **BS**

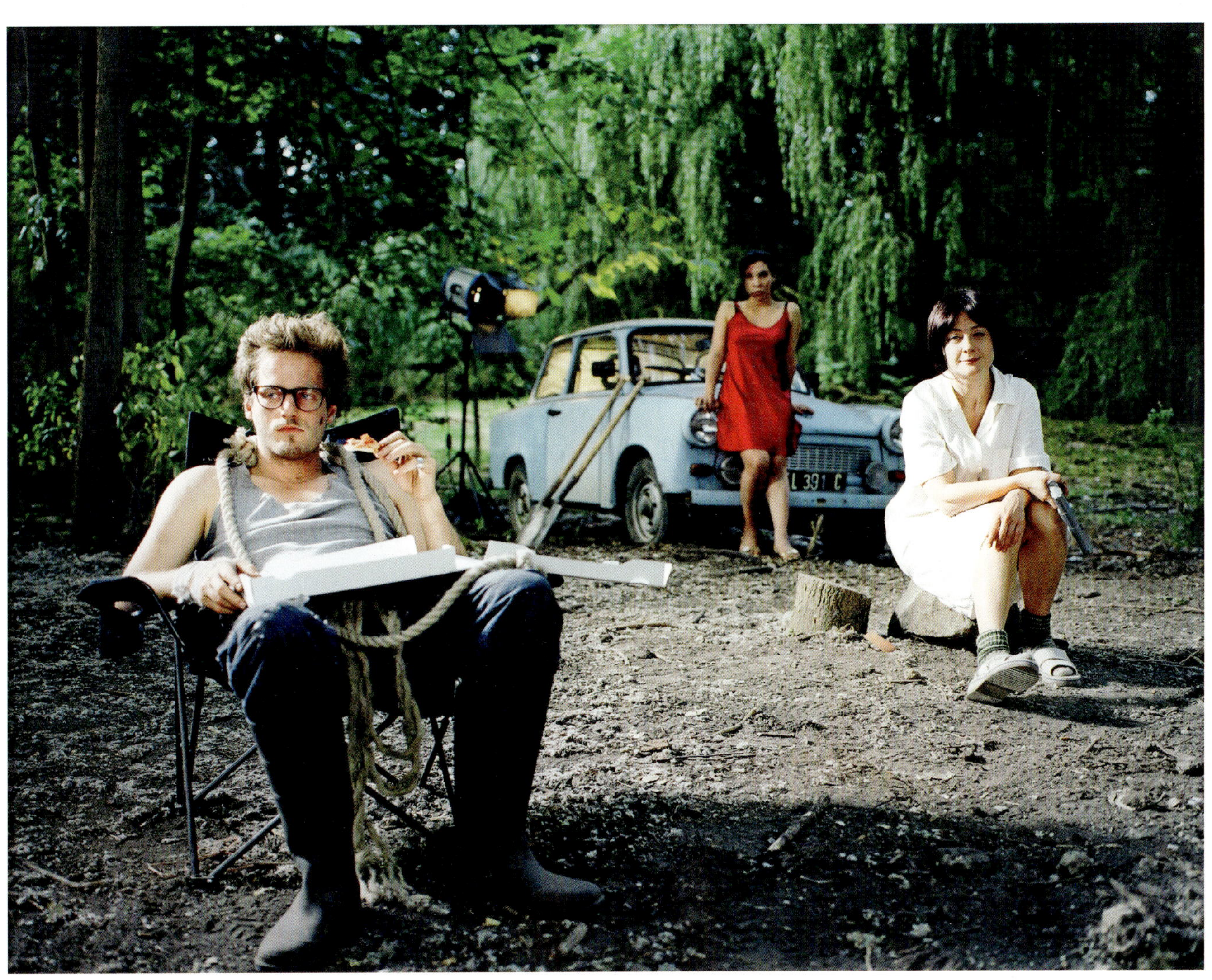

<u>Markus Schinwald</u>
Dictio Pii, 2001

The central topics of Markus Schinwald's artistic œuvre are the body and psyche of the human being and its shortcomings and imperfections. The artist regularly stages these aspects of his, in which weirdness also plays a key role.

In his film *Dictio Pii* seven protagonists stroll through a hotel. Despite its strong narrative character however, no logical or dramaturgical sequence is detetable in his somewhat Kafkaesque scenes that are connected only by their common setting, and it seems as if the key scenes were simply strung together. The film's tenor is characterized by a mysterious and ill-omened, deeply nightmarish atmosphere which is enforced by impulsive music. The people in *Dictio Pii* appear trapped and constrained; seemingly remote controlled prostheses and inhibiting implants for their bodies and clothing force them to make artificial gestures and postures. Repetitive subtitles, rather than the protagonists themselves, advise the audience of the motives behind the protagonist's cryptic actions, mental states and self-perception as they move through their non-verbal world, "[…] living in the sensation of being everything and the certitude of being nothing […] we are deranged."

Borrowing from performing arts—his prostheses and gadgets seem like masks—Markus Schinwald constructs and stages a cold reality, and charges the scenes with music and repetitively uttered enigmatic snatches of text. His various and cleverly synchronized and choreographed media create a complex symbiosis. **VA**

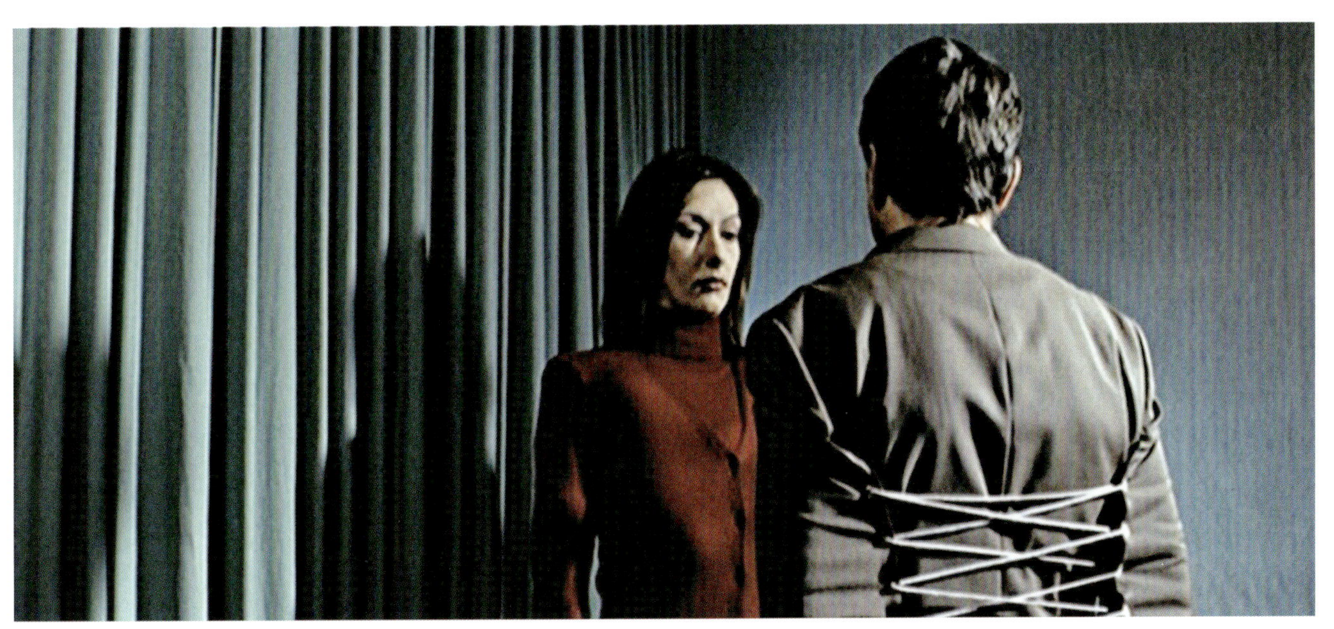

Gregor Schneider
Haus u r, Rheydt 1985 – today (Nacht – Video), 1996

From 1985 to 2001, Gregor Schneider converted his parents' home into an artistic work similar to the *Merzbau* by Kurt Schwitters, which is growing rampantly without end. It is a procedural work that spans rhizomatically over the original house to become a performance, a sculpture, an installation, a Gesamtkunstwerk or a social practice. Schneider added new rooms, he bricked up doors, raised new walls in front of old ones, lowered ceilings and floors, or tapered rooms. After a 16-year-long building phase, the original structure is not replicable anymore. The house has become a psychological space, which is physically tangible and in which archetypical fears can break out. In his video *Haus u r, Rheydt 1985 – today (Nacht – Video)* this spatial experience is reflected in the camera work. The camera observes room after room to convey the atmosphere, feelings and emotions, which are not recognizable rationally. The exaggerated breathing and sounds of movement document the physical self of the artist and his effort for the artistic production. The Gesamtkunstwerk is turned into a bio art work or, analogue to Schwitters, a "Merzgesamtkunstwerk". While Schwitters merges with his work and represents a romantically-idealist worldview, Schneider always keeps the distance. He changes his native rooms to analyse identity and difference. Doubles, interstices and pupations develop, and in the end it turns out that his self cannot elaborate a uniform picture of the entire world.[1] BS

1 Cf. Karin Orchard, „Das Haus ist vergangen", in: Angela Lammert/ Michael Diers/Robert Kudielka/Gert Mattenklott (on behalf of the Akademie der Künste, Berlin), *Topos Raum – Die Aktualität des Raumes in den Künsten der Gegenwart*, Nuremburg 2005, p. 301.

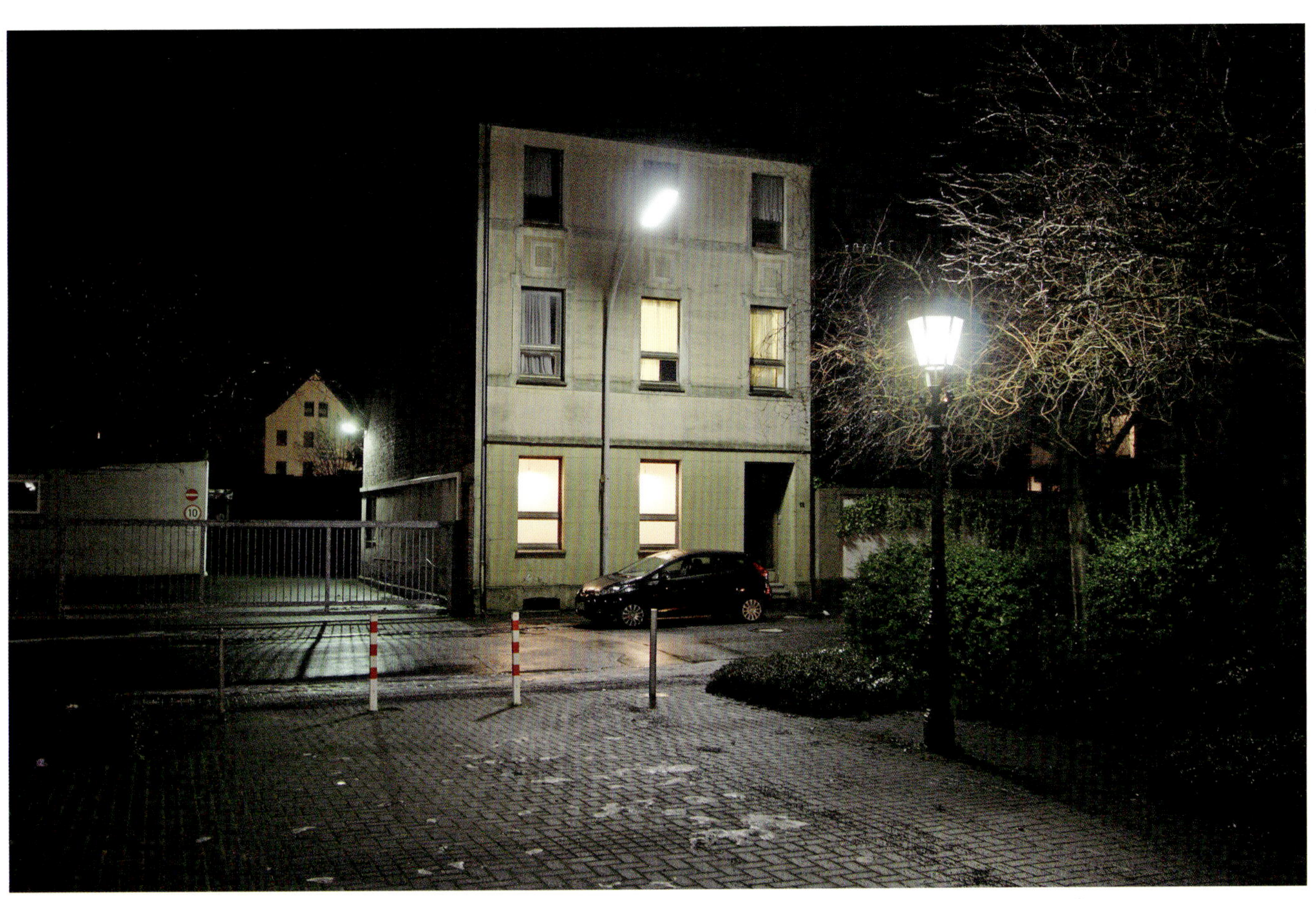

SUPERFLEX
The Financial Crisis (Session I–IV), 2009

In *The Financial Crisis (Session I–IV)* film work by the artist group SUPERFLEX the spectator is asked by a therapist to slip into different positions and scenarios against the background of the global financial crisis and economic breakdown. Thus, in the course of four hypnosis sessions (*The Invisible Hand, George Soros, You* and *Old Friends*) the spectator becomes an actor involved with the origin, outbreak and effects of the economic crisis. Using figurative and clear language, the hypnotist first leads the observer into the world of speculation, which is dominated by a thirst for power and avarice, to experience a loss of control over market mechanisms and finally the resulting social decline and existential breakdown of the individual. Various perspectives and stages of the financial collapse are experienced; through therapeutic confrontation emotions like fear, frustration and panic are reviewed. The therapist closes the sessions by snapping his fingers and uttering the line, "I want you to wake up feeling fresh, comfortable and happy," in the final session the spectator and the therapist are asked to part from their worries. Neoliberalism and capitalism, which seem to have infested the world as a psychosis, shall be battled with a therapy of confrontation and self-reflection, and demand the draft of a counter model. **VA**

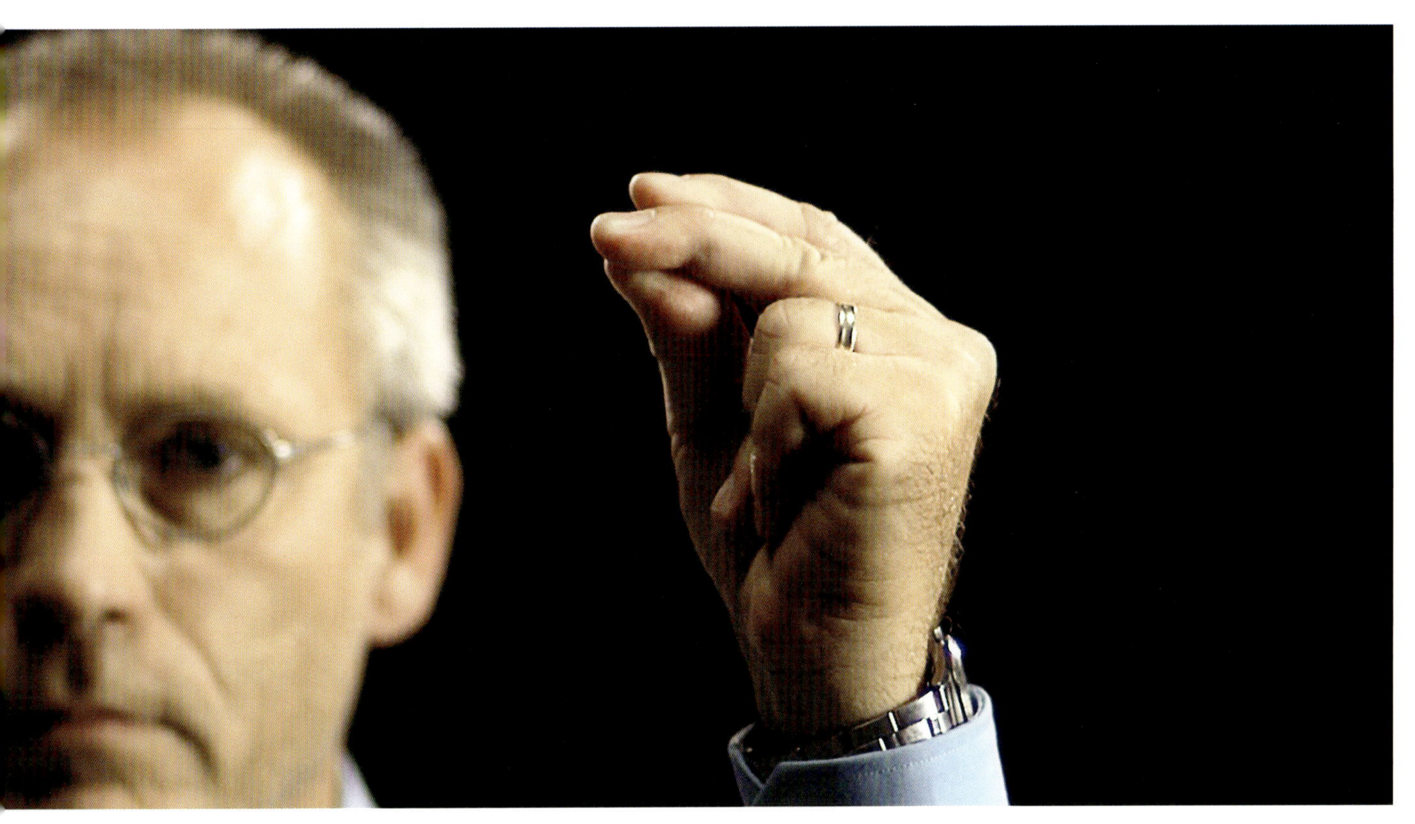

<u>Franz West</u>
***Lemure*, 2001**

In 1987 Franz West began his *Lemurenköpfe* (lemur heads) series. In ancient Rome, lemurs were deemed the spirits of the dead denied burial plots, as they made themselves liable to persecution during their lifetime. Because of their distinctive faces and large eyes indicating their nocturnal lifestyle lemurs are categorized, in zoological terms, as prosimians. Franz West began working with lemurs when he was asked by architect Hermann Czech to design gargoyles for Vienna's "Kleine Ungarbrücke". The four heads that he created were later used for the "Stubenbrücke" near the Museum of Applied Arts. Animism is the belief that all natural phenomena has a soul, and once the body is dead the soul departs to search for another host. The *Lemurenköpfe*, with their fetish-like reduced head forms and wide-open mouths can be understood as studies in animism. Among other things, West focuses on the juxtaposition between the mental interior and the material exterior worlds—like Oscar Wilde in his *The Picture of Dorian Gray*. "In the context of modernism the image of animism acted like a mirror through which modernism secured itself by seeing what it wasn't. Thus, modern means leaving animism behind and dividing the world into the dualism of body and soul, of mind and matter determined by Descartes." (Anselm Franke) In West's pieces psychoanalysis becomes socioanalysis that does not lack a slightly ironic undertone. **BS**

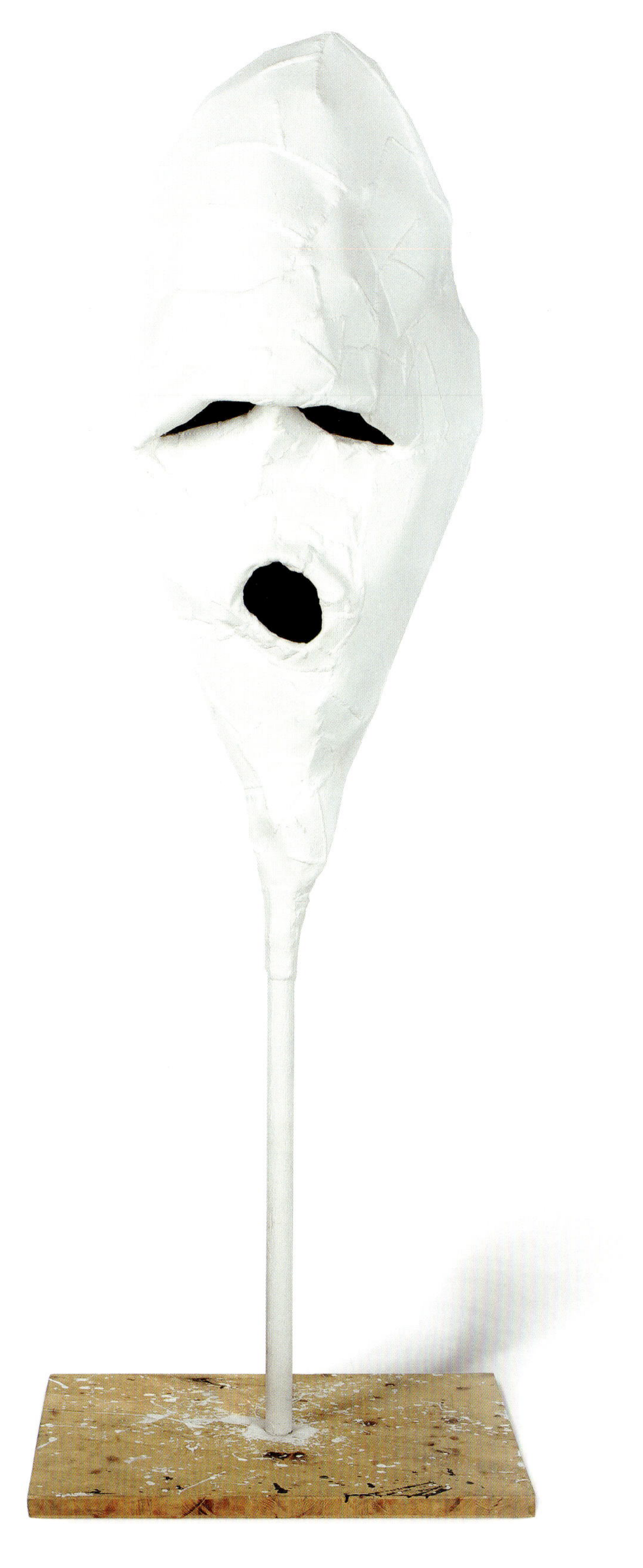

Fritz Wotruba
Scenograpy and Costumes of *Ring des Nibelungen. Ein Bühnenfestspiel aufzuführen in drei Tagen und einem Vorabend* von Richard Wagner, Deutsche Oper Berlin 1967

From January to September 1967 Richard Wagner's *Ring des Nibelungen* (Rheingold, *Walküre*, *Siegfried* and *Götterdämmerung*) was performed at the Deutsche Oper Berlin under the direction of Gustav Rudolf Sellner as, "a stage festival play for three days and an eve." Fritz Wotruba designed not only the sets, but the costumes as well—thus entire setting continuously dovetailed and was ruled by Wotruba's geometrical and abstract shapes which themselves took the cube as their basic form.

Wotruba's examination of social and political issues was groundbreaking within the field of stage design. In Fritz Wotruba's work stage design signifies his transition from sculptor to architect. The impetus for his interest in theatre was his concern with the expression of mental states, and the vast additional space with which the theatre setting presented him. The sculptural design, which replaced the role of the set as a mere background at the turn of the century, supported him in the development of this.

For the *Ring* Wotruba created an archaic scene using a sweeping cubic plateau. He often arranged the individual segments in different groupings in order to comply with Wagner's instructions for scenes that were to be set with the same design. For this reason the parts needed to be easily re- and de-mountable as well as moveable: at times the scenery should almost disappear, and at others become overwhelmingly present. Color and light played an increasingly key role in enforcing the three-dimensionality and drama of the operas. **NH**

1 **Richard Wagner worked on *Ring des Nibelungen. Ein Bühnenfestspiel aufzuführen in drei Tagen und einem Vorabend* for more than 30 years. It was first performed privately in 1876 in Bayreuth, with set design by Joseph Hoffmann.**
2 **The production marked the end of Wotruba's theatre work, which he had initiated seven years previously with Greek tragedy at the Vienna Burgtheater (The Sophocles-Cycle: *Oedipus, Electra* and *Antigone*). Before Ring Wotruba had also designed the set design for *Oedipus der König* and *Oedipus auf Kolonos* at the Salzburg Festival.**

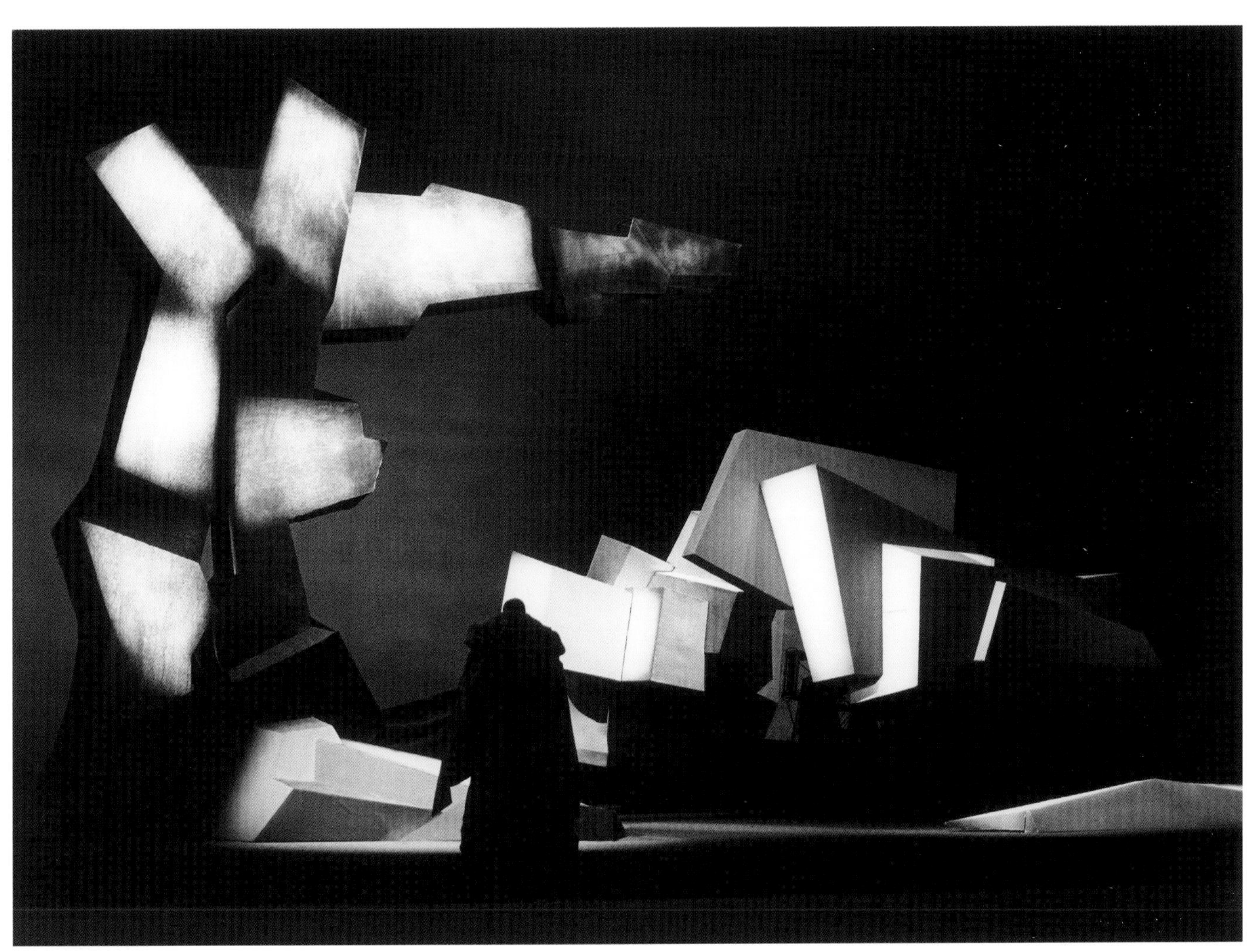

Correlatio

Plea for a conflictual Reality

**Bettina Steinbrügge in conversation
with Markus Miessen**

Bettina Steinbrügge Let's start with some definitions. How do you conceive of the terms "radicant," "relational" and "participation"?

Markus Miessen I would essentially interpret Bourriaud's notion of the 'radicant' as the interrogation of the core modernist belief that there is a single answer to a question, a kind of master-response to a given problem. One can only attempt to address complexity through and by mobilizing multi-polar responses, collaborative in nature, and imagined as a network and force field of actors rather than the single-authored protagonist. I understand his concern, which to a certain extend I share, as one that is interested in a heterogeneous and multi-faceted approach to reality, the production of ideas, and its subsequent attempt(s) towards realization, critically altering the context(s) in which we operate. To ethically produce first entails to question the very modalities of operation and how those can be translated towards a transparency in regard to a multitude of audiences.

The term 'relational' presents us with a 1990s concept of collectivization, a set of artistic practices that are interested in human relations and their social context: a description of a particular generation, a self-referential system—not collaborative across scales—but a mode of interactivity that raises interesting questions about social transformation. The notion of the relational has become a focal point of attention rather than an overarching ambition in regards to the change of realities beyond the art world. It questions the role of artists as makers and proposes (a) practice(s) of facilitating and mediation, a mode of sharing and establishing exchange between different constituencies. I am with Claire Bishop on this one, who asks: "What types of relations are being produced, for whom, and why?"

Over the past two decades, 'participation' has become a buzzword, like "sustainability" and "criticality." To attempt to understand it also means to understand the different contextual realities in which it is being used and by whom. When everyone has been turned into a participant, the often uncritical, innocent, and romantic use of the term becomes frightening. Supported by a repeatedly nostalgic veneer of worthiness, phony solidarity, and political correctness, participation has become the default position of politicians withdrawing from responsibility. I argue for an inversion of participation, a model beyond modes of consensus. Instead of reading participation as the charitable savior of political struggle, I am interested in the limits and traps of its real motivations. Rather than breeding the next generation of consensual facilitators and mediators, I would like to argue for conflict as an enabling, rather than disabling, force: conflictual participation should no longer be understood as a process by which others are invited in, but as a means of acting without mandate, as an uninvited irritant: a forced entry into fields of knowledge that arguably benefit from exterior thinking.

BS When you talk about conflictual participation as a way of building up something new, I relate it to the *Gesamtkunstwerk* (total work of art). The original idea of the *Gesamtkunstwerk* is closely connected to a harmonious and aesthetical whole. Can we say that this, today, is replaced by something conflictual? Is the new Whole something rather conflictual?

MM The notion of participation as an all-encompassing and all-inclusive practice does not interest me, as its default-mode of consensus means that the overall outcome—the common denominator so to speak— will always be fairly vague and unspecific. You can sense and trace its essential problems in projects like the current Occupy movement. Although I am generally in support of this action and would very much subscribe to the basic idea that something needs to be reconsidered within the space and structures of global capital, the notion of 99 percent (i.e., the idea that the only way that they are able to unite enough people for this cause is by being unspecific about their aims and core demands so as not to "lose" any possible supporters) also makes the whole project also quite. I think that the idea of a harmonious whole, a state of non-conflictual social cohesion, is not only romantic but also naïve. Today, the most important question in this regard is how we—talking both on the scale of, say, global capital and also on the micro-scale of the local—can learn and devise mechanisms and structures that allow us to talk to one another; not in a necessarily harmonious or inclusive way in the sense of an immediate consensual terrain, but in a dissensual arena, where difference is being understood as an asset rather than a hindrance or predicament.

BS Is the term "participation" to be taken seriously or isn't it rather a neo-liberal fighting word suggesting a kind of participation that doesn't exist anymore or isn't even wanted?

MM To start off with, I would agree that the term is certainly not neutral, and not as innocent as it is often proposed to be. To put it very bluntly, I would always be skeptical if one asks you to participate in the first place. This is both based on a certain cynicism in regard to the trustworthiness of the milieu of formal politics and a frustration in terms of the ways in which the term participation has been misused as a tactic by politicians to withdraw from their responsibility as democratically elected representatives who are supposed to not only formally represent the citizens of a respective constituency, but to also make decisions for them. This especially holds true for conditions under Tony Blair's New Labour in the UK, and the realities of the historically derived, consensus-driven Polder Model in the Netherlands. It now continues—in the UK—within David Cameron's idea of the Big Society as liberal empowerment. This again presents us with a mode of politics that utilizes neo-liberal modes of communication and public relations in order to outsource responsibility and subsequently, places the onus on the individual by playing the ball back to the citizens who have originally cast their vote as democratic stakeholders. It is a means to shield oneself from any kind of outside critique. What I am interested in—and working on at the moment—is what I would call a productive inversion of the principle of a romanticized mode of participation, one of an all-inclusive, bottom-up democratic practice. The model I am proposing—not as a replacement but as an additional mechanism for productive public unrest—is a mode of participation that starts on the scale of the individual, a first-person singular pro-active engagement that assumes responsibility and a practice of civil duty, a good sense of mistrust and an ethical position towards what I would call the post-public condition. This means that today, it is simply no longer enough to grave-dig the critique, pessimism and black-writing of the 1980s-based theories of loss, but one must actively engage in the production of space by imagining, developing, enabling, and designing new forms of irritation and corruption in order to provoke and bastardize systemic responses—be they physical or non-physical.

BS A *Gesamtkunstwerk* is closely connected to the relational. However, is it possible to connect the term *Gesamtkunstwerk* with these above-mentioned terms?

MM What we need today is a sensibility towards the specific, not in the sense of something that is necessarily contextual, but something that necessitates a specificity of approach, one that allows for a multiplicity and heterogeneity of voices, actors and agents that coexist in a genuinely pluralist space. It comes back to the Mouffian notion of agonism as a pluralist territory of action, and builds on the Rancierian concept of dissensus as a multi-polar conflictual public space. Here, totality does not exist in the sense of an overall project imagined and devised by a singular protagonist or collective, but as a countless plurality of individuals and collectives, a complex and collaborative force-field of relations.

BS How do you define artistic strategy between the two poles of plurality and totality? And can you perhaps name of some examples?

MM The request of a definition simultaneously demands a blueprint for practice, which I cannot deliver. I think there is a crucial difference between feeling obliged to work 'with everyone' i.e., following a participatory paradigm in the sense of its traditional understanding of inclusion, as opposed to a potential model of practice that focuses on a notion of publicness as a means of personal involvement, which might have an effect on the post-public condition per se. For me, what seems much more urgent today than the question of whether or not to establish more participatory structures is the question of how to assume some form of responsibility that results in projects and initiatives that somehow contribute to what I would call the realm of the common. This of course, often means that those projects, constructions or situations that this might necessitate are often not commissioned i.e., they are being set up and produced within a precarious condition and without mandate. This condition also requires one's own responsibility in terms of setting up the specific common, communal, or collaborative networks that allow for a realization of such practice. Rather than calling for a strategy that fluctuates between plurality and totality, I would like to promote a practice that places itself in this realm of the common while carefully curating a possible arena for dissensus to emerge in a productive way.

BS And coming back to the force field of relations you mentioned before, this is also a topic in psychology in the 40s and 50s which was connected to architectural theory more so than to art. How do you assess the interrelations between art, architecture and psychology, especially in regard to Frederick Kiesler, or Hans Hollein (The Visionary Architecture Project)?

MM I find this work very interesting, yet at the same time, I am interested in projects and propositions that—at the end of the day—have some form of effect in the sense that they alter, undo, rethink, or add to an existing situation. What I find quite frustrating in a lot of the so-called Visionary Architecture Projects of the 60s and 70s is their interpretation of what "the visionary condition" implies. If we are, in the end, just facing a series of paper-proposals, then there is a lack of commitment in terms of an interest and serious attempt to become a driver for change. I am not personally interested in paper architecture. It is usually a default practice by architects who never get anything built. Within the formats of the critical spatial practice that I am interested in the main concern is focusing on setting up and implementing frameworks that effect the spatial conditions in which we live, even if its actual instruments of implementation may not be physical, i.e. policies, time-codes, programming, or curatorial strategies on an urban scale. This however, does not rule out the physical dimension and my interest in constructing physical space. Nevertheless, it presents a substantially different view on practice than the notion of the visionary project.

BS Can we say that the new definitions of space in art have been impacted by the new ideas of modernist architecture?

MM Space should be understood as a medium that one works with. There is a multitude of approaches and tools that allow one to deal with space, amend it, tweak it, design and develop it, corrupt it, enhance it, simplify it, enable or disable certain processes within it, or to add to it physically. At the end of the day, the primary concern when judging a "spatial project" should be to understand, communicate, and critically reflect on its effects on space. Architecture, for example, should be understood as one of many disciplines, but also a tool with which one can contribute to the production of space. Of course architects, historically, have always thought of themselves as the single-handed masters of spatial production, which is not only a myth, but also naïve. When looking back at the second half of the 20th century, there is a very interesting historic trajectory of spatial practices and practitioners who challenged the status quo of internal beliefs of this profession—a profession, by the way, which has always been dominated by alpha-males. Observing the readings of the Situationist movement, but more importantly the work of English architect Cedric Price, one can start to draw a trajectory of a global and decentralized development called Critical Spatial Practice. What is most important to realize here is the development of a sensibility towards space, which goes beyond the physical: an understanding that only uses the physical when necessary. In architecture, for example, the physical is the default medium through which practitioners have thought about space for centuries. However, some issues, programs or problems might not favor a physical approach or solution. What I am interested in is the acknowledgment of a repertoire in architecture and spatial practice that goes beyond the physical, one that assumes customized methods for specific situations and questions. Hence, an approach to a particular given situation or brief handed over by a client would be approached in a multi-faceted way in which one, as a practitioner, develops a take on the given issue by means of a holistic package of spatial practices that result in an economy of architecture rather than a conventional architectural project in the form of purely a physical building that primarily focuses on an architectural form and aesthetic. This however, does not rule out an architectural project that comes in the form and format of a physical building, it simply offers what I would call an extended toolbox of practices, which both complicate and programmatically challenge the physical reality of a given situation.

BS Is the idea of the *Gesamtkunstwerk* just romantic?

MM I do not want to dismiss it, but I would agree with you. To claim that there is an approach that can produce a new consensual reality is something that neither interests me, nor do I think that one should attempt to tackle complexity by trying to reduce it to a common denominator. Complexity, rather than being boiled down to a middle ground, should be exploited as an asset. Viral, multitudal or rhizomatic structures should not be flattened but exacerbated. Yes, to a certain extent I think it presents a romantic notion of totality, but more importantly, I believe that it aims for a fatally misunderstood impulse that we can deal with the world in its totality. This, by default, calls for a consensus at the core of its vision, some form of reconciled mediation, some form of homogenized plurality. It is its essential idea that scares me, the belief that there could be something that understands itself as all encompassing. I would make a plea for a conflictual plurality that exploits complexity as an enriching force of everyday life.

<u>Josef Bauer</u>
Griechenbeisl Exhibition, 1971

Josef Bauer belongs to the generation of Austrian artists who presented a concrete form language to the public at the Galerie Griechenbeisl in the 1960s, together with Christa Hauer and Johann Fruhmann. At that time Bauer attempted—most likely inspired by the Italian Arte Povera, as well as by Joseph Beuys—to define a term, which intensely dealt with the cultural parameters of the production of knowledge and meaning in the arts. Also the concrete approaches of the art of the Viennese group of Gerhard Rühm and his Likes, whose use of language as a performative, but also creative material, strongly raised Bauer's interest. In the 1960s Bauer had participated in the "Bielefeld Talks" and received vital impulses from European conceptual art. His aim in his paintings and his objects was to mediate between the spheres of language and artistic material or even to impede them to develop objects, which can be understood as an accumulation of various meanings. In this context, he often used the principle of omission to preserve a bit of mystery. **HK**

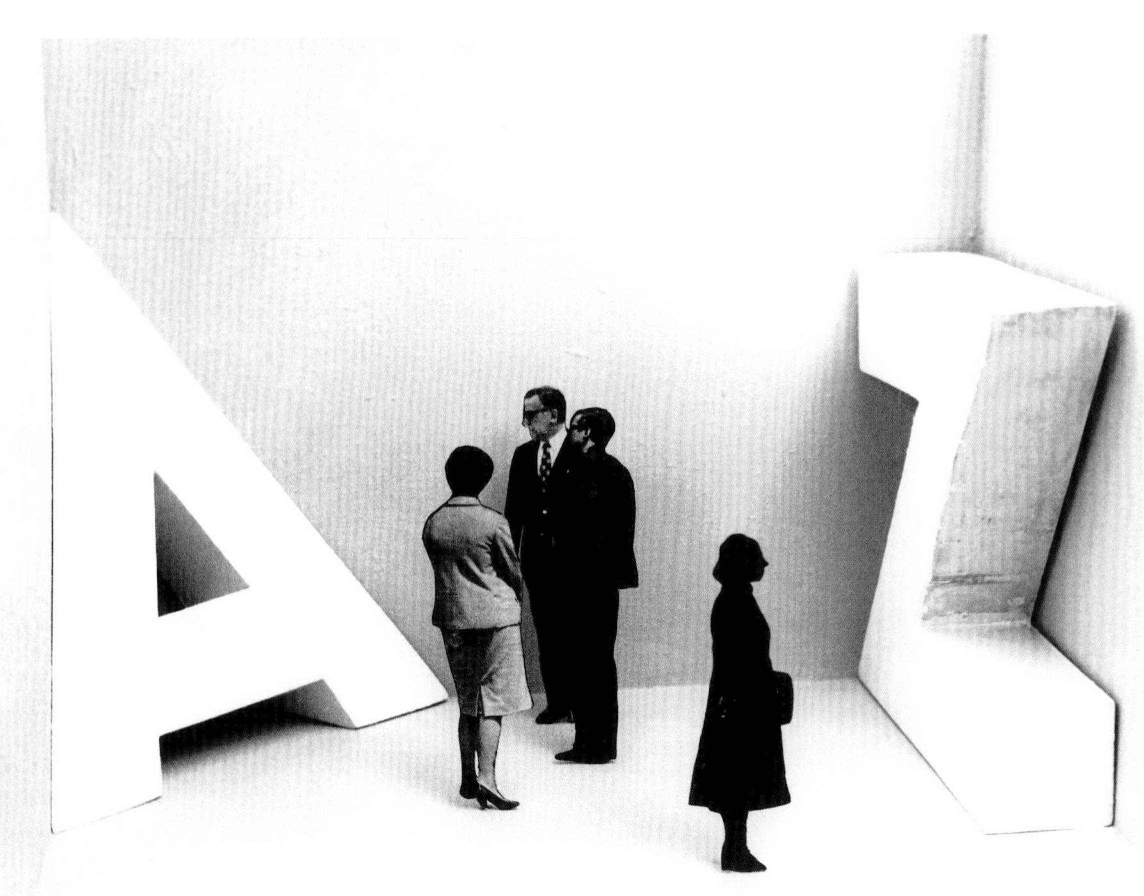

 Christian Boltanski, Ilya Kabakov and Jean Kalman
Der Ring – Fünfter Tag. Der Tag danach, **1999**

The site of the former Beelitz pulmonary sanatorium, one of the largest hospital complexes in Germany around the turn of the 1900s, hosted *Der Ring – Fünfter Tag. Der Tag danach* theatre installation which Christian Boltanski, Ilya Kabakov and Jean Kalman "understood as an extension to the programme of the Bayreuth Festival from a post-utopian viewpoint" from the 26th to the 27th of June, 1999. On the occasion of the festival *Theater der Welt* the three artists developed a piece that united museum and theatre, and formally and contextually integrated itself within the given setting. The installation was participative and framed as a walk that illustrated characteristics of *Gesamtkunstwerk* aesthetic. As its title indicates, the installation refers to Wagner's Ring of the Nibelung, in which the artists saw, "the climax of artistic megalomania [...] the

Gesamtkunstwerk." With this project they turned against Wagner's aim of anthropological, aesthetic and political totality by combining the aesthetic utopia of the composer with the social one of the sanatorium and the political one of communism: "[...] in the 20th century two great utopic concepts were developed: on the one hand that science would deliver the world from its troubles; and on the other that politics would save the world. Both utopias have failed miserably [...] On the 'day after' you have a splitting headache because of all the misery and the catastrophe that this utopia has caused." (Christian Boltanski, Jean Kalman) **BS**

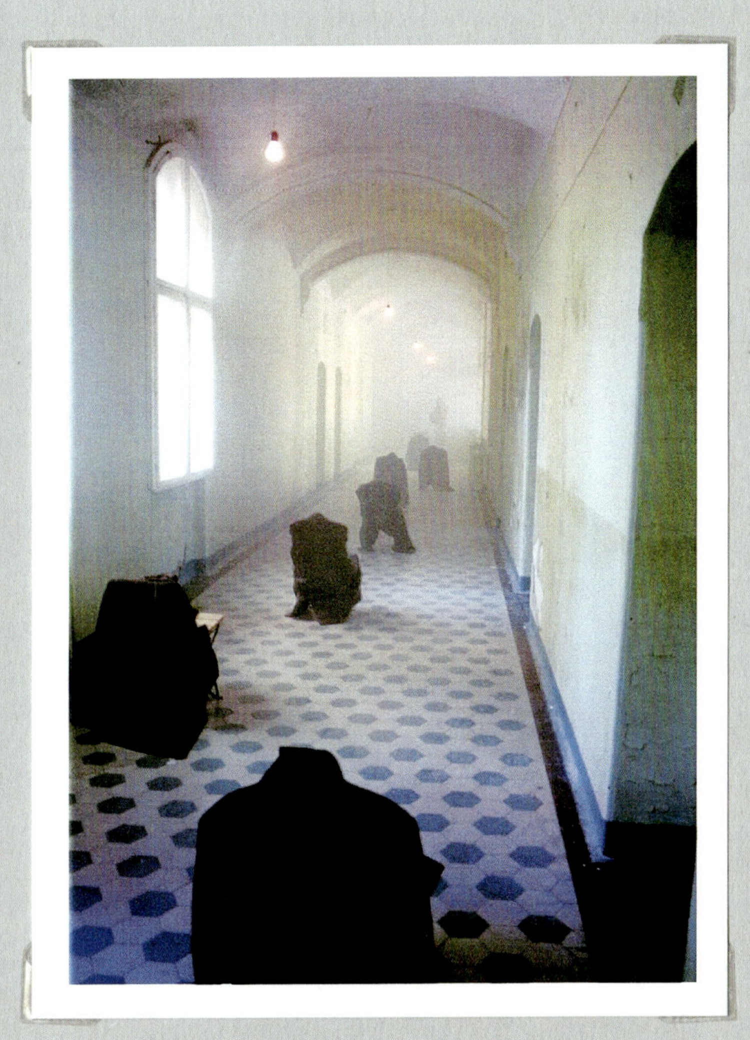

<u>Daniel Buren</u>
***Fiche technique*, 1972**

The repetition of the vertical line is a recurring motive in Daniel Buren's opus and, as Kandinsky in *Point and Line to Plane* describes, a quantitative enforcement. In 1969, Buren was invited by Joseph Beuys to Bern to Harald Szeemann's exhibition *When attitudes become form* to "use the exhibition room" together with Beuys unofficially. But Buren exhibited in the city and cluttered it up with stripes. This location-dependent working method went hand in hand with an institution-critical attitude, which challenged the museum as a venue of art and confronted a new audience with art. In *Fiche technique* Buren thematised the understanding of art pieces as consumer goods and scrutinises their perception in a museum context. By pretending blandness they criticise the institution, in which they are preserved and whose impact they are exposed to. The observers are forced to change their ways of looking at things. The stripes are Buren's visual tools, which are supposed to help alter perspectives. The mathematic precision with which Buren designs his works—each stripe is exactly 8.7 cm wide—hints at new regulations and circumstances. The image questions a rhythm guide-line, which distinguishes itself from the room by its universality and may be a pattern for many things, which an institution or an entire city offers. The title *Fiche technique* means "technical data sheet" resp. denotes information like picture rights and technical data as well as hints at a system, which confronts another one. **NH**

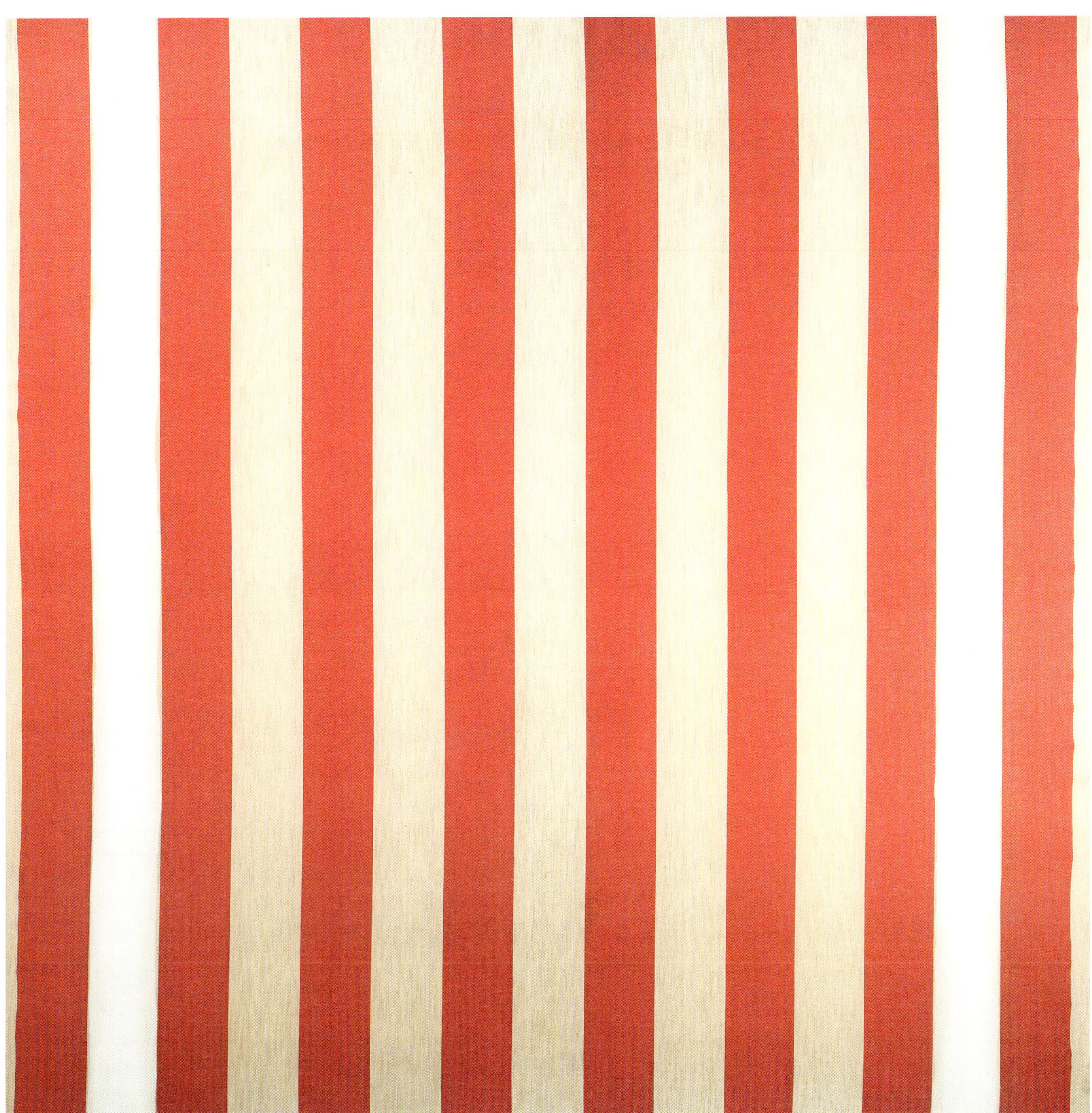

Ernst Caramelle
ohne Titel, 1986

Ernst Caramelle's work is a mobile cabinet on wheels, which was painted with red wine and equipped with two small screens. The spectator automatically identifies the horizontal line at the bottom of the cabinet as "mouth", and due to the series of cuts, the screens are perceived as winking "eyes", which form a rectangular "face". As simple as this intellectual game may seem, this object sums up the conceptual approach to sculpture at this time. The spectator also notices that the screens broadcast the current TV programs. This actualisation is the key to the work, it emphasises its media-critical dimension, and animates the face on a different level. This vitality is supported by the existence of "reality show" TV programs, which permanently attempt to cloud the distance between virtuality and reality, using subtly psychologising scripts and concepts. Coating the case with wine, whose bleaching process Caramelle bears in mind, is again a reference to temporary performative artistic processes connecting this work to (Austrian) art history. However, Caramelle's art works with mainly reserved gestures, though the formal stringency of its conceptual realisation gives sharpness and very early establishes an institution-critical stance. **HK**

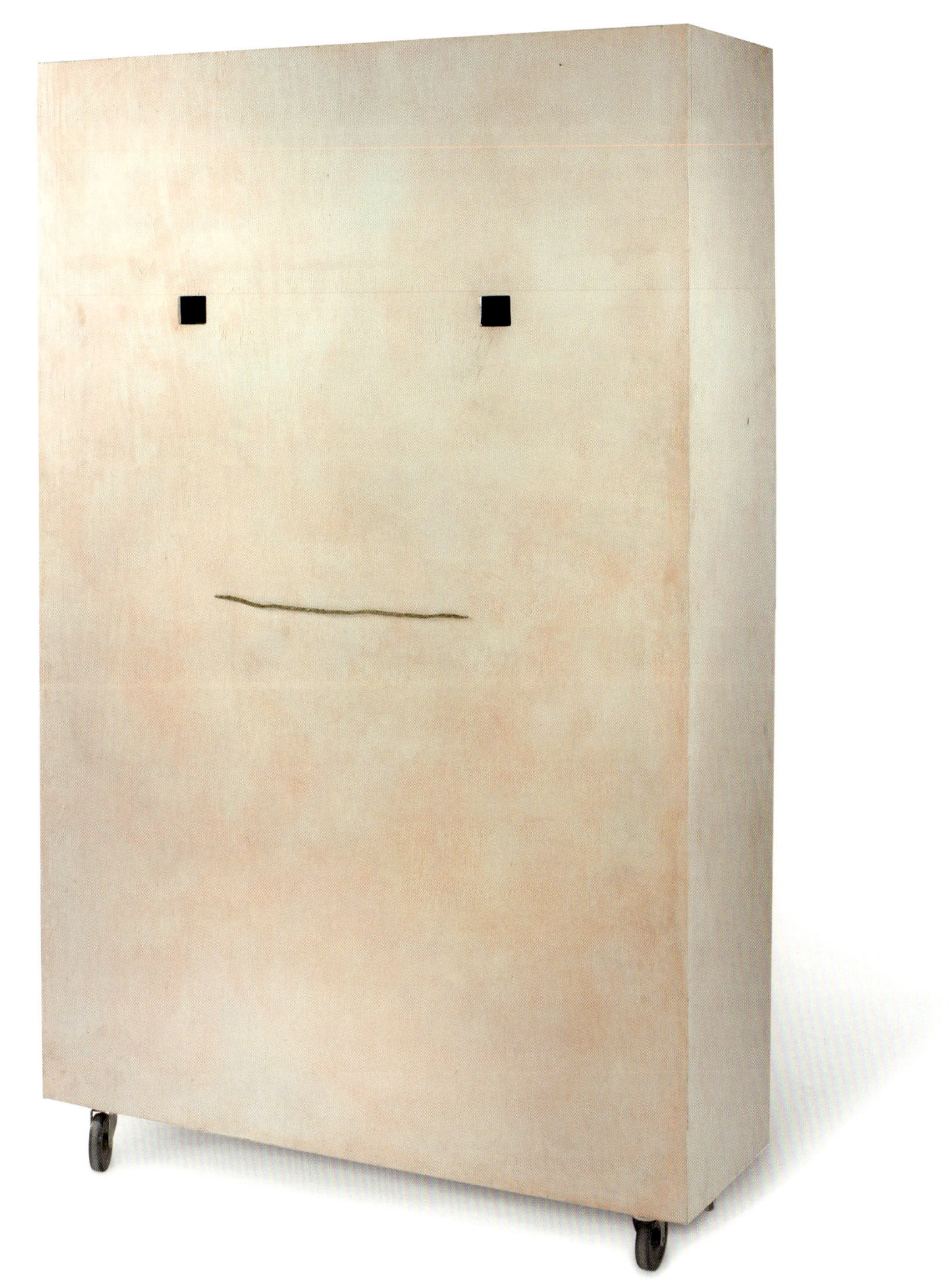

Cityrama II
Eine nichtrealisierte Stadtrundfahrt in Köln, 1962

As a collaboration between two major groups of artists or art movements, the Cityrama project surely belongs among the most advanced joint projects of the Cologne Fluxus and the representatives of Parisian Nouveau Réalisme. Arnulf Rainer and Peter Kubelka were also involved and are immersed in the concepts of this artistic city tour. The compilation of artists—Mary Bauermeister, architect Peter Neufert and collector Wolfgang Hahn—testifies to ongoing exchange within the European art scene of that day at the "Galerie der Künstler" in Cologne. *Cityrama II* is based on an idea by Nam June Paik and was designed but not realized by Wolf Vostell and Stefan Wewerka in 1961/62. Vostell and Wewerka had planned this city tour in minute detail as a group happening, and 13 artists and musicians made suggestions based on their experiences of the original *Cityrama* project. Consequently, precise instructions elaborate how these happenings should be distributed and organized whithin the metropolitan area. Several busses should deliver the visitors at the venues. The urban space serves as an expanded field of artistic activity and the group character enforces the atmosphere of an art experience that is primarily devoted to changing reality through art. Planned artistic contributions in the project from: Raphaèl Anouj, César, Christo, François Dufrêne, Gérard Deschamps, Robert Filliou, Raymond Hains, Alain Jouffroy, Peter Kubelka, Ben Patterson, Pera, Arnulf Rainer, Daniel Spoerri, Wolf Vostell, Stefan Wewerka. **HK**

aagaard achleitner anouj caesar christo deschamps dufrêne filliou hains henry jouffroy
köpcke kubelka j. j. lebel paik patterson pera niki de saint phalle rainer diter rot rühm
spoerri tinguely vostell wewerka emmett williams
laden sie herzlichst ein zu einer stadtrundfahrt cityrama in köln 3. märz 1962
abfahrt mit autobussen hotel zur post 11,30 uhr

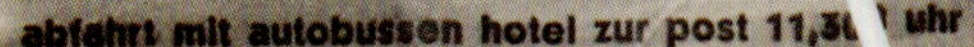

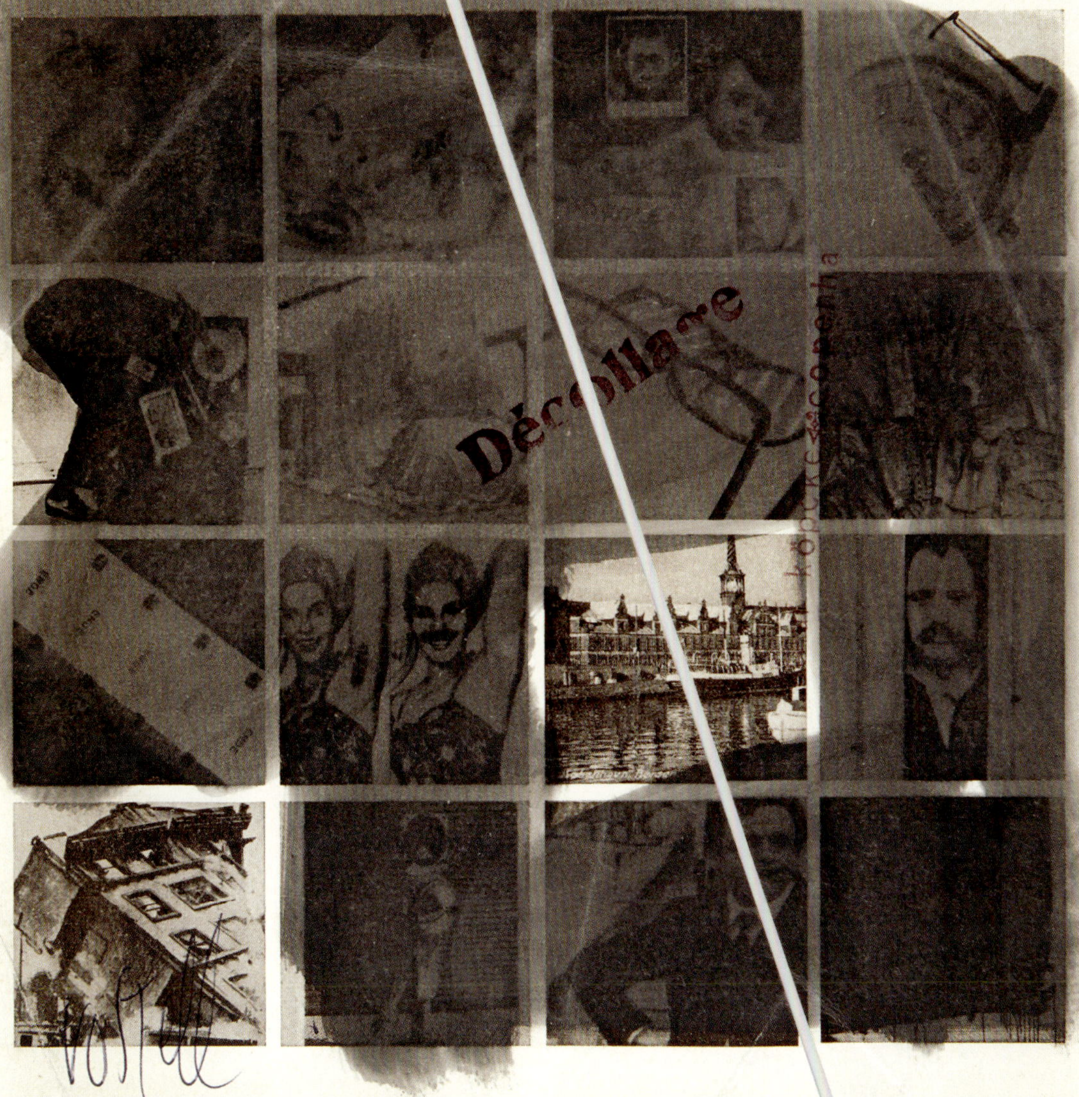

Décollage

galerie köpcke copenhagen k lille kirkestraede 1 tel. by 2698 präsentiert décollage von vostell
(annullierung der ausstellung stadtrundfahrt cityrama beabsichtigt von der galerie dumont
köln märz 1962)

Heinz Emigholz
Two Projects by Frederick Kiesler, 2006/09

Heinz Emigholz has been working on his *Architecture as Autobiography* project, in which *Two Projects by Frederick Kiesler* belongs, since 1993. The main theme of the film is the confrontation of two visionary projects by Frederick Kiesler, one of which was realized, and a second that wasn't. The *Endless House*, an architectonic design that was never constructed, is presented beside the realized *The Shrine of the Book* edifice by Armand Bartos on the site of the Israel Museum in Jerusalem. Emigholz attempts to give a comprehensive analysis of each undertaking and at the same time launches a debate on the two designs. In the film the walls of *Endless House* are used as projection surfaces that unite the analysis of the building complex in Jerusalem with narrations of rooms in New York City. Active design and projection accomplishments—i.e. incarnated imaginations—are accentuated and visualized as writing, sketches, photographs, architecture and sculptures. Emigholz prefers a cadrage in his image composition, "which establishes a phenomenological relation in the room." The predominant conventions—in relation to the documentation of architectural motives—of rectangularity and central perspective play no key role. For the spectator this means an invitation to enter into the films and break with one's own preconditioned viewing habits. The tenacious scanning of rooms and objects gradually and subtly forms an overall picture, and becomes a film on the objectification of conceptual imagination. **BS**

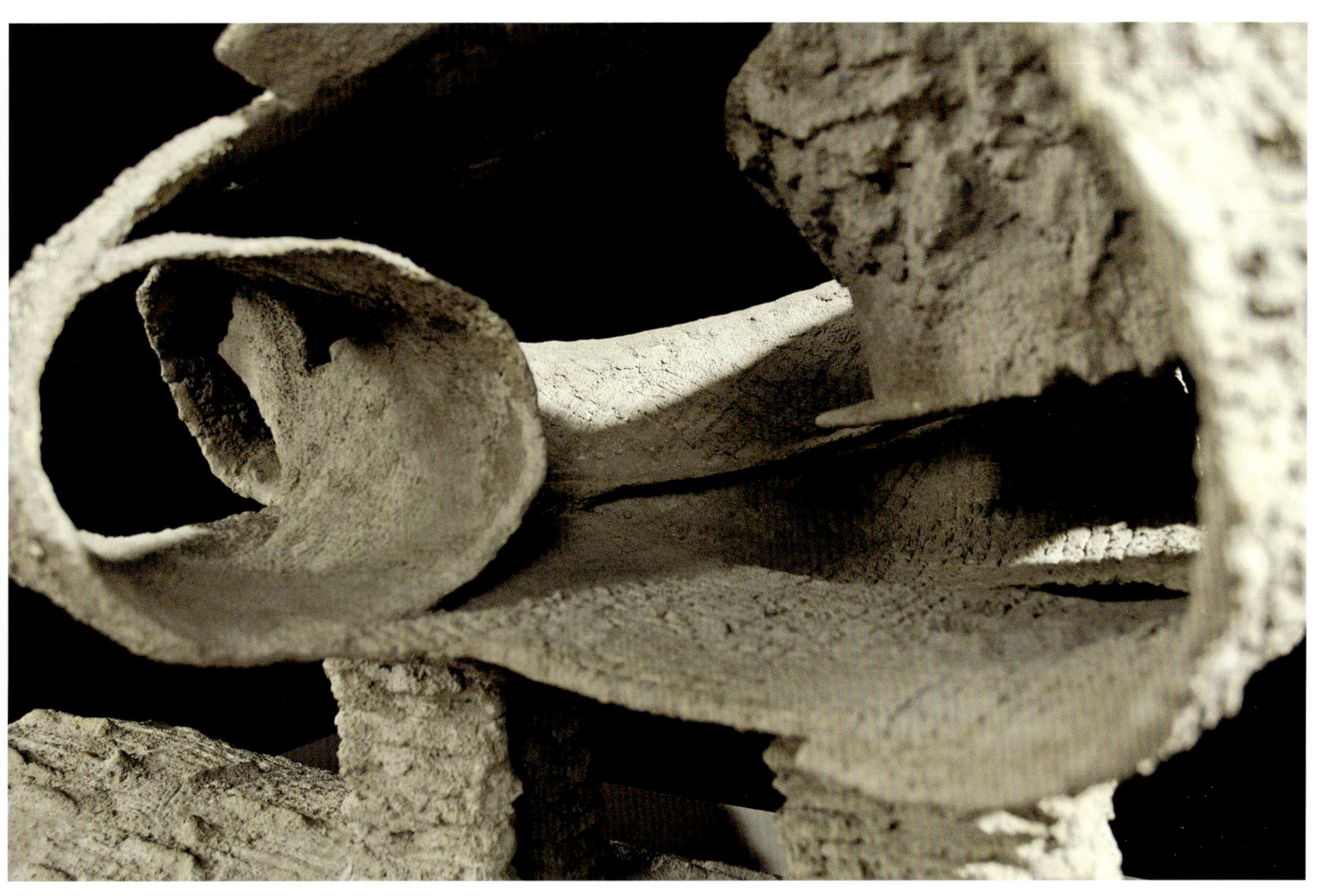

Julia Hohenwarter
Catwalk, 2009

Julia Hohenwarter's work *Catwalk* consists of nine walk-in cubes, which in their fragmentation resemble a range of moveable parts, and thus are not only visually, but also auditorily perceptible. As soon as the *Catwalk* is stepped onto, the mass centre changes, and the cube drops down with a big bang. Also the local reference determines one's perception: In a narrow passage, which makes any detour impossible, only walking on the *Catwalk* remains. The cubes decline with each step rearranging themselves, so that the structure of the row is altered. Afterwards it looks entirely different to before: The traces of the predecessor are mixed with one's own tracks, leaving an imprint of the physical engagement, which makes the object tangible and the starting point unrecognizable.

This irreversibility of experiencing the object, which is caused by the actors, is manifested in the space it occupies, and deconstructs the path separating it into parts, which are only walkable one after another. What this sequence looks like eventually is determined by the participation of the emancipated actors. Precisely their partaking turns the exhibition of an object into the exhibition of an actor and to a "Spatialization of the Subject" (Julia Hohenwarter).
Julia Hohenwarter also refers to architecture and exhibition displays, as her "way" continuously questions and adapts its function by static conditions and spatialization. **NH**

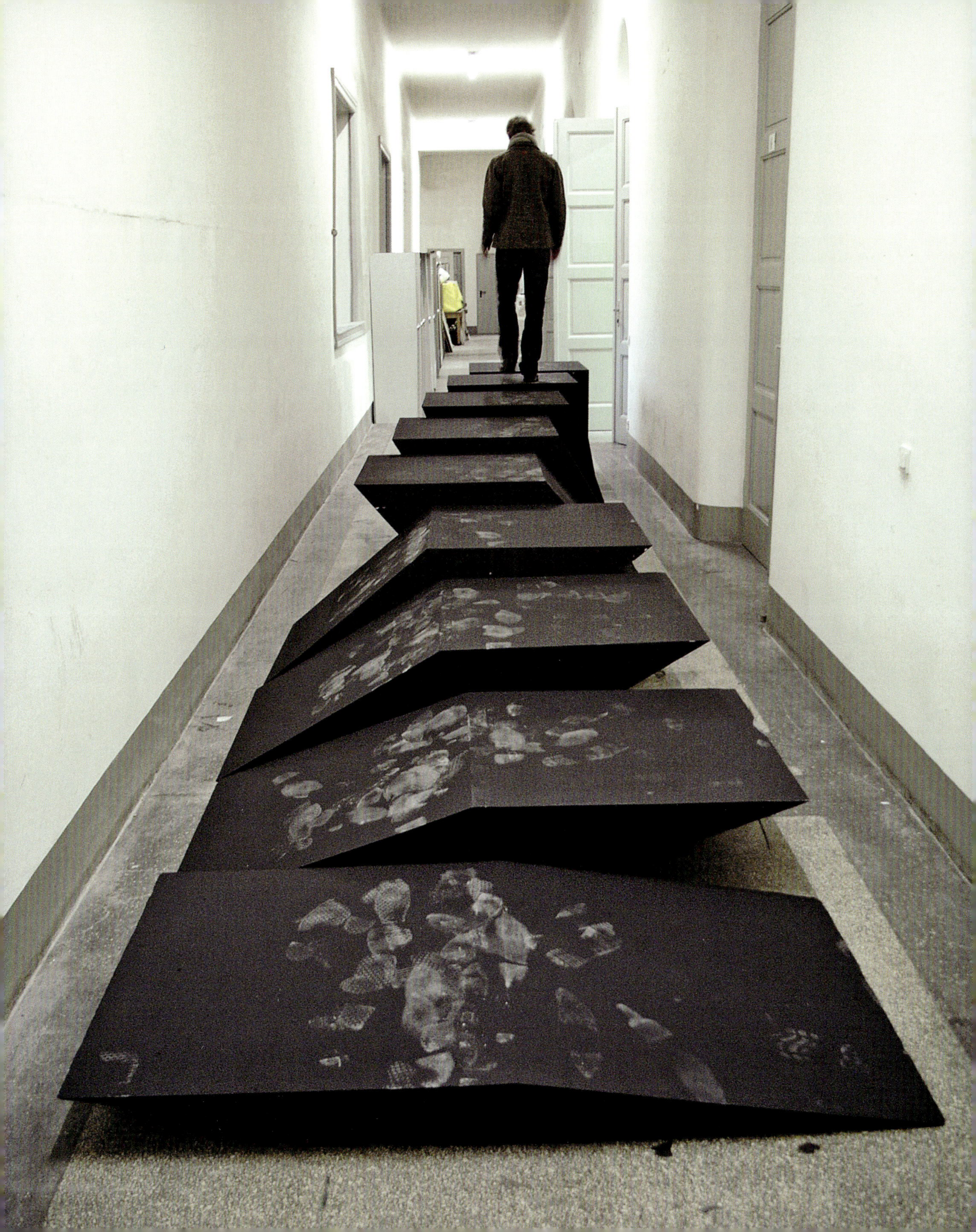

<u>Martin Kippenberger</u>
Alt Wien, Großplakat, 1991

The piece *Alt Wien* shows the traditional Viennese 1st district cafe, which artist Martin Kippenberger has turned into his temporary studio during his stays in Vienna. He developed several ideas for projects at that cafe, which he evolved that impulsively that the projects were often realised the day after. Kippenberger had coffee shop-studios in various cities all over Europe and the globe. These cafes and bars are integral components of his artistic work. Kippenberger was invited to take part in an artistic poster project launched by the *Grazer Kunstverein* for public space in 1989, his contribution was a large poster of the Viennese cafe. Kippenberger hung up a selection of posters he regarded to be interesting at the Cafe Alt Wien and had a picture taken he blew up to a large bill. His utopia of a network of different locations, his idea of a translocation of rooms and the complete dispersion of private and public areas are central aspects in his work. In his works *Ortsverschiebungen* Kippenberger reflects the redefinition of art and its newly-assigned social role as well as in his project *METRO Net* in Underground train stations as in Museum of *Modern Art Syros* (MOMAS). The project *Alt Wien* at the same time is a kind of temporary, curated exhibition, which was carried out in public, and thus shows Kippenberger's conceptual idea of a global fellowship through art. **HK**

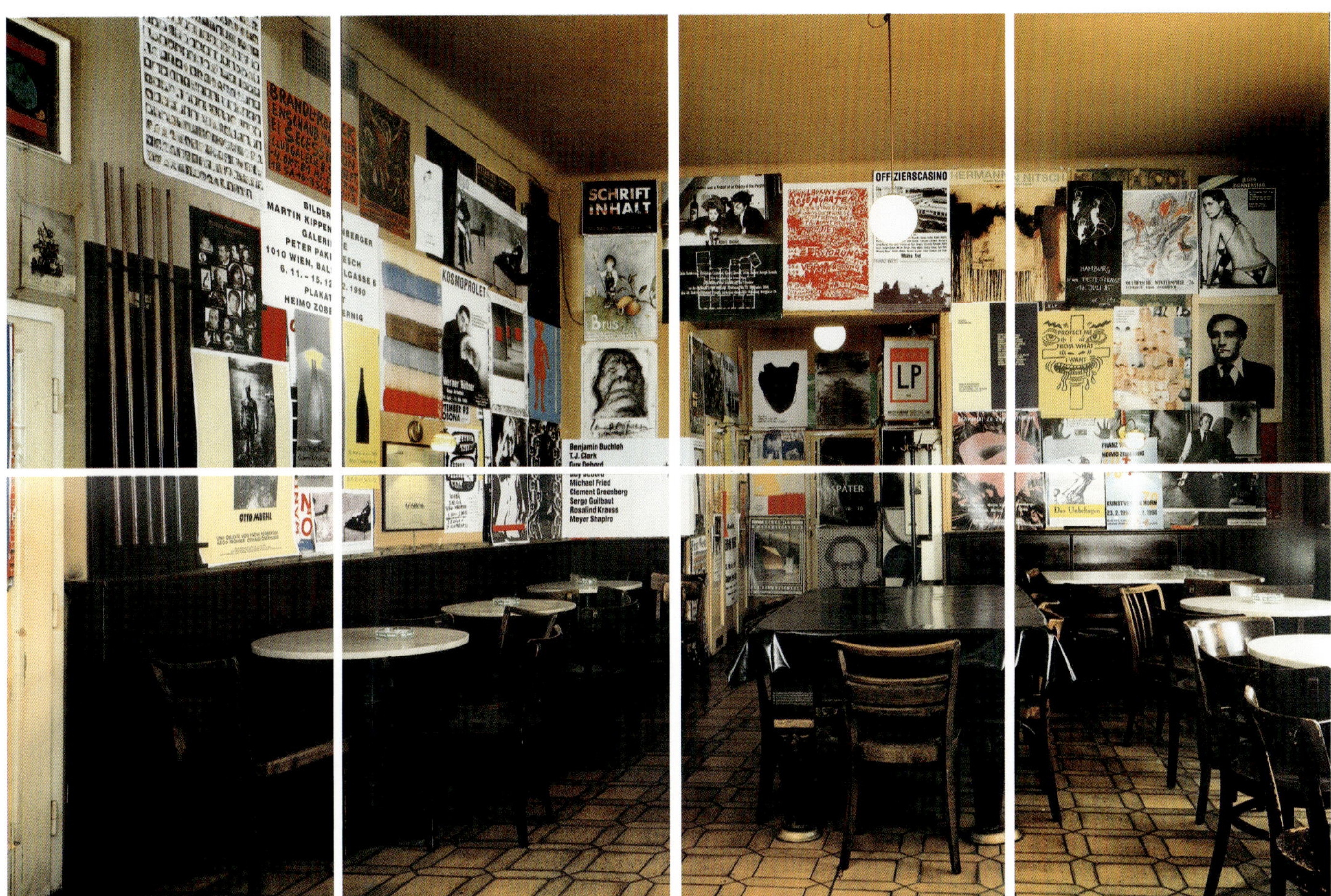

<u>Mahony</u>
o. T. (Marginale), 2011

"Everything begins with the absence of an object, which has already been both artifact and fragment. In connection and combination, designed for or of it, a collective body, which is missing, proven by its impression. The momentary gap is immediately breached as an unnecessary idea, its print remains, which is mounting and setting, substituting the context. Moreover, it enables exhibiting the object; next frame institution. Or: It is made for a museum giving the frame its context." (Mahony)

Observation is the initial point of their involvement with the topic *Gesamtkunstwerk*, produced at the anthropological museum in Mexico City. The focus was on the blanks remaining left when pieces are removed. Thereby, the mountings moved into the centre of attention, which suddenly formed a kind of cast of the exhibits. Mahony hereby uses the appropriation of something marginal, which is transformed and thus serves as a substitute of art or as a *Gesamtkunstwerk*. The collective questions it, translates it, and hence reactivates it. They set up a rhizomatic web, which connects history with the present, overcomes the borders between the banal and the artistic, and thus unlocks new potential space for the discussion of artistic and art theoretical questions. **BS**

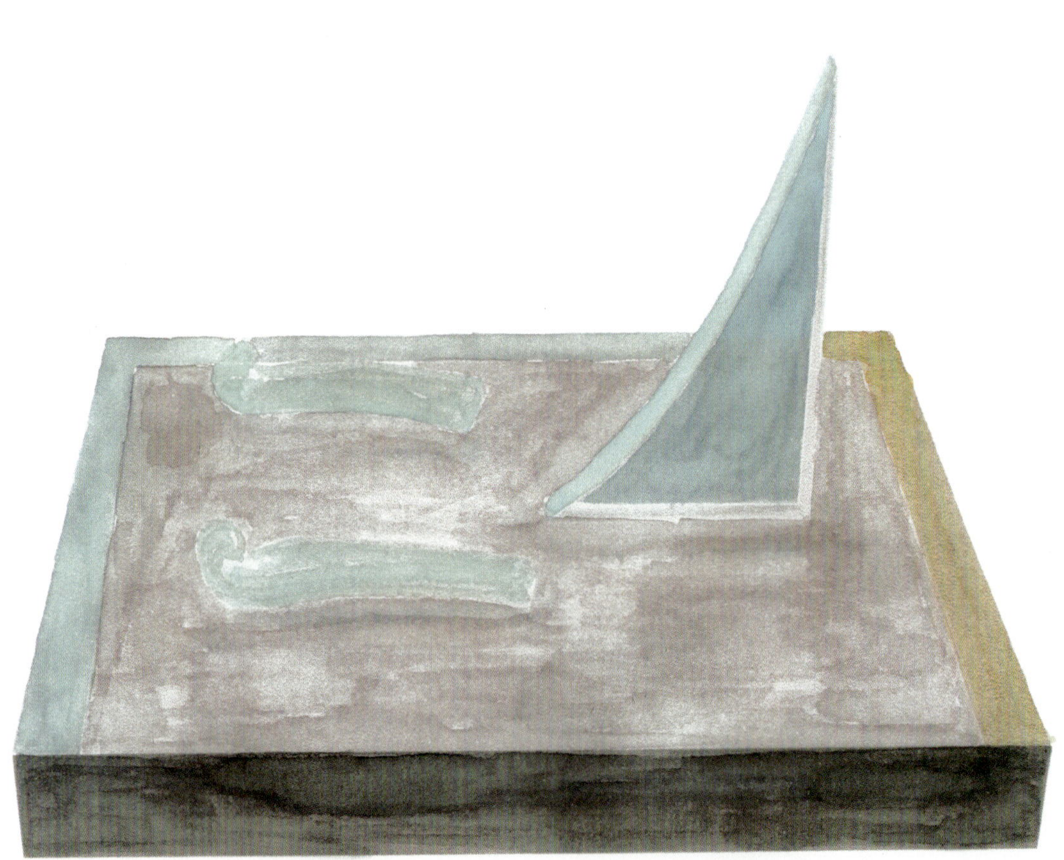

Ralo Mayer
***And turns and turns and I turn pages. (...) /
"ÜBERSETZUNG UND VERRAT", 2009/12***

Ralo Mayer's work—*And Turns and Turns and I Turn Pages. "Have another shot," the skeuomorphic whisper roared inside my ears, revealing endless fields of view, captions of geometric arrangements way beyond dimensions 3+1. It was not without rekindled enthusiasm that I thus continued reading p. 402-472: which describes footage of an automatic apparatus scanning an abandoned room full of research about Biosphere 2, and what appears to be notes for a screenplay, including the handwritten memo: Dreh?buch. All the while accompanied by melancholic sounds of robotic routines / "ÜBERSETZUNG UND VERRAT"*—the full title of which can also be thought of as its abstract description, began in 2007 during the course of Mayer's research on the Biosphere 2. In this scientific project from 1991 to 1993 eight scientists lived in a glass dome in the Arizona desert in what is regarded as the prototype of a self-sufficient ecosystem, designed to enable the colonization of our universe.

As the materialization of a utopia, Biosphere 2 becomes a system that Ralo Mayer restructures and examines performatively. The network that develops between himself and his works is founded in the temporal and spatial relation of the agents to one another and includes both objects and subjects. Mayer focuses on the question of "failure" and by means of projection and reflection to transfer this onto other media and thus renegotiate it as, among other things, the interpreter of the fictional novel *The Ninth Biospherian*.

In addition to the robotic film recordings of a camera that scans Biosphere 2 in a 360 degree shot, a text, which functions as a script, is visible, a screenplay for the image. Mayer is interested in renegotiating the mechanisms of interpretation that are released in the transfer from one medium to another and in writing a story that playfully unveils the contents and mythologization of media. **NH**

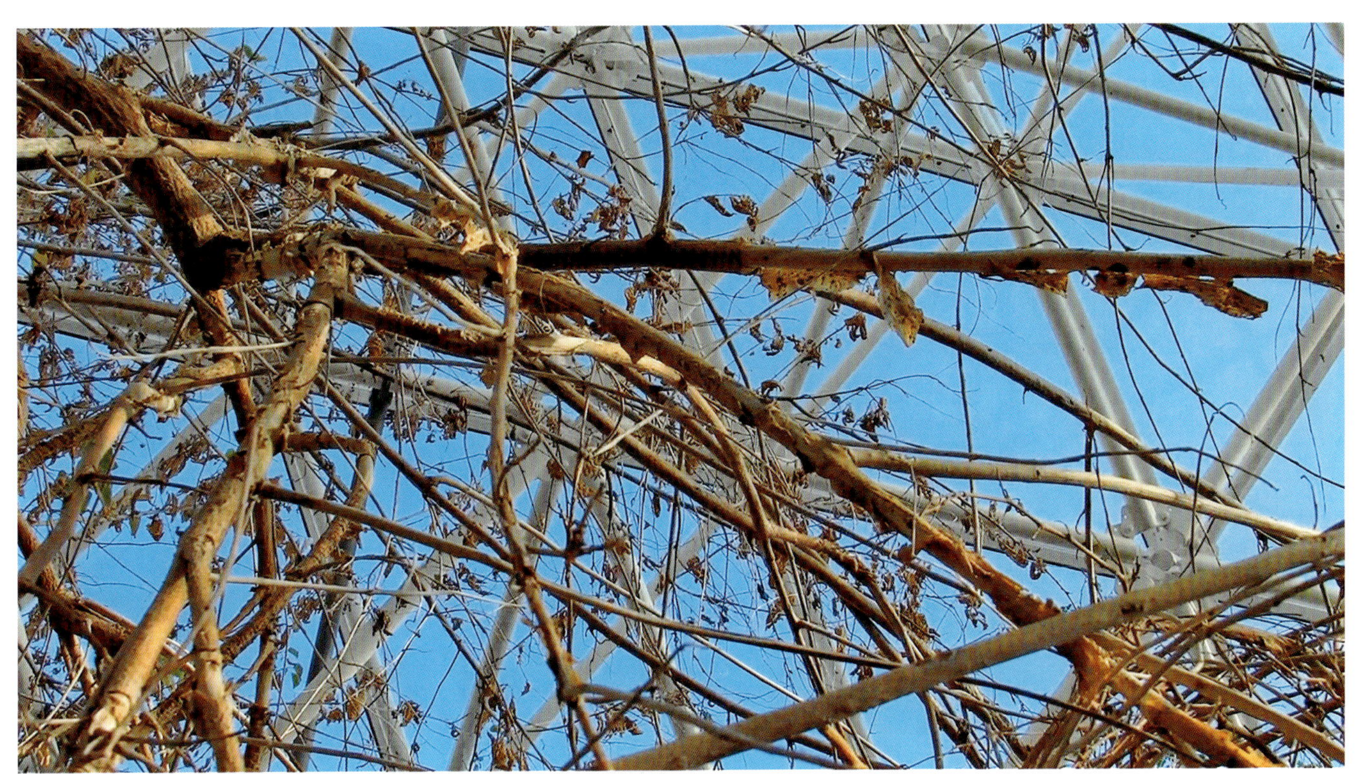

<u>Helga Philipp</u>
o. T. (Objekt 70033), Sitzmöbel, 1970

Already in 1968 Helga Philipp exhibited—together with Richard Kriesche and Marc Adrian—at the "Galerie nächst St. Stephan", Vienna. On the occasion of an exhibition at the "forum stadtpark" in Graz she founded the short-living collective "Gruppa A ustria" in collaboration with Kriesche and Jorrit Tornquist. Back then, Philipp dealt with the question of a new artistic self-conception beyond gender specification. Her steering towards an entirely geometric, formal language is a theoretical reflection on the abstraction of modernism and its effect on Eastern philosophy. The artistic discourse in her opus is directed at the concrete tendencies in Europe and America, but Philipp's utopia of a unification of art and life remains omnipresent in her work. Ratio and sensibility shall be merged to one, and the relationship between artist, object, and spectator should be set in motion in a holistic relation. Philipp developed a basic geometric structure, which she could convert freely with various materials and artistic genres. Her works are classed among the seemingly paradox field of "pure art", which deliberately chooses an abstract language in order to allow the abolition of genre definitions like sculpture, drawing, painting and design in its artistic concept. An early paper by Philipp shows, that this concept incorporates the social utopia of a new art for a democratic society: "[...] I expect [the spectator] to take responsibility for the quality of the happening by his relation, movement, his willingness to change perception and by permitting irritation of his basic condition."[1] HK

1 Quote from Brigitte Borchhardt-Birbaumer, „Mathematik der Seele", in: Carl Aigner/Gerald Bast (ed.), *Helga Philipp. Poesie der Logik*, Vienna/New York, 2010, p.56.

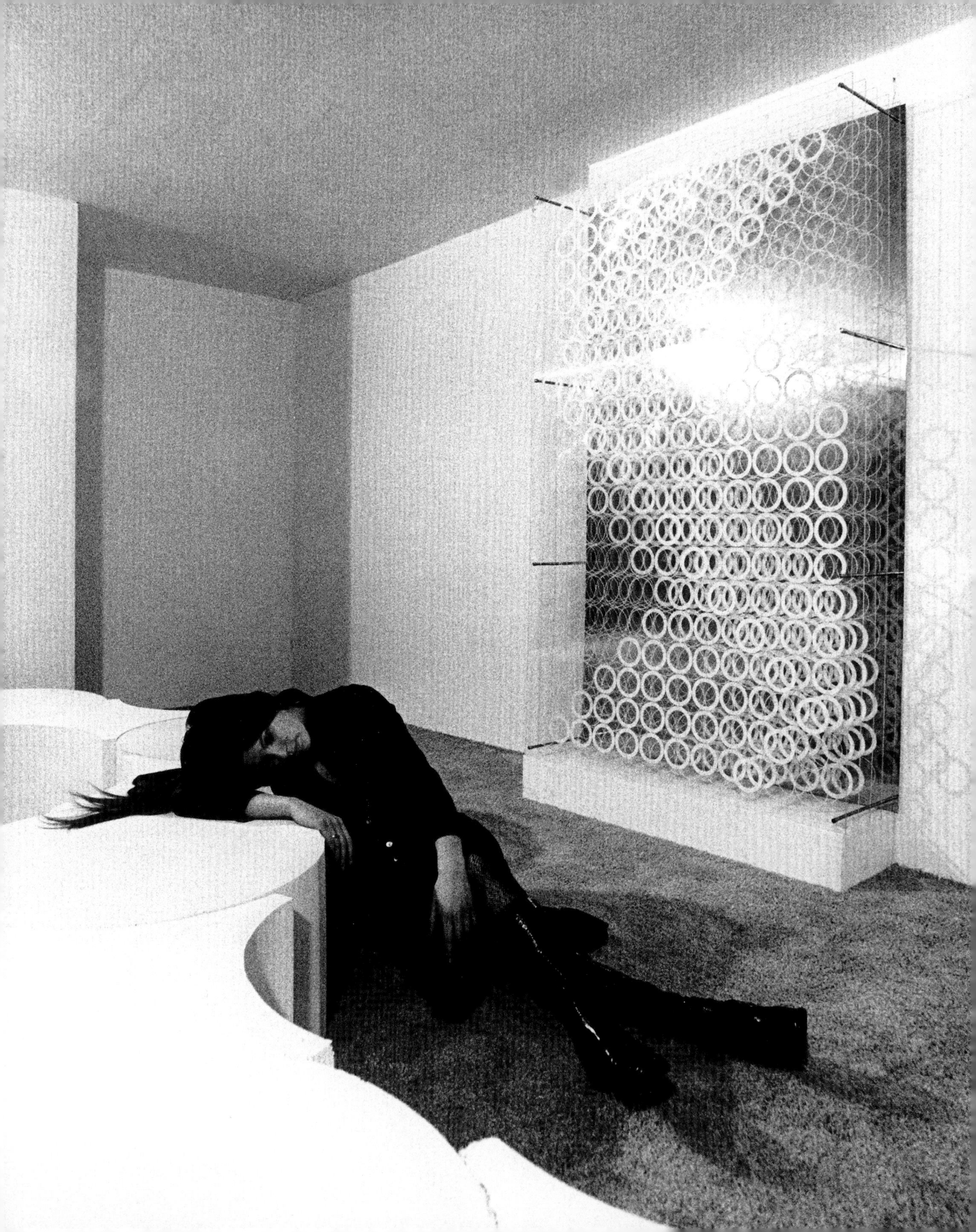

<u>Jason Rhoades</u>
Mi Saga, U Saga (Emmanuelle Saga), 2005

After the producing artist has fallen into disrepute in the late 1980s, artist Jason Rhoades started to work symbolically on the creation of new materials for art in the 2000s. He developed the material "PeaRoaFoam", setting an example against art that had seemingly retreated to mere discourse. Rhoades' art must be seen as a world machine, which by actively dealing with performative art, installation art and the illusory world of the cinema, has smashed a production of realms of experiences, expressed by the use of his own new "artistic materials". Rhoades elaborated his work at the time his colleagues Paul McCarthy and Mike Kelley attempted to unite installative elements and performance.

He questions the different realms of experience using pledges: from the funfair and the super market to the mosque, the museum or the karaoke bar. They provide the room concepts, which the artist analyses looking for moments of lived and stifled fantasies. He derived his art from the tradition of American West Coast Pop music, as well as the American film industry, and opened up these experiences to large spatial installations. In his piece *Mi Saga, U Saga (Emmanuelle Saga)* Rhoades uses simple neon signs, condenses the neon letter salad with various materials to make nonsense of the idea of the better world neon signs usually try to suggest. **HK**

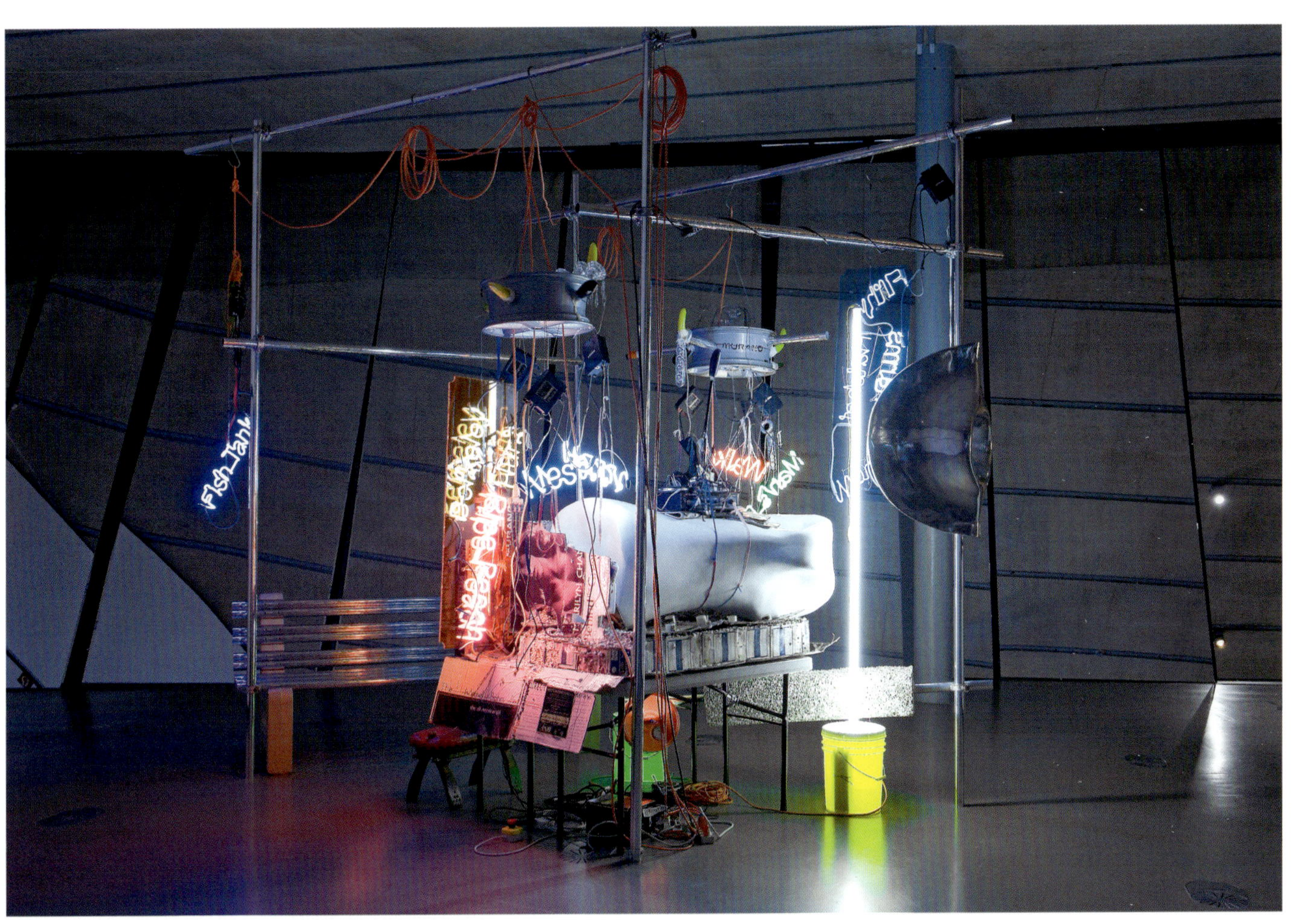

<u>Gerhard Rühm</u>
Reizwortzeichnungen, 2010

If you want to focus on a basic principle in Gerhard Rühm's opus, it would certainly be the problematisation of the dual character of language as a content and as a form, which Rühm analyses in various media and art genres. In his graphic art, Rühm is interested in a systematic exploration of writing on the image. Writing is interesting to him as a vehicle that allows an expansion of the complex of context and form in graphic art. Moreover, Rühm reflects on the use of language and its instrumentalisation, which he expresses in the late 1950s using collages and which characterises Rühm's art as profoundly socio-critical. The artistic intention is obvious: Rühm wants to get to the bottom of the poetic potential of language, which at a second glance discloses the sore spots of our society or reaches the limits of artistic and social taboos.

Rühm's artistic career proceeded simultaneously in various fields. Very early the poet, artist, director and performer held readings together with H. C. Artmann, Friedrich Achleitner and Konrad Bayer, attended performative events and produced theatre plays. Being friends with Marc Adrian, he also worked on artistic forms of expression in language. He belongs to the first representatives of concrete poetry in Austria. Against the background of the interest in those days in cybernetics, the communication theory and psychology of perception, in the 1960s Rühm mooved to Berlin and positioned himself in the German concrete poetry scene. His work in visual poetry started with early typogrammes and has extended to the *Reizwortzeichnungen*, that unveil a concrete, but also a poetic dimension of perception in language and writing. His activities as an author and director, as well as a performer of his own poems and his music are to be rated similarly highly. His art works are machines of meaning, which enter a complex game with the psychological constitution of the recipient, as they always also convey a reference to reality. **HK**

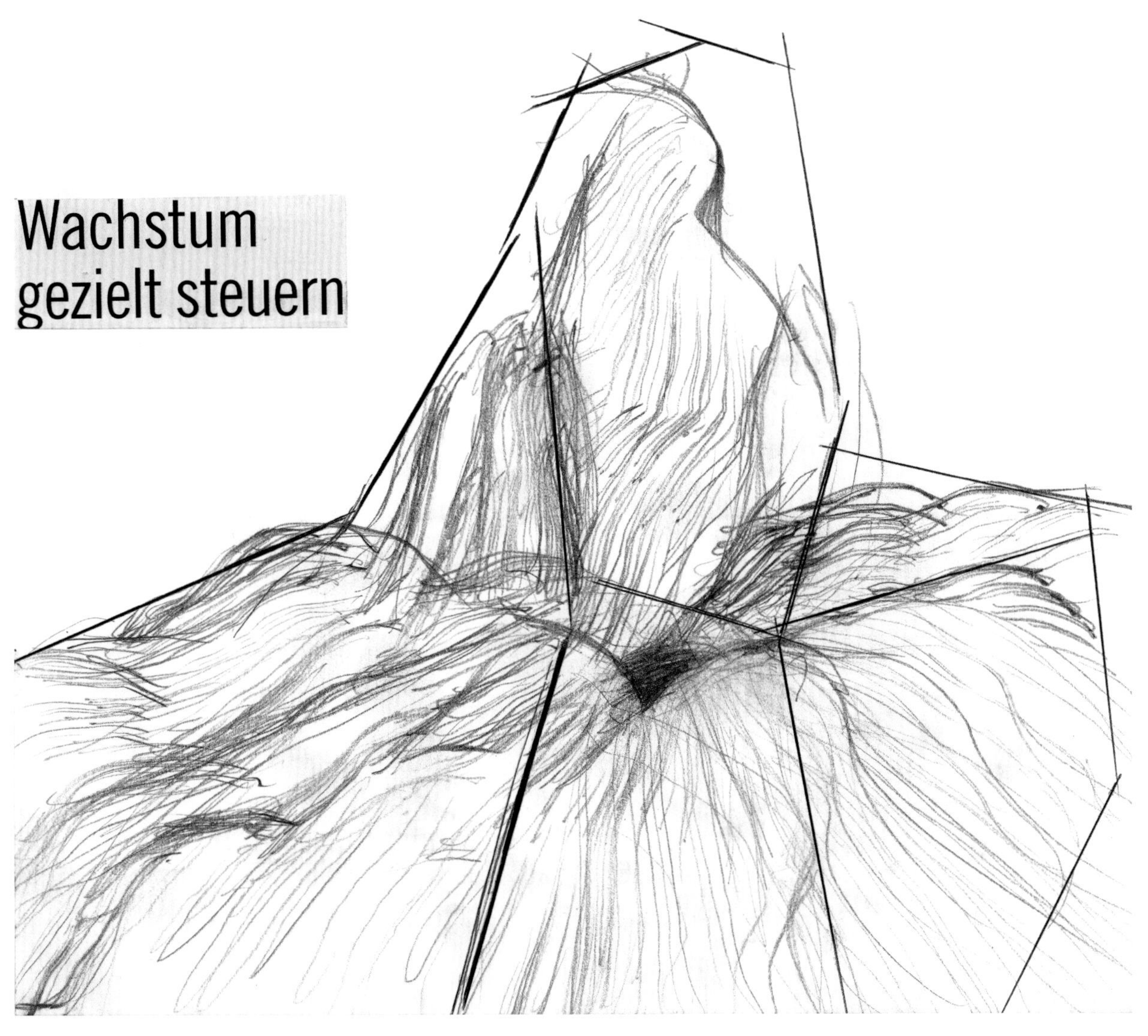

Wachstum
gezielt steuern

<u>Jörg Schlick</u> and <u>Günter Brus</u>
Langspielkreise, 2004

The joint piece of Jörg Schlick and Günter Brus was first presented in an exhibition in Cologne in 2004. A year before Brus had seen Schlick's latest work in Berlin, and afterwards approached the artist together with his wife. Brus has always been interested in the contemporary art scene he critically observed. In Schlick he had found a complex thinker, who he was happy to confront with his work in joint projects. Anni Brus launched the initiative for the cooperation with the Graz-based multi artist.

The pieces combine Schlick's virtually scientific approach within his artistic method he had consistently expanded reflecting on gene technology, perceptional psychology and the mechanisms of the art world. The graphic contribution of Brus on the convex mirrors looks like a "particle accelerator", an extension of the anti-septic painting of Schlick with Brus' artistic struggle for form and his complex constructions of an enhanced understanding of the world. Their work results in a critical reflection of the modernism of Josef Albers or Heimo Zobernig's reference aesthetics, being impeded by Ego-reflection and by a new, subjective graphic gestus. The figures, sketched onto the convex mirror, unite with the mirrored image of the spectator, while at the same time the mirror, which reflects the entire exhibition room and demonstrates the absurdity of spatial coordinates between observer and work, creates an absolute distance. The total adoption of rational-scientific dimensions and the constructive unveiling of unconscious holistic human processes are signs of this critical analysis of the various levels of our life worlds and worlds of thought. **HK**

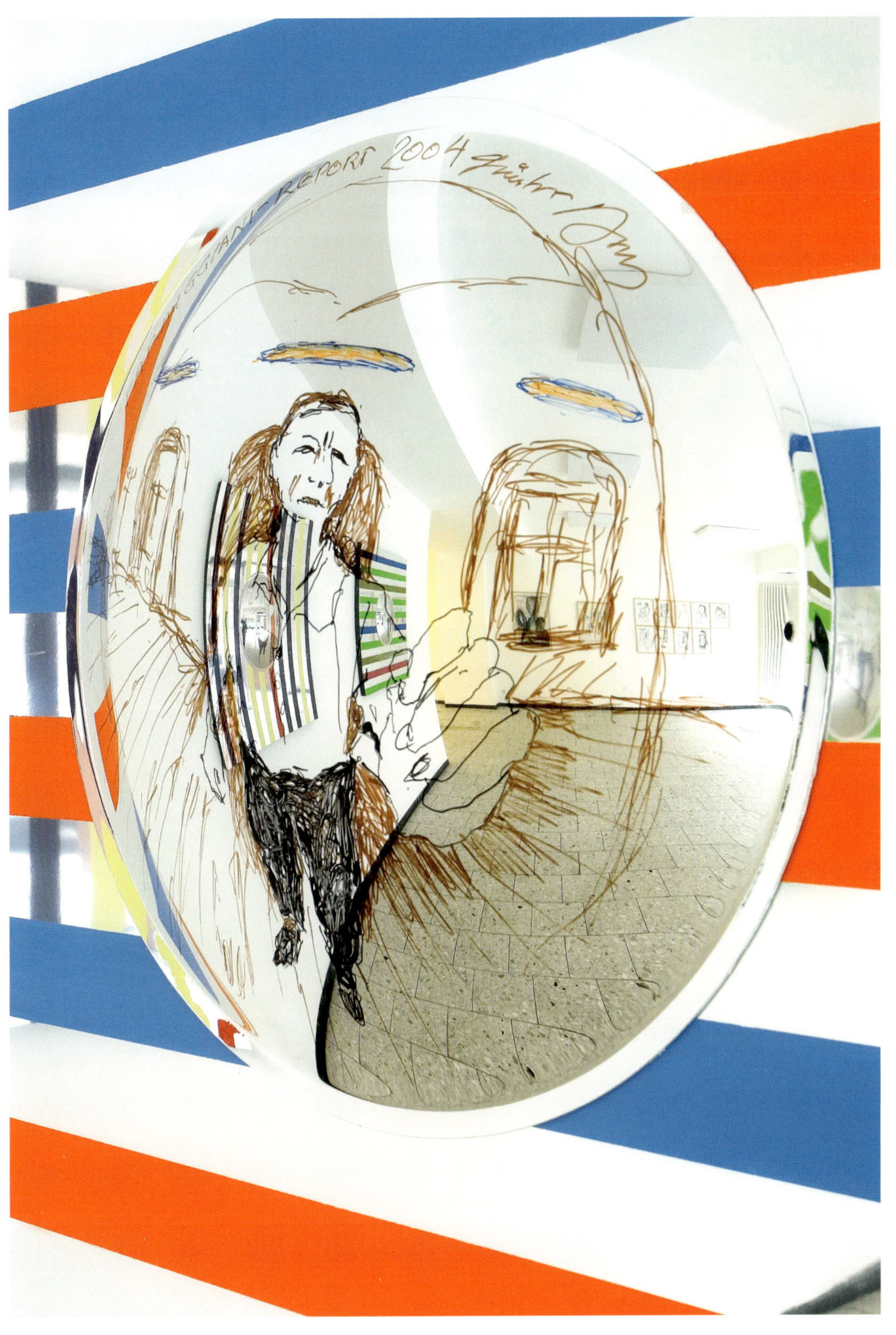
REPORT 2004

Appendix

Marc Adrian (1930 Vienna—2008 Vienna) studied under Fritz Wotruba at the Academy of Fine Arts Vienna. He created a.o. verre eglomise montages, typographies, computer graphics, extensive mobiles, films, theatre plays and poems. In 1965 Adrian took part in *The Responsive Eye* (MoMA, New York), one of the most important exhibitions to Op-Art. Adrian was collaborator at the Center for Advanced Visual Studies of the Massachusetts Institute of Technology (MIT) in Cambridge. Teachings at the Hochschule für bildende Künste Hamburg and the Academies for Applied and Fine Arts Vienna.
Lit.: Galerie Hofstätter (ed.), *Marc Adrian. Hinterglasmontagen, Computergrafik, Mobiles, photography & Film 1954–1979*, exhibition catalogue, Galerie Hofstätter Vienna, Vienna, 2003

Klaus Auderer (*1968 Ehenbichl) has studied visual arts at the Bezalel Academy of Arts and Design in Tel Aviv and at the Academy of Fine Arts in Munich. Among his exhibitions and screenings were *Independence*, South Gallery, London (2003), *Utopia Station*, Haus der Kunst, Munich (2004), *OK-Videofestival*, National Gallery of Indonesia, Jakarta (2005), *Favoriten 08*, Städtische Galerie at the Lenbachhaus, Munich (2008); The New York International Independent Film and Video Festival (2008), *The Towers of Silence*, Kunsthalle Vienna (2009).
Lit.: Klaus Auderer, Robert Gfader, *Chessdrawings*, Berlin, 2009

Josef Bauer (*1934 Wels) lives in Linz. From 1956 until 1964 Bauer attended the Art School Linz, since 1962 he took part in solo and group exhibitions, a.o. at the Galerie at the Griechenbeisl, Vienna, the Joanneum, Graz, the Galerie nächst St. Stephan, Vienna (1975), and the Landesgalerie, OÖ Landesmuseum, Linz. Important exhibitions were *Kunst aus Sprache* at the Museum of the 20th Century, Vienna, *Das offene Bild—Aspekte der Moderne in Europa nach 1945* at the Westfälischen Landesmuseum Münster and the Museum der bildenden Künste Leipzig (1993) as well as *Objekte—sculpture in Österreich nach 1945* at the Belvedere, Vienna (2001). www.josef-bauer.net
Lit.: Josef Bauer, *Hinstellungen*, Vienna, 1968

Joseph Beuys (1921 Krefeld—1986 Dusseldorf) was a sculptor, illustrator and a conceptual artist. From 1961 to 1972 Beuys held the chair for monumental sculpture at the State Art Academy Dusseldorf. In 1964, 1968, 1972, 1977, 1982 and 1987 he collaborated in the documenta in Kassel.
Lit.: Veit Loers, Pia Witzmann (ed.), *Joseph Beuys. documenta-Arbeit*, Stuttgart, 1993

In his work, **Christian Boltanski** (*1944 Paris) creates new references through fictional and real relics. Numerous solo and group exhibitions, a.o. documenta, Kassel (1972, 1977), Biennale di Venezia (1975, 1980, 1993, 1995, 2011), Museum of the 20th Century, Vienna (1982), Guggenheim Museum, New York (2010).
Ilya Kabakov (*1933 Dnepropetrovsk) lives and works in New York. Kabakov studied Graphic Design and Book illustration. Together with Emilia Kabakov he received several awards, a.o. the awarded diploma of the Biennale di Venezia in 1993. Numerous group exhibitions, a.o. Biennale di Venezia (1977, 1988, 1993, 1997, 2001, 2003) and documenta in Kassel (1992). Solo exhibitions a.o. Reykjavík Art Museum (2006) and Setagaya Art Museum, Tokio (2008).
Lit.: Barbara Gronau, *Theaterinstallationen. Performative Räume under Beuys, Boltanski and Kabakov*, Munich, 2010
Jean Kalman (*1945, Paris) has been working worldwide at noteable theatres, a.o. Salzburger Festspiele, Milan Scala, Metropolitan Opera New York, Opéra national de Paris, etc. since 1979. In 2004 he received the Evening Standard Award. for best Light-Design. In 2005 he was the artistic director (together with Andrea Breth and Christian Boltanski) of the scenic installation *Nächte unter Tage* at RuhrTriennale.

Monica Bonvicini (*1965 Venice) lives and works in Berlin and since 2003 she is professor for performative art and sculpture at the Academy of Fine Arts Vienna. She held numerous solo and group exhibitions, a.o. Berlin Biennale für Zeitgenössische Kunst (1998, 2004) and Biennale di Venezia (1999, 2005, 2011). In 2007, Bonvicini received the order for the sculpture *HUN LIGGER—SHE LIES*, which is floating in the water in front of the new Oslo Opera.
Lit.: Andrea Linnenkohl (ed.), *Monica Bonvicini. Both Ends*, exhibition catalogue, Kunsthalle Fridericianum, Kassel, Cologne, 2010

Marcel Broodthaers (1924 Brussels—1976 Cologne) worked as a bookseller and poet, before he turned to visual arts. In 1968 Broodthaers founded his *Musee d'Art Moderne, Department des Aigles* in Brussels. A year later, he moved to Cologne and Dusseldorf. In 1971 he continued his project *Musée d'Art Moderne, Département des Aigles, Section Cinéma* in Dusseldorf. In 1972, 1977, 1982 and 1997 he showed at the documenta in Kassel.
Lit.: Marcel Broodthaers, *Section Littéraire du Musée d'Art Moderne, Département des Aigles: Ceci est une pipe*, Brussels, 2001

Daniel Buren (*1938 Boulogne-Billancourt) lives in Paris and exhibits in various museums and galleries all over the world. Since 1972 he has participated in the documenta in Kassel three times. Buren was invited to the Biennale di Venezia a couple of times, where he was awarded the Golden Lion for the best pavilion in 1986. Since then Buren has realised a large number of works in public space worldwide.
Lit.: Hildegund Amanshauser (ed.), *Daniel Buren. Im Raum. Die Farbe. Arbeit in situ*, exhibition catalogue, Secession Vienna, Vienna, 1989

Tom Burr (*1963 New Haven, Conn.) lives and works in New York. After graduating from the School of Visual Arts in New York he attended a study programme at the Whitney Independent in 1987/88. He looks back on numerous international exhibitions, a.o. *What Happened to the Institutional Critique*, American Fine Arts, Co., New York (1993) and Whitney Museum, New York (2002). Recently the Kunstmuseum Basel (2009/10) and the FRAC Champagne-Ardennes in Reims (2011) dedicated solo exhibitions to Burr.
Lit.: Anette Freudenberger (ed.), *Tom Burr. Moods*, exhibition catalogue, Secession Vienna, Cologne, 2007

Günter Brus (*1938 Ardning), who was part of the Viennese Actionism in the late 1960s. In his expressive *Bilddichtungen, he* turned from performance art to illustration and literature. Brus exhibited together with Jörg Schlick in 2004 at the Galerie Christian Nagel, Cologne, and 2005 at the Galerie Bleich-Rossi, Graz, aus.
Lit.: Günter Brus/Jörg Schlick, *In besseren Kreisen*, exhibition catalogue, Galerie Bleich Rossi, Graz, Graz/Cologne, 2005

Ernst Caramelle (*1952 Hall in Tirol) studied from 1970 until 1976 at the University of Applied Arts Vienna. He participated in numerous exhibitions, a.o. documenta 9, Kassel, Secession Vienna, ARC Musée d'Art Moderne de la Ville de Paris and New York Kunsthalle. Caramelle was visting professor for graphics at the University of Applied Arts Vienna and professor at the Academy of Fine Arts in Karlsruhe.
Lit.: Ernst Caramelle, *Image Bank*, exhibition catalogue, Bawag Foundation Vienna, Vienna, 2001

Bernhard Cella (*1969 Salzburg) lives in Vienna and studied at the Academy of Fine Arts Vienna and the Hochschule für bildende Künste Hamburg as well as at the Kunstuniversität Linz (stage design and liberal arts). His exhibitions include a.o. *H. U. Obrist neben H. U. Obrist*, 69 illustrations in scale 1:1, Vienna Art Week (2011), *Salon für Kunstbuch*, 1:1 model of a bookshop, multi media installation, 21er Haus Vienna (2011), *Gruppenbild mit Dame ohne Gesichtserkennung*, Festival of the Regions (EA, 2011), *The Future will be*, 3-D clouds, Open Space/Art Cologne (2011), *NO-ISBN*, Galerie für zeitgenössische Kunst Leipzig (EA, 2010). www.cella.at
Lit.: Bernhard Cella, *and learning english has no use*, Salzburg, 2011

Cityrama II was a happening in Cologne in 1961 by César (1921–1998), Ben Patterson (*1934; lives and works in NY and Wiesbaden), Wolf Vostell (1932–1998), Christo (*1935), Arnulf Rainer (*1929), Robert Filliou (1926–1987) and Stefan Wewerka (*1928). Vostell's and Wewerka's planned sightseeing tour *Cityrama* in Cologne, to which many artists of the Nouveau Réalisme were invited, never took place.
Lit.: Susanne Neuburger (ed.), *Nouveau Réalisme*, exhibition catalogue museum moderner kunst stiftung ludwig wien, Vienna, 2005

Heinz Emigholz (*1948 Achim) has been working as an international film maker, artist, author and producer since 1973 on numerous films, exhibitions, retrospectives and publications. Since 1993 he is lecturing at the Berlin University of the Arts. In 1974 Emigholz began working on his encyclopedic animation series *Die Basis des Make-Up*, while he commenced his film series *Photographie und jenseits*, which consists of 70 short and long films, and also includes the sub division *architecture als Autobiographie* der *Friedrich-Kiesler*-Film, ten years later. More at www.pym.de.
Lit.: Museum für Gegenwart No. 11 – Heinz Emigholz, exhibition catalogue, Hamburger Bahnhof, Cologne, 2008

VALIE EXPORT (*1940 Linz) lives and works in Vienna. Her artistic work includes a.o. video environments, digital photography, installations, body-performances, experimental films, conceptual photography, body-material-interaction, texts on contemporary art history and on feminism. Since 1968, she has continuously participated in international art exhibitions, a.o. at the Biennale di Venezia and the documenta in Kassel, as well as at film and video festivals.
Lit.: Agnes Husslein-Arco/Angelika Nollert/Stella Rollig (ed.): *VALIE EXPORT. Zeit und Gegenzeit*, exhibition catalogue, Belvedere Vienna and Lentos Kunstmuseum Linz, Cologne, 2010

Claire Fontaine live and work in Paris since 2004. Her neoconceptual works, similar to other artists' work, consist of video, sculpture, painting and text. She particularly focuses on political impotence and the crisis of the individual, two topics important to contemporary art today. Most recently Claire Fontaine exhibited at *Arbeit Macht Kapital, Kubus* at the Städtischen Galerie at the Lenbachhaus and Kunstbau, Munich (2008), as well as at *They Hate Us For Our Freedom*, Contemporary Art Museum St. Louis (2008). Currently Claire Fontaine works on a book on the concepts of the "readymade" and the crisis of society.
Lit.: Ruba Katrib/Tom McDonough, *Claire Fontaine. Economies*, exhibition catalogue, Museum of Contemporary Art North Miami, Miami, 2010

Peter Friedl (*1960 Oberneukirchen) lives in Berlin. Friedl's artistic practice deals with the tension between aesthetical and political consciousness. In 2006 he organised the retrospective *Peter Friedl: Work 1964–2006* at the Museu d'Art Contemporani de Barcelona, which was also on display in Miami and Marseille. Friedl took part at the documenta X (1997) and XII (2007) as well as the 48th Biennale di Venezia (1999). Since the 1980s Friedl has published several essays and books.
Lit.: Anselm Franke (ed.), *Peter Friedl: Secret Modernity. Selected Writings and Interviews 1981–2009*, Berlin, 2010

The artistic group **gelatin**, consisting of Wolfgang Gantner, Ali Janka, Florian Reiter and Tobias Urban, first met in 1978 during a summer camp. Back then their cooperation and the joint performances began, since 1993 they exhibit internationally, a.o. at the Musée d'Art Moderne de la Ville, Paris (2008), the Tomio Koyama Gallery, Tokio (2009), or the Biennale di Venezia (2001, 2007, 2011). Their work includes numerous performances, installations and lectures in Vienna, London, Paris, New York, Island, Bulgarien etc.
Lit.: gelitin (ed.), *gelatin's acb*, Cologne, 2008

Isa Genzken (*1948 Bad Oldesloe) studied from 1969 till 1973 at the Hochschule für Bildende Künste in Berlin and in Hamburg, as well as from 1973 till 1977 at the Kunstakademie Dusseldorf. She lives and works in Berlin. Genzken's works range from sculpture, photography, installations, film, video, and painting to works on paper and artistic books. Numerous solo exhibitions worldwide, a.o. in 1996 at the Generali Foundation in Vienna and in 2006 at the Secession Vienna. In 1982, 1993, 2003 and 2007 she took part at the Biennale di Venezia, in 1982, 1992 and 2002 at the documenta in Kassel.
Lit.: Alex Farquharson, Diedrich Diederichsen, Sabine Breitwieser, *Isa Genzken*, London/New York, 2006

Liam Gillick (*1964, Aylesbury) lives and works in New York. solo exhibitions a.o. *The Wood Way*, Whitechapel Gallery, London (2002), *A short text on the possibility of creating an economy of equivalence*, Palais de Tokyo, Paris (2005), and the retrospective *Three Perspectives and a short scenario*, Witte de With, Rotterdam, Kunsthalle Zurich, Kunstverein Munich and MCA, Chicago (2008–2010). Gillick was nominated for the Turner Prize in 2002 and for the Vincent Award des Stedelijk Museums in Amsterdam in 2008.
Lit.: Kunst- and Ausstellungshalle der Bundesrepublik Deutschland (ed.), *Liam Gillick. ein langer Spaziergang … zwei kurze Stege … (one long walk … two short piers …)*, Cologne, 2010

Franz Graf (*1954 Tulln) lives and works in Vienna. From 1997 till 2006 he was visiting professor at the Academy of Fine Arts Vienna. solo exhibitions a.o. Secession Vienna (1995), Bonner Kunstverein (1995), Rupertinum Salzburg (2001) and MAK, Vienna (2009). In 2007, on the occasion of *Kunst am Bau* at the Mozarteum Salzburg, he realised a floor design in the entry hall of the Universität am Mirabellplatz.
Lit.: Hans-Peter Wipplinger (ed.), *Franz Graf. SCHWARZ HEUTE JETZT HABE DASS SCHON FAST VERGESSEN*, exhibition catalogue, Kunsthalle Krems, Nuremburg, 2010

Thomas Hirschhorn (*1957 Bern) lives and works in Paris. Solo exhibitions a.o. Musée d'art contemporain, Montreal (2007), Secession Vienna (2008), Museo Tamayo Arte Contemporáneo, Mexiko City (2008). Works in public space include, a.o. a block of flats in Glasgow (*Raymond Carver-Altar*, 2000) and the underground station Berlin Alexanderplatz (*Ingeborg Bachmann-Altar*, 2006). Thomas Hirschhorn was a.o. present at the 48., 50. and 54. Biennale di Venezia (1999, 2003, 2011), the documenta 11 (2002) as well as the 27. Bienal de São Paulo (2006).
Lit.: Thomas Hirschhorn, Bataille Maschine, Berlin, 2003

Julia Hohenwarter (*1980 Vienna) studied architecture at the TU Vienna and at the TU Graz as well as visual arts at the Academy of Fine Arts Vienna with Monica Bonvicini and at the Royal Danish Academy of Fine Arts Copenhagen with Gerard Byrne. Hohenwarter's works are between performance and installation. Exhibitions a.o. at the Tanzquartier Vienna (2006), the UNAgaleria in Bucarest (2008), in Copenhagen (2010) and the KIT Dusseldorf (2011).
Lit.: KIT—art at the Tunnel Dusseldorf (ed.), *WIENER GLUT. Junge aus Wien und Düsseldorf*, exhibition catalogue, KIT—Kunst im Tunnel Düsseldorf, Dusseldorf, 2011

Hans Hollein (*1934 Vienna) lives and works in Vienna. He has lectured at several universities and was Austrian board member at the Biennale di Venezia for art (1978–1990) and for architecture (1991–2000). Solo exhibitions a.o. 1963 at the Galerie nächst St. Stephan (with Walter Pichler) in Vienna, in 1967 at the MoMA, New York (with Walter Pichler and Raimund Abraham), and in 1987 at the Museum of the 20th Century, Vienna. In 1977 and 1987 Hollein took part at the documenta in Kassel, in 1972 at the Biennale di Venezia. In 2006 he presented his *Flugzeugträger* in the Austrian pavilion at the X. architecture-Biennale in Venice.
Lit.: Walter Pichler/Hans Hollein, *Hollein – Pichler – Architektur*, Vienna, exhibition catalogue, Galerie nächst St. Stephan, Vienna, Vienna, 1963

Inspection Medical Hermeneutics (Sergei Anufriev, Yuri Leiderman, Pavel Pepperstein) was founded in 1987. Solo exhibitions a.o. in 1990 at the Kunsthalle Dusseldorf as well as in 1993 at the Swiss Institute, New York, and at the Kunstverein Hamburg. Group exhibitions took place a.o. in 1996 and 2001 at the Biennale di Venezia as well as the Kunsthalle Vienna and the Stedelijk Museum Amsterdam, also in 1996.

Pavel Pepperstein (*1966 Moscow) lives and works in Moscow. His most recent solo exhibitions include *Landscapes of the Future—The Venice Biennale installation*, Kewenig Galerie, Cologne, Leviathan, Sutton Lane, Paris, Pavel Pepperstein, artothek, Cologne, and *A Suprematist Study of Ancient Greek Myths*, Galerie Kamm, Berlin. He took part a.o. at the 53. Biennale di Venezia and the 3. Moscow Biennale for Contemporary Art.

Sergei Anufriev (*1964 Odessa) lives and works in Moscow and Kiev. He participated a.o. in the 2. and 3. Moscow Biennale for Contemporary Art.
Lit.: Matthias Haldemann (ed.), *Pavel Pepperstein and Gäste*, exhibition catalogue, Kunsthaus Zug, Ostfildern, 2004

Christian Jankowski (*1968 Göttingen) works in installation, performance, film, video, photography and sculpture. The graduate of the Hochschule für bildende Künste Hamburg first hit the headlines in 1999 at the 48. Biennale di Venezia, curated by Harald Szeemann. Since then his works have been displayed in solo and group exhibitions in Europe, the US and Asia.
Lit.: Marion Ackermann (ed.), *Christian Jankowski. Dienstbesprechung*, Ostfildern, 2008

Tillman Kaiser (*1972 Graz) studied at the Academy of Fine Arts Vienna with Hubert Schmalix and Friedensreich Hundertwasser. In 2010 he exhibited at the 14. Vilnius Painting Triennial and at the Belvedere, Vienna, as well as in 2011 at Honor Fraser, Los Angeles, and the Galerie Emanuel Layr, Vienna.
Lit.: Tillman Kaiser, *Ready add-ons*, exhibition catalogue, Neue Galerie Graz, Graz, 2008

Ian Kiaer (*1971 London) lives and works in London. Solo exhibitions a.o. Galleria Civica d'Arte Moderna e Contemporanea, Turin (2009), Bloomberg Space, London (2009), Kunstverein Munich (2010), Aspen Art Museum (2012). Group exhibitions a.o. *British Art Show 7: In the Days of the Comet*, Nottingham, London, Glasgow, Plymouth (2011), *All of This and Nothing: 6thHammer Invitational*, Hammer Museum, Los Angeles (2011), Arte essenziale, Collezione Maramotti, Reggio Emilia (2011), 54. Biennale di Venezia (2011).
Lit.: The British School at Rome (ed.), *Ian Kiaer: Endless House Projects*, exhibition catalogue, The British School at Rome, Rome, 2005

Friedrich Kiesler (1890 Czernowitz—1965 New York) studied, but did not graduate in painting and print. He was awarded the Therese-Dessauer-Preis and granted an artistic scholarship, and kept travelling to Berlin. In the 1920s Kiesler started designing stage sets and participating in exhibitions. Kiesler wrote trendsetting texts on stage design and museum display. When the MoMA bought his *Endless House* model in 1951, he eventually made his breakthrough.
Lit.: Dieter Bogner, *Friedrich Kiesler 1890–1965. inside the endless house*, exhibition catalogue, Historisches Museum der Stadt Wien, Vienna/Cologne/Weimar, 1997

Martin Kippenberger (1953 Dortmund—1997 Vienna) studied at the Hochschule für bildende Künste Hamburg. He was a lecturer at several universities in Germany, the US, France and the Netherlands. Solo and group exhibitions worldwide, a.o. Solomon R. Guggenheim Museum, New York (1993), documenta X (1992, 1997), Biennale di Venezia (2003) and *Martin Kippenberger. Utopien für alle*, Kunsthalle Graz (2007).
Lit.: Peter Pakesch (ed.), *Modell Martin Kippenberger. Utopien für alle*, exhibition catalogue, Kunsthaus Graz am Landesmuseum Joanneum, Cologne, 2007

The artistic group **Mahony** was formed in 2002 and consists of Stephan Kobatsch (*1975), Clemens Leuschner (*1976) and Jenny Wolka (*1978), who live and work in Vienna. Until 2010 also Andreas Duscha was part of the group. Mahony use different media like video, text, sculpture, or performance. They have participated in countless exhibitions, a.o.: 2nd Bienal del fin del mundo, Ushuaia (2009), 4th Beijing International Art Biennale (2010), Kunsthalle Vienna (2010, 2011), CRAC Alsace (2011), Proyectos Monclova, Mexiko-Stadt (2011). Solo exhibitions a.o.: Galerie Emanuel Layr (2007, 2009, 2010), Factory—Kunsthalle Krems (2010), The Artist's Institute, New York (2012).
Lit.: Mahony, *seeing wrong and not seeing*, exhibition catalogue, Galerie Emanuel Layr, Vienna, 2011

Gordon Matta-Clark (1943 New York—1978 New York) studied French literature from 1962 till 1963 at the Sorbonne, Paris as well as architecture at the Cornell University, Ithaca, USA, from 1962 to 1968. His knowledge of space and architecture strongly influenced his performances, paintings, sculptures, photographs and films. He took part in many projects and group exhibitions, a.o. at the Documenta V, Kassel as well as the 9. Biennale of Paris. After his death in 1978 comprehensive retrospectives were shown a.o. at the Museum of Contemporary Art, Chicago, Centro Julio Gonzalez, Valenzia, the Serpentine Gallery, London as well as the Generali Foundation in Vienna.
Lit.: Pamela M. Lee, *Object to Be Destroyed: The Work of Gordon Matta-Clark*, Cambridge/London, 2000.

Ralo Mayer (1976) mostly lives and works in Vienna. Performative research on the history of space travel and Science Fiction in installation, film and performance, characterise his work. In 2006 he began his research series *HOW TO DO THINGS WITH WORLDS* at the Manoa Free University. Solo exhibitions a.o. Secession, Vienna (2008), Argos, Brussels (2010), Lentos Kunstmuseum, Linz (2011), Kunsthaus Baselland, Basel (2012).
http://was-ist-multiplex.info
Lit.: Ralo Mayer, *Obviously a major malfunction/KAGO KAGO KAGO BE (Woran glauben die Motten, wenn she zu den Lichtern streben)*, exhibition catalogue, Lentos Kunstmuseum Linz and Kunstmuseum Baselland, Nuremburg, 2011

Paul McCarthy (*1945 Salt Lake City) lives and works in Los Angeles. He studied at the UCLA as well as at the San Francisco Art Institute and the University of Utah. McCarthy's works include illustrations, sculptures, actions and performances, performance videos, films and installations, in which he often mixes technical, sexual and naturalist elements. Numerous international exhibitions, a.o. in Belgium, Austria, Italy, New York, Amsterdam, etc.
Lit.: Paul McCarthy, *Piccadilly Circus, Bunker Basement*, Zurich, 2004

Jonathan Meese (*1970 Tokio) lives and works in Berlin and Hamburg. His works mainly consist of installations and performances. Meese took part in several solo and group exhibitions, a.o. Essl Museum, Klosterneuburg (2008), Arp Museum, Remagen (2009), Museum of Contemporary Art Miami (2010), Alte Nationalgalerie Berlin (2011) and GEM Museum Voor Actuele art, Den Haag (2011). In 2005 he performed *jonathan meese ist mutter parzival* at the Magazat the Staatsoper Berlin.
Lit.: Jonathan Meese, *Diktatur der Kunst*, Cologne, 2011

Hermann Nitsch (*1938 Vienna) is a conceptual artist. Together with Günter Brus, Otto Muehl and Rudolf Schwarzkogler, he was part of the Viennese Actionism. Since having acquired Schloss Prinzendorf in 1971, he uses the palace as his studio and laboratory, especially for his *Orgien Mysterien Theater*. In 1982, Nitsch exhibited at the documenta and also took part in Harald Szeemann's exhibition *Der Hang zum Gesamtkunstwerk* in 1983. In 2007 the Hermann Nitsch Museum in Mistelbach was opened, followed by the Museo Nitsch in Naples a year later.
Lit.: Hermann Nitsch, *Das O. M. Theater*, Darmstadt, 1969

Oswald Oberhuber (*1931 Merano) was rector at the University of Applied Arts Vienna, gallerist, curator and author of many publications. In his works Oberhuber abrogates laws and regulations: As the co-founder of the Austrian informal painting and sculptor (around 1949), he formulated his theory of the constant change of art already in the mid 1950s, rejecting any formation of a genre since.
Lit.: Oswald Oberhuber, Mutazione. *Permanente Veränderung. Ein Gespräch mit Ursula Riederer*, Vienna/Bozen, 2004

Hermann Painitz (*1938 Vienna) lives in Vienna and Kirchstetten. He first worked as a goldsmith in Bern, London and Vienna. In 1962 he started his career as a painter, sculptor and poet, and was soon later signed on by Herbert Tasquil as his assistant at the Academy of Applied Arts in Vienna. In 1964, Painitz held his first solo exhibition at the Galerie im Griechenbeisl in Vienna, and in 1967 he participated in the exhibition *Kinetika* by Werner Hofmann at the Museum of the 20th Century. From 1977 to 1983 Painitz was the president of the Secession Vienna.
Lit.: Hermann Josef Painitz, *H. J. Painitz. Mehr als die Summe der Teile. 55 Stufen und 378 Bilder*, exhibition catalogue, Neue Galerie Graz. Graz 1998

Seb Patane (*1970 Italy) lives and works in London. Patane studied at the Central Saint Martins College of Art & Design, London, and at Goldsmiths University, London. Solo exhibitions a.o. Tate Britain, London (2007), Art Basel (2009) and La Kunsthalle Mulhouse (2011). Group exhibitions a.o. migros Museum für Gegenwartskunst, Zürich (2006), MoMA, New York (2008), and Royal Academy of Art in London (2010). In 2006 Patane curated the exhibition *Sweet Home Under White Clouds*, Peles Empire, London.
Lit.: Bettina Steinbrügge (ed.), *Seb Patane*, exhibition catalogue La Kunsthalle Mulhouse, Berlin 2011

Helga Philipp (1939 Vienna—2002 Vienna) studied sculpture with Hans Knesl at the Academy for Applied Arts Vienna. Through the Biennale di Venezia 1958 and friends like Marc Adrian, she came in contact with the Op-Art-Avantgarde and the concrete art movement in 1961, and was soon integrated in the Wiener Gruppe. Philipp lectured from 1965 to 2002 at the University of Applied Arts Vienna as an assistant professor. In 1967 she took part in the exhibition *Kinetika* by Werner Hofmann at the Museum of the 20th Century.
Lit.: Carl Aigner/Gerald Bast (ed.), *Helga Philipp. Poesie der Logik*, exhibition catalogue, Niederösterreichisches Landesmuseum, St. Pölten, Vienna, 2010

Walter Pichler (*1936 Deutschnofen) graduated from the Academy for Applied Art in Vienna in 1956. From sculpture in the 1960s he turned to architecture and in 1963 he exhibited in *Architektur* (with Hans Hollein) at the Galerie nächst St. Stephan. Together with Hans Hollein from 1965 to 1967 he was publisher of the architecture magazine *Bau. Schrift für Architektur und Städtebau*. In 1967 Pichler took part in the exhibition *Visionary Architecture* at the MoMA in New York with Hans Hollein and Raimund Abraham. Pichler also exhibited at the documenta in Kassel in 1968 and 1977.
Lit.: Walter Pichler/Hans Hollein, *Hollein – Pichler – Architektur*, exhibition catalogue, Galerie nächst St. Stephan, Vienna, 1963

Marjetica Potrč (*1953 Ljubljana) studied architecture and sculpture at the University of Ljubljana. Group exhibitions a.o. Biennale di Venezia (1993, 2003 and 2009) and Bienal de São Paulo (1996 and 2006). Solo exhibitions at the Guggenheim Museum, New York (2001), and at the de Appel Foundation, Amsterdam (2004). One of her latest works in public space is *The Cook, the Farmer, his Wife and their Neighbour* (Stedelijk goes West, Amsterdam 2009). Since 2011 Potrč is professor at the Hochschule für bildende Künste Hamburg.
Lit.: Lívia Páldi (ed.), *Marjetica Potrč. Next Stop, Kiosk/Naslednja postaja Kiosk*, exhibition catalogue, Moderna galerija Ljubljana, Frankfurt/Main, 2003

Jason Rhoades (1965 Newcastle—2006 Los Angeles) studied at the California College of Arts and Crafts, Oakland, the San Francisco Art Institute, the Skowhegan School of Painting and Sculpture and the University of California. Numerous solo exhibitions, a.o. Musueum of Modern Art Stiftung Ludwig Vienna (2002), CAC Málaga (2006), Hauser & Wirth, London (2010). Group exhibitions a.o. Van Abbemuseum, Eindhoven (2008), Kunsthaus Graz (2008), Whitney Biennial (2008), MoMA, New York (2009), and Kunsthalle Göppingen (2010). In 1997, 1999 and 2007 Rhoades exhibited at the Biennale di Venezia.
Lit.: Eva Meyer-Hermann (ed.): *Jason Rhoades – Volume. A Rhoades Referenz*, Cologne, 1998

Thiago Rocha Pitta (*1980 Tiradentes) lives and works in São Paulo. He studied painting at the Federal University in Rio de Janeiro as well as Politics, Aesthetics and Philosophy at the Pontifical Catholic University of Rio de Janeiro and the Museu da República in Rio de Janeiro. In 2007, Rocha Pitta designed his sculpture *Uma Trilogia* for the Vale do Anhangabaú, Pavilhão Ascensão, in São Paulo. Exhibitions a.o. MoMA PS1, New York (2006), Art Basel (2008), Museum on the Seam, Jerusalem (2009), migros Museum für Gegenwartskunst, Zürich (2011).
Lit.: Thiago Rocha Pitta, *Notas de um desabamento*, exhibition catalogue, Escola de Artes Visuais do Parque Lage, Rio de Janeiro, Rio de Janeiro, 2010

Gerwald Rockenschaub (*1952 Linz) lives and works in Berlin. In 1993, he showed at the 1993 the Austrian pavilion at the Biennale di Venezia together with Andrea Fraser and Christian Philipp Müller and was present at the documenta 12 in Kassel in 2007. A year later, Rockenschaub led the first outdoor performance at the temporary Kunsthalle Berlin and presented three large installations at the Kunsthalle Bern. Recently, his works were exhibited at *multidial* at the Kunstmuseum Wolfsburg.
Lit.: Chantal Mouffe, Ulli Moser, *Gerwald Rockenschaub. Kunst, Kontext, Kritik*, exhibition catalogue, Secession Vienna, Vienna, 1994

Constanze Ruhm (*1965 Vienna) lives in Vienna and works in film, video and installation. She is author and curator, and was vice president of the Secession Vienna from 1999 to 2001. Since 2006, she is professor for digital art and media at the Academy of Fine Arts Vienna.
Lit.: Diedrich Diederichsen/Constanze Ruhm (ed.), *Immediacy and Non-Simultaneity: Utopia of Sound*, Vienna, 2010

Gerhard Rühm (*1930 Vienna) studied piano and composition at the Vienna Music Academy, and privately with Josef Matthias Hauer. In the mid 1950s, he was a co-founder of the Wiener Gruppe. A large retrospective was dedicated to them at the Biennale di Venezia in 1997. Other exhibitions were a.o. in 1979 at the museum moderner kunst stiftung ludwig wien and in 1992 at the Galerie beim Steinernen Kreuz Brigitte Seinsoth, Bremen. Rühm lectured as a professor at the Hochschule für bildende Künste in Hamburg from 1972 to 1995 as well as at the International Sommeracademy for visual arts in Salzburg. He lives in Cologne and Vienna.
Lit.: Ferdinand Altnöder (ed.), *Gerhard Rühm. Sichtwechsel*, exhibition catalogue, Galerie Altnöder, Salzburg, Weitra, 2010

Markus Schinwald (*1973 Salzburg) lives and works in Vienna and Los Angeles. Solo exhibitions a.o. Kunsthaus Bregenz (2009), Műcsarnok Kunsthalle Budapest (2010), *Orient* at the Kunstverein Hannover (2011), Lentos Kunstmuseum Linz (2011). In 2011, Markus Schinwald represented Austria at the 54. Biennale di Venezia. Group exhibitions a.o. Liverpool Biennial (2010), Bonniers Konsthall, Stockholm (2010).
Lit.: Markus Heinzelmann/Nicolaus Schafhausen (ed.), *Markus Schinwald*, exhibition catalogue, Frankfurter Kunstverein, Berlin, 2004

Jörg Schlick (1951 Graz—2005 Graz) studied Art History, lectured at the TU Graz and the Joanneum, Graz, and was a.o. curator of "steirischer herbst". Together with Wolfgang Bauer, Albert Oehlen and Martin Kippenberger he founded the Lord Jim Loge in 1985, whose magazine *Sonne, Busen, Hammer* was published by Schlick. Together Günter Brus, Schlick exhibited at the Galerie Christian Nagel, Cologne, in 2004 and at the Galerie Bleich-Rossi, Graz, the following year.
Lit.: Günter Brus/Jörg Schlick, *In besseren Kreisen*, exhibition catalogue, Galerie Bleich Rossi, Graz, Graz/Cologne, 2005

Christoph Schlingensief (1960 Oberhausen—2010 Berlin) worked internationally with his actionist projects as well as his theatre and opera productions. His first production was staged at the Volksbühne am Rosa-Luxemburg-Platz in Berlin in 1993 *100 Jahre CDU—Spiel ohne Grenzen*. Others followed a.o. in 2000 the Container performance *Bitte liebt Österreich* in the course of the Wiener Festwochen and in 2004 Wagner's *Parsifal* in Bayreuth. Schlingensief also worked as a lecturer and founded the initiative Festspielhaus Afrika. In 2011, a retrospective was held at the Biennale di Venezia.
Lit.: Susanne Gaensheimer (ed.), *Schlingensief: Deutscher Pavillion 54. Biennale Venedig*, Venice, 2011.

Gregor Schneider (*1969 Rheydt) lives and works in Rheydt. Since 2000, he has been lecturing at the Berlin University of the Arts as a professor for sculpture. In 2001 Schneider won the Golden Lion with his solo exhibition *Haus u r, Rheydt 1985 – today (Nacht – Video)* at the 49. Biennale di Venezia. Solo exhibitions a.o. Secession Vienna (2000), Hamburger Kunsthalle (2003), Gallery Wako Works of Art, Tokio (2010). Group exhibitions a.o. Moderna Museet (2002), Bonner Kunstverein (2005), Museum für Moderne Kunst Frankfurt/Main (2010).
Lit.: Anita Shah/Susanne Titz (ed.), *Gregor Schneider. END*, exhibition catalogue, Museum Franz Gertsch, Burgdorf, and Museum Abteiberg Mönchengladbach, Cologne, 2010

Esther Stocker (*1974 Schlanders) has studied at the art academies in Vienna and Brera as well as the Art Center College of Design in Pasadena. She has been exhibiting worldwide regularly since, a.o. CCNOA, Brussels (2008), museum moderner kunst stiftung ludwig wien (2008), South London Gallery (2009), solo exhibition Destino Comune, MACRO, Rom (2011).
Lit.: Rainer Fuchs (ed.), *Esther Stocker. geometrisch betrachet*, exhibition catalogue, museum moderner kunst stiftung ludwig Vienna, Nuremburg, 2008

SUPERFLEX is a collective consisting of Bjørnstjerne Reuter Christiansen (*1969), Jakob Fenger (*1968) and Rasmus Nielsen (*1969) since 1993. All three studied at the Royal Academy in Copenhagen, where she also lives and works. Solo exhibitions a.o. Van Abbe Museum, Eindhoven (2010) as well as Museum der Kunst der Westküste, Alkersum (2011). Group exhibitions a.o. Kunsthaus Graz (2011), Singapore Biennale (2011) and Tokyo Metropolitan Museum of Photography (2011). www.superflex.net
Lit.: Barbara Steiner (ed.), *SUPERFLEX TOOLS*, Cologne, 2003

Una Szeemann (*1975 Locarno) has been working as an artist since the late 1990s. Since 2006, she collaborates with Bohdan Stehlik. Numerous solo exhibitions, a.o. Kodama Gallery, Tokio (2005), CACT, Bellinzona (2008), Haswellediger & Co. Gallery, New York (2008). Group exhibitions a.o. Münchner Kunstverein (2004), *00s—The history of a decade that has not yet been named*, Biennale de Lyon (2007), Malmö Konsthall (2008), Nam June Paik Art Center, Seoul (2009), Art Basel (2011).
Lit.: *The Hamsterwheel*, exhibition catalogue Biennale di Venezia, Printemps de Septembre—à Toulouse, Arts Santa Mònica, Barcelona, and Malmö Konsthall, Vienna, 2007

Peter Weibel (*1944 Odessa) had numerous solo exhibitions a.o. at the Neue Galerie Graz (2004), at the Slought Foundation, Philadelphia (2009), and at the Palais du Rhin, Strasbourg (2011). He has lectued at several institutions, a.o. at the Academy for Applied Arts Vienna, the College of Art and Design in Halifax and at the Gesamthochschule Kassel. From 1993 to 1999 he curated the Austrian pavilion at the Biennale di Venezia. As a scientist, Weibel has published numerous texts, essays and books.
Lit.: Peter Weibel/Bruno Latour (ed.), *Making Things Public. Atmospheres of Democracy*, Karlsruhe, 2005

Franz West (*1947 Vienna) lives and works in Vienna. He dedicated himself to sculpture, installation as well as video and graphics. West studied at the Academy of Fine Arts Vienna and was professor at the Städelschule in Frankfurt/Main. He took part at the Biennale di Venezia in 1988, 1990, 1993, 1997, 2003, 2007 and 2011 as well as at the documenta in Kassel in 1992 and 1997.
Lit.: Kasper König (ed.), *Franz West. Autotheater*, exhibition catalogue, Museum Ludwig, Cologne, MADRE—Museo d'Arte Contemporanea Donnaregina, Naples, Kunsthaus Graz, Cologne, 2009

The artistic group **WochenKlausur** has been holding social interventions since 1993. By invitation of art institutions, the group has realised more than 30 proposals for the change of socio-political shortcomings in a.o. Berlin, Venice, Fukuoka, Zurich, Stockholm and Chicago. WochenKlausur are based in Vienna. www.wochenklausur.at
Lit.: Wolfgang Zinggl (ed.), *WochenKlausur: Sociopolitical Activism in Art*, Vienna, 2001

Fritz Wotruba (1907 Vienna—1975 Vienna) studied at the Wiener Kunstgewerbeschule with Anton Hanak. During his teachings at the Academy of Fine Arts Vienna, he influenced an entire generation of artists e.g. Oswald Oberhuber and Alfred Hrdlicka. Wotruba's works include sculpture and scenography, but also illustrations as well as architecture, e.g. church in Vienna-Mauer. He first participated at the Biennale di Venezia in 1932. In 1967 Wotruba designed the stage set for Richard Wagner's *Ring des Nibelungen* at the Deutsche Oper Berlin.
Lit.: Agnes Pistorius, *Fritz Wotruba. Das szenische Werk*, Vienna/Cologne/Weimar, 1995

Heimo Zobernig (*1958 Mauthen) lives and works in Vienna. He studied in Vienna at the Academy of Fine Arts and at the Academy for Applied Arts. Following two spells as visiting professors in Germany, he started lecturing at the Academy of Fine Arts Vienna in 2000. Numerous exhibitions, a.o. documenta IX and X in Kassel (1992,1997), museum moderner kunst stiftung ludwig wien (2002/03), Kunsthalle Basel (2003), K21 Dusseldorf (2003), Galleria Civica di Modena (2008), Tate St. Ives (2008/2009), Fundação Calouste Gulbenkian, Lissabon (2009), CAPC, Bordeaux (2009), Kunsthalle Zürich (2011), Essl Museum, Klosterneuburg (2011)
Lit.: Günther Oberhollenzer (ed.), *Heimo Zobernig*, exhibition catalogue, Essl Museum Klosterneuburg, Vienna, 2011

Véronique Aichner studied art history and romanistic studies at the University of Innsbruck. In 2007, she completed a postgraduate course in "Art & Economy" at the University of Applied Arts Vienna. From 2007 till 2010 she worked at the Gabriele Senn Galerie, Vienna, and since 2010 she is curatorial assistant for contemporary art at the Belvedere.

Simon Baier studied art history and philosophy in Heidelberg, Karlsruhe and New York and was a scholarship holder at the Independent Study Program at the Whitney Museum for American Art from 2005 to 2006. Since 2008 Baier has worked as an associate at the NFS Bildkritik of the University of Basel, where he has been scientific assistant at the chair of Modern Art History since 2009.

Holger Birkholz (born in 1968 in Soest, Germany) studied art history, German philology and philosophy in Kassel. He graduated in 2002 with a paper on *Kontext. Ein Problem kunstwissenschaftlicher Methodenliteratur und künstlerischer Praxis*. Since 2000, he has been chief curator of the exhibition *Monitoring* at the "Kasseler Dokumentarfilm- und Videofest". As a scientific associate in Art History at the Academy of Fine Arts, he has been working and living in Dresden since 2004.

Anselm Franke is curator and critic in Berlin. He was curator of the KW Institute for Contemporary Art in Berlin until 2006 and director of the Extra City Kunsthal Antwerpen until 2010, as well as co-curator of the Manifesta 7 in Italy in 2008. Franke curated exhibitions like *Territories* (2003–2004), *Mimétisme* (2008) and *Animism* (2010–2012) and is editor of publications as well as author of texts a.o. to Amos Gitai, Peter Friedl and Jimmie Durham. In 2012 he will be chief curator of the Taipei Biennal, Taiwan.

Boris Groys (born in 1947 in East-Berlin) studied philosophy and mathematics in Leningrad. Since 1975 he has been co-editor of the underground magazine *37* and has published numerous essays on non-conformist contemporary culture. In 1981, he left the USSR and lectured philosophy and aesthetics at the Hochschule für Gestaltung in Karlsruhe. International teachings followed, from 2001 to 2004 he was principal of the Academy of Fine Arts Vienna. His latest publication was *Einführung in die Anti-Philosophie* (2009, Verlag Hanser).

Nina Herlitschka studies art history and cultural sciences as well as fine arts focusing on performative art at the Academy of Fine Arts in Vienna. Her works are positioned at the border between theory and practice. She participated in exhibitions at the Secession Vienna in 2009 as well as the Kunstraum Niederösterreich Vienna in 2011. In 2010, Nina Herlitschka was study assistant of Carola Dertnig and collaborated in the symposium "This Sentence is Now Being Performed" at the Academy of Fine Arts Vienna.

Agnes Husslein-Arco, since 2007 director of the Belvedere in Vienna, is art historian and curator of numerous exhibitions on classic modernism and contemporary art as well as an author and editor of scientific publications. In 1981, she opened the Vienna affiliate of Sotheby's, which she managed until the year 2000. In addition, she presided over Sotheby's branches in Budapest and Prague in 1988. In the 1990s Husslein-Arco was Director of European Development at the Solomon R. Guggenheim Museum, from 2001 till 2003 Director of the Rupertinum in Salzburg and from 2003 until 2005 co-founder and Director of the Museum der Moderne Salzburg. From 2002 until 2004 she also organised the build-up of the Museum Moderner Kunst Kärnten (MMKK).

Eva Kernbauer is senior researcher at the Academy of Fine Arts Vienna. Kernbauer studied art history in Vienna, Berlin and Trier, and was curatorial and scientific associate at the mumok and the Kunsthalle Vienna as well as assistant at the Institute of Art History at the University of Bern from 2008 to 2011. Current fields of work are historic and contemporary audience models, artistic research, sculpture and installation since the 1960s, and historicity in contemporary art.

Harald Krejci studied art history, artistic pedagogy and Italian philology at the Universities of Augsburg and Munich. From 2000 onwards, he was a freelancer at the Galerie Krobath, the mumok and the Kunsthalle Vienna, before being named scientific head of the archive of the Kiesler Foundation Vienna, where he examined the inheritance of Friedrich Kiesler. In 2008, he became an assistant at the chair of architectural theory to Kari Jormakka for the exhibition *archidiploma2008*. Krejci curated and organised exhibitions on Kiesler at the MMK Frankfurt/Main and the Drawing Center in New York as well as on Maurizio Sacripanti at the Kiesler Stiftung Vienna. Since 2009 he works at the Belvedere, where he curated the exhibition *DYNAMIK! Kubismus, Futurismus, KINETISMUS* in 2011. His research focuses on interwar art, abstraction in Vienna, exile research centring on New York and London, and the elaboration of catalogues of works for Marc Adrian and Curt Stenvert.

Markus Miessen is an architect and author, and has published in various collaborations, most recently *The Nightmare of Participation* (Sternberg, 2010). His works are published and exhibited internationally, and in 2008 he founded the Winter School Middle East (Dubai/Kuwait). At present, he is lecturing for Critical Spatial Practice at the Städelschule in Frankfurt as well as at HEAD Geneva and the USC Los Angeles. www.studiomiessen.com, www.criticalspatialpractice.org, www.winterschoolmiddleeast.org, www.nOffice.eu

João Ribas is curator at the MIT List Visual Arts Center. Most recently, he has curated the exhibitions of *Stan VanDerBeek: The Culture Intercom* (Contemporary Art Museum, Houston, 2011) and *Manon de Boer* (Contemporary Art Museum, St. Louis, 2011). Ribas' texts are published in countless art and culture publications, and from 2008 to 2010 he won the International Association of Art Critics (AICA) Award in three consecutive years. He was visiting professor at various institutions and organisations worldwide.

Bettina Steinbrügge studied art history, English philology and comparative literature in Kassel. From 2001 to 2007 she was the artistic director of the Halle für Kunst Lüneburg. Following teachings at the University of Lüneburg and the art space of the University of Lüneburg, she started lecturing at the Haute École d'Art et de Design in Geneva in 2009. Since 2007 she has also been a member of the curatorial team of the Forum Expanded at the Berlin International Film Festival (Berlinale). Until autumn 2011 she curated for La Kunsthalle Mulhouse, where she realised exhibitions like *The End of the World as we know it* and *L'Idée de Nature*. Since 2011 she is curator for contemporary art at the Belvedere. Bettina Steinbrügge regularly publishes on topics in contemporary art; her current focus is on museum concepts of the 21st century, forms of artistic criticism and particularly the intersection of art and film.

Primary Literature

Antonin Artaud, *Das Theater und sein Double*, Frankfurt/Main, 1979.

Jean Baudrillard, *Simulacra und Simulation*, Ann Arbor, 1994.

Michel de Certeau, *Die Kunst des Handelns*, Berlin, 1988.

Jacques Derrida, *Eine gewisse unmögliche Möglichkeit vom Ereignis zu sprechen*, Berlin, 2003.

Michel Foucault, *Die Ordnung der Dinge*, Frankfurt/Main, 1971.

Jürgen Habermas, *Die Moderne—Ein unvollendetes Projekt*, Leipzig, 1994.

Ottokar Hostinský, *Das Musikalisch-Schöne und das Gesammtkunstwerk vom Standpuncte der formalen Ästhetik*, Leipzig, 1877.

Ilya Kabakov, *Über die totale Installation*, Ostfildern, 1995.

Wassily Kandinsky, *Über das Geistige in der Kunst*, Bern, 1952.

Thomas Mann, *In defense of Wagner. A letter on the German culture that produced both Wagner and Hitler*, in: Common Sense, January 1940, p. 11–14.

Hermann Nitsch, *Das Sein. Zur Theorie des Orgien-Mysterien-Theaters*, Vol. 1–3, Vienna, 2009.

Pierre-Joseph Proudhon, Von den Grundlagen und der sozialen Bestimmung der Kunst, ed. Klaus Hertling, Berlin, 1988.

Christoph Schlingensief, *Der Animatograph—Odins Parsipark*, Programme Stiftung Schloss Neuhardenberg, August 2005.

Karlheinz Stockhausen, *Texte zur Musik 1963-1970, Vol. III: Einführungen und Projekte, Kurse, Sendungen, Standpunkte, Nebennoten*, ed. Dieter Schnebel, Cologne, 1971.

Karlheinz Stockhausen, Texte zur Musik 1970-1977, Vol. IV: *Werk-Einführungen, Elektronische Musik, Weltmusik, Vorschläge und Standpunkte, Zum Werk anderer*, Cologne, 1978.

Bruno Taut, *Eine Notwendigkeit*, in: Der Sturm, 4th edition. February 1914.

Bruno Taut, *Zum neuen Theaterbau*, in: Das Hohe Ufer, Vol. 1, No. 8, August 1919.

Bruno Taut, *Architektur neuer Gemeinschaft*, in: Die Erhebung. Jahrbuch für neue Dichtung und Wertung, hg. von Alfred Wolfenstein, Vol. 2, Berlin, 1920.

Karl Friedrich Eusebius Trahndorff, *Aesthetik oder Lehre von der Weltanschauung und Kunst*, Berlin, 1827.

Richard Wagner, *Richard Wagners gesammelte Schriften und Dichtungen*, 4 Volumes, Leipzig, 1887.

Oswald Wiener, *Die Verbesserung von Mitteleuropa*, Reinbek, 1969.

Secondary Literature

Hans Adler/Ulrike Zeuch (ed.), *Synästhesie. Interferenz, Transfer, Synthese der Sinne*, Würzburg, 2002.

Theodor W. Adorno, *Versuch über Wagner*, in: id., Gesammelte Schriften, Vol. 13, ed. Rolf Tiedemann, Frankfurt/Main, 1971, p. 7-148.

Theodor W. Adorno, *Die Kunst und die Künste*, in: id., Kulturkritik und Gesellschaft, Frankfurt/Main, 1975, p. 432-453.

Daniel Albright, *Untwisting the Serpent. Modernism in Music, Literature, and Other Arts*, Chicago, 2000.

Amanda Anderson/Joseph Valente (ed.), *Disciplinarity at the Fin de Siècle*, Princeton, 2002.

Heinz Ludwig Arnold (ed.), *Aufbruch ins 20. Jahrhundert. Über Avantgarden*, Munich, 2001.

Wolfgang Ashold/Walter Fähnders (ed.), *Manifeste und Proklamationen der europäischen Avantgarde (1909-1938)*, Stuttgart, 1995.

Wolfgang Ashold/Walter Fähnders (ed.), *Der Blick vom Wolkenkratzer. Avantgarde—Avantgardekritik—Avantgardeforschung*, Amsterdam, 2000.

Karin Bauer, *Adorno's Nietzschean Narratives. Critiques of Ideology, Readings of Wagner*, Albany, 1999.

Daniela Baumann, *Gesamtkunstwerk. Aus der Sicht von Bazon Brock, Odo Marquard, Kurt Schwitters und Joseph Beuys*, diploma thesis, Mozarteum, Salzburg, 2003.

Ralf Beil, (ed.), *Gesamtkunstwerk Expressionismus 1905–1925*, exhibition catalogue. Institut Mathildenhöhe Darmstadt, Stuttgart, 2010.

Udo Bermbach, *Der Wahn des Gesamtkunstwerks. Richard Wagners politisch-ästhetische Utopie*, Frankfurt/Main, 1994.

René Block, (ed.), *Der Hang zum Gesamtkunstwerk. Europäische Utopien seit 1800*, Berlin, 1983.

Manfred Boetzkes, *Max Klinger. Wege zum Gesamtkunstwerk*, exhibition catalogue Roemer- und Pelizaeus-Museum Hildesheim, Mainz, 1984.

Dieter Borchmeyer, *Das Theater Richard Wagners. Idee, Dichtung, Wirkung*, Stuttgart, 1982.

Gabriele Brandstetter/Helga Finter/Markus Wesendorf (ed.), *Grenzgänge. Das Theater und die anderen Künste*, Tübingen, 1998.

Kai Buchholz/Rita Latocha/Hilke Peckmann/Klaus Wolbert (ed.), *Die Lebensreform-Entwürfe zur Neugestaltung von Leben und Kunst um 1900*, 2 Volumes, Darmstadt, 2001.

Peter Bürger, *Theorie der Avantgarde*, Frankfurt/Main, 1974.

Matei Călinescu, *Five Faces of Modernity. Modernism, Avant-Garde, Decadence*, Kitsch, Postmodernism, Durham, 1987.

Lucien Dällenbach/Christiaan L. Hart Nibbrig (ed.), *Fragment und Totalität*, Frankfurt/Main, 1984.

Sara Danius, *The Senses of Modernism. Technology, Perception, and Aesthetics*, Ithaca, 2002.

Robert Donington, *Opera and Its Symbols. The Unity of Words, Music, and Staging*, New Haven, 1990.

Sybil Dümchen, *Das Gesamtkunstwerk als Auflösung der Einzelkünste. Zur subversiven Ästhetik*, Alain Robbe-Grillets, Marburg, 1994 (artefact 4).

Christina Eichel, "*Vom Ermatten der Avantgarde zur Vernetzung der Künste. Perspektiven einer interdisziplinären Ästhetik im Spätwerk*", Theodor W. Adornos, Frankfurt/Main, 1993.

Samuel N. Eisenstadt, *Die Vielfalt der Moderne*, Weilerswist, 2000.

William R. Everdell, *The First Moderns. Profiles in the Origins of Twentieth-Century Thought*, Chicago, 1997.

Astradur Eysteinsson, *The Concept of Modernism*, Ithaka, 1990.

Torsten Feldmann, *Addition, Synthese und Utopie. Stationen des Gesamtkunstwerks zwischen Romantik und Postmoderne*, dissertation. Ruhr-University Bochum, 2000.

Luisa-Marie Fillitz, *Bühne—Bildende Kunst—Gesamtkunstwerk. Jean Tinguely*, diploma thesis. University of Vienna, 2010.

Anke Finger, *Das Gesamtkunstwerk der Moderne*, Göttingen, 2006.

Gloria Flaherty, *Opera in the Development of German Critical Thought*, Princeton, 1978.

Gabriele Förg (ed.), *Unsere Wagner: Joseph Beuys. Heiner Müller. Karlheinz Stockhausen. Hans Jürgen Syberberg. Essays*, Frankfurt/Main, 1984.

Roger Fornoff, *Die Sehnsucht nach dem Gesamtkunstwerk. Studien zu einer ästhetischen Konzeption der Moderne*, Hildesheim, 2004.

Rainer Franke, *Richard Wagners Zürcher Kunstschriften. Politische und ästhetische Entwürfe auf seinem Weg zum „Ring des Nibelungen*, Hamburg, 1983.

Sven Friedrich, *Das auratische Kunstwerk. Zur Ästhetik von Richard Wagners Musiktheater-Utopie*, Tübingen, 1996.

Silvia Gauss, Joseph Beuys „Gesamtkunstwerk, Freie und Hansestadt Hamburg*, Wangen, 1995.

Roman Gleissner, *Die Entstehung der ästhetischen Humanitätsidee in Deutschland*, Stuttgart, 1988.

Manuela Göhner, *Rhetorische Ästhetik des Gesamtkunstwerks. Joseph Beuys. Ein Beispiel zur Methode der Kunstkritik aus der Sicht der rhetorischen Anthropologie*, Oberhausen, 2000.

Christian Godin, *La Totalité*, 6 Volumes, Seyssel, 1998–2003.

Gerhard von Grävenitz (ed.), *Konzepte der Moderne*, Munich, 1999.

Martin Gregor-Dellin, *Richard Wagner. Die Revolution als Oper*, Munich, 1973.

Barbara Gronau, *Theaterinstallationen. Performative Räume bei Beuys, Boltanski und Kabakov*, Munich, 2010.

Boris Groys, *Gesamtkunstwerk Stalin. Die gespaltene Kultur in der Sowjetunion*, Vienna, 1988.

Uta Grund, *Zwischen den Künsten. Edward Gordon Craig und das Bildertheater um 1900*, Berlin, 2002.

Hans Günther (ed.), *Gesamtkunstwerk. Zwischen Synästhesie und Mythos*, Bielefeld, 1994.

Guido Hiß, *Synthetische Visionen. Theater als Gesamtkunstwerk von 1800 bis 2000*, Munich, 2009 (Aesthetica theatralia; 1).

Detlev Hoffmann (ed.), *Der Traum vom Gesamtkunstwerk*, Rehberg-Loccum, 1989 (Loccum protocols; 9/98).

Werner Hofmann, *Die Grundlagen der modernen Kunst. Eine Einführung in ihre symbolischen Formen*, Stuttgart, 1987.

Fredric Jameson, *Postmodernism or The Cultural Logic of late Capitalism*, Durham, 1991.

Cornelia Klinger, *Flucht, Trost, Revolte. Die Moderne und ihre ästhetischen Gegenwelten*, Munich, 1995.

Heinrich Klotz (ed.), *Vision der Moderne. Das Prinzip der Konstruktion*, Munich, 1986.

Thomas Koebner, *Handlungen mit Musik. Die Oper als Zeitspiegel, Leidenschaftsdrama, Gesamtkunstwerk*, Salzburg, 1993.

Juliet Koss, *Modernism after Wagner*, Minneapolis, 2008.

Stefan Kunze, *Der Kunstbegriff Richard Wagners. Voraussetzungen und Folgerungen*, Regensburg, 1983.

Chung-Sun Kwon, *Studie zur Idee des Gesamtkunstwerks in der Frühromantik. Zur Utopie einer Musikanschauung von Wackenroder bis Schopenhauer*, Frankfurt/Main, 2003.

Friedhelm Lach, *Der Merz Künstler Kurt Schwitters*, Cologne, 1971.

Frank E. Manuel/Fritzie P. Manuel, *Utopian Thought in the Western World*, Cambridge, 1979.

Karin Maur (ed.), *Vom Klang der Bilder*, Munich, 1985.

Angela Merte, *Totalkunst. Intermediale Entwürfe für eine Ästhetisierung der Lebenswelt*, Bielefeld, 1998.

Richard Noble (ed.), *Utopias*, London, 2009 (Documents of Contemporary Art).

Eberhard Ostermann, *Das Fragment. Geschichte einer ästhetischen Idee*, Munich, 1991.

Randall Packer/ Ken Jordan, *Multimedia: From Wagner to Virtual Reality*, New York, 2002.

Gerald Raunig, *Kunst und Revolution. Künstlerischer Aktivismus im langen 20. Jahrhundert*, Vienna, 2005.

Florian Rötzer/Peter Weibel (ed.), *Cyberspace. Zum medialen Gesamtkunstwerk*, Munich, 1993.

Alex Ross, *The Rest Is Noise: Listening to the Twentieth Century*, London, 2009.

Daniel Schneller, *Richard Wagners „Parsifal" und die Erneuerung des Mysteriendramas in Bayreuth. Die Vision des Gesamtkunstwerks als Universalkultur der Zukunft*, Bern, 1997.

Richard Sheppard, *Modernism—Dada—Postmodernism*, Evanston, 2000.

Peter Simhandl, *Bildertheater. Bildende Künstler des 20. Jahrhunderts als Theaterreformer*, Berlin, 1993.

Matthew Wilson Smith, *The Total Work of Art: From Bayreuth to Cyberspace*, New York, 2007.

Reto Sorg/Stefan Bodo Würffel (ed.), *Totalität und Zerfall im Kunstwerk der Moderne*, Munich, 2005.

Barbara Steffen (ed.), *Vienna 1900—Klimt, Schiele und ihre Zeit. Ein Gesamtkunstwerk*, exhibition catalogue. Fondation Beyeler, Riehen/Basel, Stuttgart, 2010.

Harald Szeemann (ed.), *Der Hang zum Gesamtkunstwerk. Europäische Utopien seit 1800*, exhibition catalogue., Frankfurt/Main, 1983.

Harald Szeemann, *Individuelle Mythologien*, Berlin, 1985.

Charles Taylor, *Sources of the Self. The Making of the Modern Identity*, Cambridge, 1989.

Konrad Tobler, *Hodler, Stauffer, Wölfli. Eine Berner Parallelgeschichte*, Zurich, 2011.

Silvio Vietta/Dirk Kemper (ed.), *Ästhetische Moderne in Europa. Grundzüge und Problemzusammenhänge seit der Romantik*, Munich, 1989.

Boris Voigt, *Richard Wagners autoritäre Inszenierungen. Versuch über die Ästhetik charismatischer Herrschaft*, Hamburg, 2003.

Jeff Wallace, *Beginning Modernism*, Manchester/New York, 2011.

Wolfgang Welsch, *Unsere postmoderne Moderne*, Berlin, 1993.

Ian Boyd White, *Bruno Taut, Baumeister einer neuen Welt. Architektur und Aktivismus 1914-1920*, Stuttgart, 1981.

George p. Williamson, *The Longing for Myth in Germany. Religion and Aesthetic Culture from Romanticism to Nietzsche*, Chicago, 2004.

Essays

Inge Baxmann, "Verbindung der Künste und Verknüpfung der Sinne. Zur Wagner-Rezeption der Avantgarde in Frankreich", in: Annegret Fauser/Manuela Schwartz (ed.), *Von Wagner zum Wagnérisme. Musik, Literatur, Kunst, Politik*, Leipzig, 1999, p. 513-534.

Hans-Peter Bayerdörfer, "Wege des Mythos ins ‚Theater der Zukunft'. Richard Wagner und die Theaterreformbewegung der Jahrhundertwende", in: Dieter Borchmeyer (ed.), *Wege des Mythos in der Moderne. Richard Wagner ‚Der Ring des Nibelungen'*, Munich, 1987, p. 182-201.

Udo Bermbach, "Mythos als Zivilreligion. Zu einem Aspekt der Idee des Gesamtkunstwerks", in: *Programmhefte der Bayreuther Festspiele VII (Parsifal)*, 1992.

Udo Bermbach, "Von der Oper zum Gesamtkunstwerk. Der Fall Richard Wagner", in: Udo Bermbach/Wulf Konold (ed.), *Der schöne Abglanz*, Berlin/Hamburg, 1992.

Udo Bermbach, "Reine Kunst, persönliche Lebensmacht, nationale Kulturmacht. Wagner, seine Epigonen und die Instrumentalisierung einer großen Idee", in: Hermann Danuser/Herfried Münkler (ed.), *Zukunftsbilder. Richard Wagners Revolution und ihre Folgen in Kunst und Politik*, Schliengen, 2002, p. 61-73.

Udo Bermbach, "Richard Wagner und Joseph Beuys. Über die Fortdauer einer offenbar zeitlosen Idee: das Gesamtkunstwerk", in: *Oper aktuell. Die Bayerische Staatsoper 2002/2003*, ed. Gesellschaft zur Förderung der Münchner Opern-Festspiele, Munich, 2002.

Markus Bernauer, "Les parfums, les couleurs et les sons se confondent. Überlegungen zum ‚Wagnérisme'", in: Hermann Danuser/Herfried Münkler (ed.), *Zukunftsbilder. Richard Wagners Revolution und ihre Folgen in Kunst und Politik*, Schliengen, 2002, p. 192-210.

Jutta Boehe, "Theater und Jugendstil—Feste des Lebens und der Kunst", in: Gerhard Bott (ed.), *Vom Morris zum Bauhaus. Eine Kunst gründet auf Einfachheit*, Hanau, 1977, p. 143-158.

"Christian Boltanski und Jean Kalman im Gespräch mit Michael Haerdter", in: Joachim Fiebach (ed.), *Theater der Welt—Arbeitsbuch*, Berlin, 2/1999, p. 55-60.

Detlef Borchers, "Windows als Gesamtkunstwerk", in: *Die Zeit*, Nr. 10, 1999, p. 29.

Dieter Borchmeyer, "Gesamtkunstwerk", in: id./Victor Žmegač (ed.), *Moderne Literatur in Grundbegriffen*, Tübingen, 1994, p. 181-184.

Dieter Borchmeyer, "Gesamtkunstwerk", in: Ludwig Finscher (ed.), *Die Musik in Geschichte und Gegenwart*, Sachteil (3), Kassel, 1995, p. 1282-1290.

Manfred Brauneck, "Das Theaterfest als soziale Utopie. Richard Wagners Entwurf eines ‚Kunstwerks der Zukunft'", in: *Neue Rundschau*, 94th edition, issue 4, 1983, p. 60-78.

Stefan Breuer, "Richard Wagner Fundamentalismus", in: *Deutsche Vierteljahrsschrift für Literaturwissenschaft und Geistesgeschichte*, 73rd edition, issue 4, 1999, p. 643-664.

Stefan Breuer, "Religion—Kunst—Politik", in: Eckehard Kiem/Ludwig Holtmeier (ed.), *Richard Wagner und seine Zeit*, Laaber, 2003.

Bazon Brock, "Der Hang zum Gesamtkunstwerk. Pathosformeln und Energiesymbole zur Einheit von Denken, Wollen und Können", in: Harald Szeemann (ed.), *Der Hang zum Gesamtkunstwerk. Europäische Utopien seit 1800*, exhibition catalogue, Frankfurt/Main, 1983, p. 22-39.

Bill Brown, "The Dark Wood of Postmodernity (Space, Faith, Allegory)", in: *PMLA*, 120th edition, issue 3, 2005, p. 734-750.

Klaus-Detlef Bruse, "Die griechische Tragödie als ‚Gesamtkunstwerk'. Anmerkungen zu den musikästhetischen Reflexionen des frühen Nietzsche", in: *Nietzsche-Studien*, Vol. 13, 1984, p. 156-176.

Gabriele Bryant, "Timely Untimeliness. Architectural modernism and the idea of the Gesamtkunstwerk", in: Mari Hvathum/Christian Hermansen (ed.), *Tracing Modernity: Manifestations of the Modern in Architecture and the City*, New York, 2004.

Christopher Butler, "Innovation and the Avant-Garde, 1900–1920", in: Nicholas Cook/Anthony Pople, *The Cambridge History of Twentieth Century Music*, Cambridge, 2004.

Miroslav Cerny, "Otakar Hostinsky über Richard Wagners Gesamtkunstwerk", in: *Beiträge zur Musikwissenschaft*, 28th edition, issue 4, 1986, p. 320-323.

Jean Clair, "Das dritte Reich als Gesamtkunstwerk des pervertierten Abendlandes", in: Harald Szeemann (ed.), *Der Hang zum Gesamtkunstwerk. Europäische Utopien seit 1800*, exhibition catalogue, Frankfurt/Main, 1983, p. 93-104.

Paul Coates, "Cinema, Symbolism and the Gesamtkunstwerk", in: *Comparative Criticism*, 4th edition, 1982, p. 213-229.

John Daverio, "'Total Work of Art' or ‚Nameless Deeds of Music'. Some Thoughts on German Romantic Opera", in: *Opera Quarterly*, 4th edition, issue 4, 1986, p. 61-74.

Wolfgang Dömling, "Eine zukünftige Vereinigung der Musik und Malerei", in: *Programmhefte der Bayreuther Festspiele* VII, 1991.

Klaus Englert, "Der Traum vom Gesamtkunstwerk. Das ästhetische Dispositiv der Moderne?", in: *Zeitschrift für Ästhetik und Allgemeine Kunstwissenschaft*, 44th edition, issue 1, 2000, p. 5-25.

Bernd Euler-Rolle, "Wege zum ‚Gesamtkunstwerk' in den Sakralräumen der österreichischen Spätbarocks am Beispiel der Stiftskirche von Melk", in: *Zeitschrift des Deutschen Vereins für Kunstwissenschaft*, 1989, p. 25-48.

Bernd Euler-Rolle, "Kritisches zum Begriff des ‚Gesamtkunstwerks' in Theorie und Praxis", in: Götz Pochat/Renate Wagner-Rieger (ed.), *Barock. regional-international*, Graz, 1993, p. 365-374 (Kunsthistorisches Jahrbuch Graz; 25).

Sabine Fabo, "Konzepte des Gesamtkunstwerk in den Neuen Medien", in: *LAB. Jahrbuch 1995/96 für Künste und Apparate*, Cologne, 1996, p. 76-87.

Annette Frank, "Das Gesamtkunstwerk", in: Michael Metzeltin/Margit Thir (ed.), *GesamtMediale Anthropologie*, Vienna, 2000, p. 29-86.

Carl Freytag, "Die Beste aller Welten als Konstruktion. Raumträume bei Paul Scheerbart und Bruno Taut", in: Sigrid Lane (ed.), *Raumkonstruktionen der Moderne. Kultur—Literatur—Film*, Bielefeld, 2001, p. 159-192.

Jens Malte Fischer, "Das ‚Kunstwerk der Zukunft' und seine theatralischen Folgen", in: Hermann Danuser/Herfried Münkler (ed.), *Zukunftsbilder. Richard Wagners Revolution und ihre Folgen in Kunst und Politik*, Schliengen, 2002, p. 211-225.

Erika Fischer-Lichte, "Das ‚Gesamtkunstwerk'. Ein Konzept für die Kunst der achtziger Jahre?", in: Maria Moog-Grünwald/Christoph Rodiek (ed.), *Dialog der Künste. Intermediale Fallstudien zur Literatur des 19. und 20. Jahrhunderts. Festschrift für Erwin Koppen*, Frankfurt/Main, 1989, p. 61-74.

Rüdiger Görner, "Über die ‚Trennung der Elemente'. Das Gesamtkunstwerk—ein Steinbruch der Moderne?", in: *Maske und Kothurn*, 29th edition, 1983, p. 98-122.

Antje von Graevenitz, "Erlösungskunst und Befreiungspolitik. Wagner und Beuys", in: Gabriele Förg (ed.), *Unsere Wagner: Joseph Beuys, Heiner Müller, Karlheinz Stockhausen, Hans-Jürgen Syberberg*, Frankfurt/Main, 1984, p. 11-49.

Rolf Grimminger, "Das imperiale Gesamtkunstwerk. Gabriele d'Annunzios Roman Il Fuoco, Venedig und Richard Wagner", in: Hans Günther (ed.), *Gesamtkunstwerk. Zwischen Synästhesie und Mythos*, Bielefeld, 1994, p. 91-106.

Tag Gronberg, "Performing Modernism", in: Christopher Wilk (ed.), *Modernism 1914-1939: Designing a New World*, London, 2006.

Agnes Hannes, "Ausstellungstechnologie und Avantgarde. Das interaktive Gesamtkunstwerk „Bloodflames 1947" von Friedrich Kiesler*, diploma thesis. University of Vienna, 2006.

Sabine Hänsgen, "Die Installation als Gesamtkunstwerk. Zu einem Genre in der zeitgenössischen russischen Kunst", in: Elisabeth Cheauré (ed.), *Kultur und Krise. Rußland 1987-1997*, Berlin, 1997, p. 105-119.

Werner Hofmann, "Gesamtkunstwerk Vienna", in: Harald Szeemann (ed.), *Der Hang zum Gesamtkunstwerk. Europäische Utopien seit 1800*, exhibition catalogue, Frankfurt/Main, 1983, p. 84-92.

Norbert Hopster, "Das ‚Dritte Reich'. ‚Gesamtkunstwerk' oder ästhetisch inszenierte ‚Ganzheit'?", in: Hans Günther (ed.), *Gesamtkunstwerk. Zwischen Synästhesie und Mythos*, Bielefeld, 1994, p. 241-258.

Eckehard Jesse, "Die Totalitarismusforschung und ihre Repräsentanten. Konzeptionen von Carl J. Friedrich, Hannah Arendt, Eric Voegelin, Ernst Nolte und Karl Dietrich Bracher", in: *Aus Politik und Zeitgeschichte*, insert in the weekly *Das Parlament*, 8. Mai 1998.

Dominik Keller, "‚Gesamtkunstwerk' in der amerikanischen Kinolandschaft der zwanziger Jahre", in: Harald Szeemann (ed.), *Der Hang zum Gesamtkunstwerk. Europäische Utopien seit 1800*, exhibition catalogue, Frankfurt/Main, 1983, p. 395-400.

Friedrich Kittler, "Weltatem. Über Wagners Medientechnologie", in: Manfred Schneider/Samuel Weber (ed.), *Diskursanalysen*, Opladen, 1986, p. 94-107.

Richard Klein, "Wagners plurale Moderne", in: Claus-Steffen Mahnkopf (ed.), *Richard Wagner. Konstrukteur der Moderne*, Stuttgart, 1999

Cornelia Klinger, "Die Utopie der Versöhnung von Kunst und Leben. Die Transformation einer Idee im 20. Jahrhundert. Vom Staat als Kunstwerk zum life-style des Individuums", in: Dies./Wolfgang Müller-Funk (ed.), *Das Jahrhundert der Avantgarden*, Munich, 2004, p. 211-246.

Heinrich Klotz, "Für ein mediales Gesamtkunstwerk. Im Gespräch mit Florian Rötzer", in: Florian Rötzer (ed.), *Digitaler Schein. Ästhetik der elektronischen Medien*, Frankfurt/Main, 1991, p. 356-370.

Eduard Krüger, "Beziehungen zwischen Kunst und Musik", in: *Allgemeine Musikalische Zeitung*, ed. Franz Brendel, Leipzig, 1848.

Till R. Kuhnle, "Anmerkungen zum Begriff ‚Gesamtkunstwerk'—die Politisierung einer ästhetischen Kategorie?", in: *Germanica*, Nr. 10, 1992, p. 35-50.

Stefan Kunze, "Richard Wagners Idee des ‚Gesamtkunstwerks'" in: Helmut Koopmann/J. Adolf Schmoll (ed.), *Beiträge zur Theorie der Künste im 19. Jahrhundert*, Vol. 2, Frankfurt/Main, 1972, p. 196-229.

Marcella Lista, "Les ‚compositions scéniques' de Kandinsky. La quête moderne du Gesamtkunstwerk", in: *Cahiers du Musée national d'art moderne*, Nr. 63, 1998, p. 38-57.

Odo Marquard, "Gesamtkunstwerk und Identitätssystem. Überlegungen im Anschluss an Hegels Schellingkritik", in: Harald Szeemann (ed.), *Der Hang zum Gesamtkunstwerk. Europäische Utopien seit 1800*, exhibition catalogue, Frankfurt/Main, 1983, p. 40-49.

Annette Michelsen, "Where is your rupture?: Mass Culture and the Gesamtkunstwerk", in: *October*, No. 56, Frühjahr 1991, p. 43-63.

Jurij Murasov, "‚Das Auge des Gehöres'. Gesamtkunstwerk und Schriftlichkeit", in: Hans Günther (ed.), *Gesamtkunstwerk. Zwischen Synästhesie und Mythos*, Bielefeld, 1994, p. 29-54.

Scott D. Paulin, "Richard Wagner and the Fantasy of Cinematic Unity: The Idea of the Gesamtkunstwerk in the History and the Theory of Film Music", in: James Buhler/Caryl Flinn/David Neumeyer (ed.), *Music and Cinema*, Hannover, 2000, p. 58-84.

H. Martin Puchner, "Polyphonous Gestures. Wagnerian Modernism from Mallarmé to Stravinsky", in: *Criticism*, No. 41, issue 1, 1999, p. 25-39.

Willem van Reijen, "Im Labyrinth. Gesamtkunstwerk und Postmoderne", in: Wilhelm Donner (ed.), *Moderne Labyrinthe*, Frankfurt/Main, 1992, p. 11ff.

Franz Rauhut, "Die Idee der Einheit oder Verwandtschaft und der Vereinigung oder Verschmelzung der Künste", in: *Wissenschaftliche Zeitschrift der Karl-Marx-Universität Leipzig*, 6th edition. issue 5, 1956/57, p. 553-575.

Peter Rummenhöller, "Romantik und Gesamtkunstwerk", in: Walter Salmen (ed.), *Beiträge zur Geschichte der Musikanschauung im 19. Jahrhundert*, Regensburg, 1965, p. 161-170.

Alain Satgé, "L'Œuvre d'Art Totale et les Symbolistes Français: L'Exemple de la ‚Revue Wagnérienne' (1885-1888)", in: Elie Konigson (ed.), *L'œuvre d'Art Totale*, Paris, 1995, p. 47-58.

Jeffrey Schnapp, "Border Crossings. Italian/German Peregrinations of the Theater of Totality", in: *Critical Inquiry*, Herbst 1994, p. 80-123.

Irmela Schneider, "Von der Vielsprachigkeit zur ‚Kunst der Hybridation'. Diskurse des Hybriden", in: Dies./Christian W. Thomson (ed.), *Hybridkultur. Medien, Netze, Künste*, Cologne, 1997, p. 13-66.

Jochen Schulte-Sasse, "Carl Einstein; or, The Postmodern Transformation of Modernism", in: Andreas Huyssen/David Bathrick (ed.), *Modernity and the Text. Revisions of German Modernism*, New York, 1989.

Peter Simhandl, "Gesamtkunstwerk", in: Manfred Brauneck/Gérard Schneilin (ed.), *Theaterlexikon 1. Begriffe und Epochen, Bühnen und Ensembles*, Reinbek, 2007.

Jürgen Söring, "Gesamtkunstwerk", in: Klaus Weimar (ed.), *Reallexikon der deutschen Literaturwissenschaft*, Vol. 1, Berlin, 1997, p. 710–712.

George Steiner, "Das totale Fragment", in: Lucien Dällenbach/Christiaan L. Hart Nibbrig, (ed.), *Fragment und Totalität*, Frankfurt/Main, 1984, p. 18–29.

Rainer Stollmann, "Faschistische Politik als Gesamtkunstwerk. Tendenzen der Ästhetisierung des politischen Lebens im Nationalsozialismus", in: Horst Denkler/Karl Prumm (ed.), *Die deutsche Literatur im Dritten Reich. Themen, Traditionen, Wirkungen*, Stuttgart, 1976, p. 83–101.

Wolfgang Storch, "Gesamtkunstwerk", in: *Ästhetische Grundbegriffe*, Vol. 2, Stuttgart, 2001, p. 731–791.

Charles Swoope, "Kandinsky and Kokoschka. Two Episodes in the Genesis of Total Theatre", in: *yale/theatre*, 3rd edition, issue 1, 1970, p. 11–18.

Peter Vergo, "The origins of expressionism and the notion of the Gesamtkunstwerk", in: Shulamith Behr (ed.), *Expressionism reassessed*, Manchester, 1993, p. 11–19.

Elodie Vitale, "De l'œuvre d'Art totale à l'œuvre totale. Art et Architecture au Bauhaus", in: *Cahiers du Musée national d'art moderne*, No. 39, 1992, p. 62–77.

Albert Wellek, "Zur Geschichte und Kritik der Synästhesie-Forschung", in: *Archiv für die gesamte Psychologie*, issue 79, 1931, p. 325–384.

Johannes Werner, "Das Gesamtkunstwerk als Utopie", in: *Universitas*, 36th edition, issue 3, 1981.

Gottfried Willems, "Die Künste, ihre Medien und die Fallen der Spezialisierung. Das Gesamtkunstwerk als Gegenstand der Wissenschaft", in: Dirck Linck/Stefanie Rentsch (ed.), *Bildtext—Textbild*, Freiburg im Breisgau, 2007, p. 53–71.

Marc Adrian
Großes Sylvesterbild, 1977
Verre eglomise montage
190 × 145 cm
Belvedere, Vienna (permanent loan private collection)

Klaus Auderer
Groundzerosystems: Baghdad 2003, Phnom Penh 2005
9 colour pigment prints, each 111 × 166.5 cm
Edition 2 + 1
Courtesy of Galerie Sabine Knust, Munich and the artist

Gott, Maria, Joseph, das Christkind and ihr Küchenkruzifix
(from the series *Psychoplasma*), 2003–2013
5 colour pigment prints, each 111 × 166.5 cm
Edition 2 + 1
Courtesy of Galerie Sabine Knust, Munich and the artist

Psychopath Park
Global research and sketching project, since 2003
in various war and military museums: Cairo 2010, London
2008, Istanbul 2007, Vienna 2009, Berlin 2004, Munich
2009, Latrun (IL) 2003, Berscheva (IL) 2005, Haifa 2005,
Warsaw 2007, Füssen (D) 2005, Tel Aviv 2002, Budapest
2009
5 books with 70 sketches and photographies each;
each 21 × 29.7 cm
Courtesy of Galerie Sabine Knust, Munich and the artist

Josef Bauer
Ausstellung Griechenbeisl: Buchstaben, 1971
Installation
Courtesy of the artist

Ausstellung Griechenbeisl: Bild mit Wolke, 1971
Installation
Courtesy of the artist

Ausstellung Griechenbeisl: Ecken-A, 1971
Installation
Courtesy of the artist

Ausstellung Griechenbeisl: Gabel, 1971
Installation
Courtesy of the artist

Ausstellung Griechenbeisl: Stein, 1971
Installation
Courtesy of the artist

Ausstellung Griechenbeisl: Abguss 1:1, 1971
Installation
Courtesy of the artist

Ausstellung Griechenbeisl: Fläche 1:1, 1971
Installation
Courtesy of the artist

Ausstellung Griechenbeisl: Umrisslinie 1:1, 1971
Installation
Courtesy of the artist

Ausstellung Griechenbeisl: Photo 1:1, 1971
Installation
Courtesy of the artist

Joseph Beuys
7000 Eichen, 1982–1987
Documentation materials of the performance:
Pflanzung eines Baumes der Poesie, 4 Seiten 21 × 29.7 cm
Pflanzaktion 84 20.–24. März, 2 Seiten, 21 × 27.9 cm
Jeder Baum hat seinen Preis, Postkarte Spendenaufruf
...denn wir wollen die Pflanzaktion ja NIE mehr beenden!,
1 Seite Joseph Beuys 1982
Joseph Beuys 7000 Eichen, 1 working paper of Freie Interna-
tionale Universität (FIU) Leaflet 14 pages
Courtesy of private collection, documenta Archiv and Dieter
Schwerdtle Archiv

Monica Bonvicini
We Finally Built Walls, 2010
Wood construction, 30 safety glass windowpanes, black
enamel paint
379 × 1207.5 × 6.8 cm (dimensions variable)
Courtesy of the artist and Galerie Max Hetzler, Berlin

Christian Boltanski/Ilya Kabakov/Jean Kalman
Der Ring—Fünfter Tag. Der Tag danach, 1999
A project of the Hebbel-Theater, Berlin and the Theater der
Welt
Portfolio, 29 pieces
Belvedere, Vienna
Fotos © Martina Schmücker/ David Zink Yi

Marcel Broodthaers
Musée d'art moderne, Abteilung der Adler, 1969
Print, invitation
17.5 × 11.5 cm
Double-sided print in French and German
Marcel Broodthaers prie ... de bien vouloir assister à la céré-
monie de clôture de la Section XIXème S. ... (Marcel Brood-
thaers ... requests taking part in the closing ceremony of the
department for the 19th century...)
Courtesy of Generali Foundation, Vienna

Daniel Buren
Fiche technique, 1972
Acrylic on red and white textile
142 × 137.5 cm
Belvedere, Vienna (permanent loan Dr. Ernst Ploil)

Tom Burr
Derailed 2, 2005
Plywood, decorative wood railing, paint
101 × 300 × 80 cm
Courtesy of the artist and Galerie Neu

Worn Out, 2005
Plywood, galvanized hinges, paint, carpet
106 × 60 × 259 cm
Collection of Alexander Schröder, Berlin

Ernst Caramelle
ohne Titel, 1986
TV-Screens, wood, wine
194.5 × 124 × 39 cm
Rudi Molacek Collection, Vienna

Bernhard Cella
Salon für Kunstbuch im 21er Haus, since 2011
(ongoing project)
Sculpture
Courtesy of Belvedere, Vienna and the artist

Cityrama II
1 cabinet containing the following articles:
Christo (artist)/Stefan Wewerka (Photographer), *Cityrama II*,
1961, Photo
César, *Compression Dirigée-Dauphine*, 1961, 25.4 × 20.3
cm
Christo, *Projekt für die Verhüllung eines öffentlichen Gebäu-
des*, 1961, 27 × 20.9 cm
Robert Filliou, *Brief an Köpke*, 1962, 26.9 × 20.9 cm
Wolf Vostell / Stefan Wewerka, *Konzept zu „Cityrama II"*,
1962, 29.7 × 21 cm
Ben Patterson, *Brief an Vostell and Wewerka*, 1962, newspa-
per clippings: 29 × 23.4 cm/letter: 21.4 × 20,9 cm
Arnulf Rainer, *Brief an Stefan Wewerka*, 1962, 29.7 × 21 cm
Arnulf Rainer, *Schwarze Architektur*, 1967,
closed: 29.7 × 21 cm, measure when open: 29.7 × 42 cm
Arnulf Rainer, *Schwarze Architektur*, 29.7 × 21 cm
Wolf Vostell, Stefan Wewerka, Galerie Dumont, *Einladung zu
Cityrama II*, 1962, 25.7 × 19 cm
Courtesy of mumok, museum moderner kunst stiftung ludwig
wien, previously Sammlung Hahn, Cologne

Heinz Emigholz
Two projects by Frederick Kiesler (Austria/Germany), 2006/09
HDV, 4:3, 16'
Courtesy of the artists and Amour Fou, Vienna

VALIE EXPORT
Restringierter Code, 1979
Performance, video performance
Video, 30' 39"
Courtesy of Charim Galerie, Vienna

Claire Fontaine
I, 2009
HDV, 16:9, 4' 20"
Courtesy of the artist and T293, Naples/Rome

Peter Friedl
Bilbao Song, 2010
Video installation 16:9, 5' 53", Loop
Courtesy of the artists and Galerie Meyer Kainer, Vienna

gelatin
World Trade Center, 2000
Photography (Fujiflex)
162 × 126 cm
Belvedere, Vienna (State subsidy for galleries)

B-Thing (from the series *World Trade Center*), 2000
Photography (Fujiflex)
40 × 60cm
7 pieces
Belvedere, Vienna (State subsidy for galleries)

Isa Genzken
empire vampire III, 19, 2004
plastic, metal, glass, textile, coating, paper, wood
320 × 100 × 75 cm
Courtesy of Thyssen-Bornemisza Art Contemporary, Vienna

Liam Gillick
Volvo Bar, 2008
Wood, laminated chipboard, jute covering, vinyl letters
Measures variable
Courtesy of Esther Schipper, Berlin and Galerie Eva Presen-
huber, Zurich

Franz Graf
*DERR SCHRECKEN JEDOCH VERMEERTE MEIN INTER-
ESSE*, 2011
Cabinet with glass objects and various materials
Courtesy of the artist

Thomas Hirschhorn
Tool Family, 2007
Wood, card board, podium, mannequins, brown and transparent adhesive tape, different tools, enlarged tools, enlarged
book, yellow transparent foil, prints, integrated text
290 × 290 × 290 cm
Courtesy of the artists and ARNDT Berlin

Julia Hohenwarter
Catwalk, 2009
Sculpture
Wood, dispersion paint
Belvedere, Vienna

Hans Hollein/Walter Pichler
Plakatentwurf für die Ausstellung Architektur in der Galerie nächst St. Stephan, 1963
China ink on paper
45 × 55 cm
Courtesy Hans Hollein/Walter Pichler

Hans Hollein
Gebäude, 1959
China ink on paper
45 × 55cm
Courtesy of Hans Hollein

Stadt, 1962
China ink on paper
45 × 55 cm
Courtesy of Hans Hollein

Suspended city-structure with transportion-interchange, 1963
Pencil on paper
60 × 80 cm
Courtesy of Hans Hollein

**Inspection Medical Hermeneutics
(Pavel Pepperstein/Sergei Anufriev)**
PARAMEN # 1
1994, acrylic paint/canvas, 65 × 50 cm
Courtesy of the artists, Galerie Kamm, Berlin and Nahodka Arts Ltd, London

PARAMEN # 3
1994, acrylic paint/canvas, 65 × 50 cm
Courtesy of the artists, Galerie Kamm, Berlin and Nahodka Arts Ltd, London

PARAMEN # 4
1994, acrylic paint/canvas, 65 × 50 cm
Courtesy of the artists, Galerie Kamm, Berlin and Nahodka Arts Ltd, London

PARAMEN # 6
1994, acrylic paint/canvas, 65 × 50 cm
Courtesy of the artists, Galerie Kamm, Berlin and Nahodka Arts Ltd, London

PARAMEN # 7
1994, acrylic paint/canvas, 65 × 50 cm
Courtesy of the artists, Galerie Kamm, Berlin and Nahodka Arts Ltd, London

PARAMEN # 8
1994, acrylic paint/canvas, 65 × 50 cm
Courtesy of the artists, Galerie Kamm, Berlin and Nahodka Arts Ltd, London

PARAMEN # 9
1994, acrylic paint/canvas, 65 × 50 cm
Courtesy of the artists, Galerie Kamm, Berlin and Nahodka Arts Ltd, London

PARAMEN # 10
1994, acrylic paint/canvas, 65 × 50 cm
Courtesy of the artists, Galerie Kamm, Berlin and Nahodka Arts Ltd, London

PARAMEN # 11
1994, acrylic paint/canvas, 65 × 50 cm
Courtesy of the artists, Galerie Kamm, Berlin and Nahodka Arts Ltd, London

PARAMEN # 12
1994, acrylic paint/canvas, 65 × 50 cm
Courtesy of the artists, Galerie Kamm, Berlin and Nahodka Arts Ltd, London

PARAMEN # 13
1994, acrylic paint/canvas, 65 × 50 cm
Courtesy of the artists, Galerie Kamm, Berlin and Nahodka Arts Ltd, London

PARAMEN # 14
1994, acrylic paint/canvas, 65 × 50 cm
Courtesy of the artists, Galerie Kamm, Berlin and Nahodka Arts Ltd, London

PARAMEN # 15
1994, acrylic paint/canvas, 65 × 50 cm
Courtesy of the artists, Galerie Kamm, Berlin and Nahodka Arts Ltd, London

PARAMEN # 16
1994, acrylic paint/canvas, 65 × 50 cm
Courtesy of the artists, Galerie Kamm, Berlin and Nahodka Arts Ltd, London

PARAMEN # 17
1994, acrylic paint/canvas, 65 × 50 cm
Courtesy of the artists, Galerie Kamm, Berlin and Nahodka Arts Ltd, London

PARAMEN # 18
1994, acrylic paint/canvas, 65 × 50 cm
Courtesy of the artists, Galerie Kamm, Berlin and Nahodka
Arts Ltd, London

PARAMEN # 20
1994, acrylic paint/canvas, 65 × 50 cm
Courtesy of the artists, Galerie Kamm, Berlin and Nahodka
Arts Ltd, London

PARAMEN # 21
1994, acrylic paint/canvas, 65 × 50 cm
Courtesy of the artists, Galerie Kamm, Berlin and Nahodka
Arts Ltd, London

PARAMEN # 22
1994, acrylic paint/canvas, 65 × 50 cm
Courtesy of the artists, Galerie Kamm, Berlin and Nahodka
Arts Ltd, London

PARAMEN # 24
1994, acrylic paint/canvas, 65 × 50 cm
Courtesy of the artists, Galerie Kamm, Berlin and Nahodka
Arts Ltd, London

PARAMEN # 25
1994, acrylic paint/canvas, 65 × 50 cm
Courtesy of the artists, Galerie Kamm, Berlin and Nahodka
Arts Ltd, London

PARAMEN # 27
1994, acrylic paint/canvas, 65 × 50 cm
Courtesy of the artists, Galerie Kamm, Berlin and Nahodka
Arts Ltd, London

Christian Jankowski
Telemistica, 1999
Video, 22'
Courtesy of Galerie Martin Klosterfelde and Lisson Gallery,
London

Tillman Kaiser
Innenblick Kirche, 2011
Cardboard, China ink, glass, butterfly wings, iron
200 × 129 × 61 cm
Belvedere, Vienna

Ian Kiaer
Grey Cloth Project: Glashaus, 2005
Paperwork, card board, acrylic on linen, acryl rod
Paperwork: 49 × 64 cm; Model: 25 × 30 × 22 cm
Collection of Gregory R. Miller and Michael Weiner, New York

Friedrich Kiesler
Manifeste du Corréalisme, in: *L'Architecture d'Aujourd'hui*,
No. 2, special edition, June 1949.
Courtesy of Österreichische Friedrich and Lillian Kiesler
Privatstiftung

Martin Kippenberger
Alt Wien, Großplakat, 1991
Poster, 8 pieces
Each 84.1 × 118.9 cm
Private collection

Mahony
O.T. (Marginale), 2011
Different objects, various materials, several sizes
Courtesy of the artist and Galerie Emanuel Layr

Gordon Matta-Clark
Bronx Floors: Floor Above, Ceiling Below, 1972
3 black & white photos, framed, 21.5 × 28 cm
Belvedere, Vienna (permanent loan Dr. Ernst Ploil)

Ralo Mayer
*And turns and turns and I turn pages. (Und kommt nicht on
den Punkt, nicht weil es keinen Punkt gäbe, nein; nein, es gibt
so viele.) "Have another shot," the skeuomorphic whisper roared inside my ears, revealing endless fields of view, captions
of geometric arrangements way beyond dimensions 3+1. It
was not without rekindled enthusiasm that I thus continued
reading p. 402-472: which describe footage of an automatic apparatus scanning an abandoned room full of research
about Biosphere 2, and what appears to be notes for a
screenplay, including the handwritten memo: Dreh?buch. All
the while accompanied by melancholic sounds of robotic routines / "ÜBERSETZUNG UND VERRAT"*, 2009/2012
2-Kanal HD-Video mit Sound, 40'
Fresnel lens, acrylic glass
Based on the novel *The Ninth Biospherian* and the film project with the same name, developed in cooperation with Oliver
Gemballa
Courtesy of the artists

Paul McCarthy
*Basement Bunker: Looking Down at the Queen and the Green
Hat*, 2003
Photo, Cibachrome on aluminium, 183 × 122 cm
Belvedere, Vienna (permanent loan Wolfgang Anselmino)
Photo: Ann-Marie Rounkle

Basement Bunker: Painting Queens in the Red Carpet Hall 3,
2003
Photo, Cibachrome on aluminium, 183 × 122
Belvedere, Vienna (permanent loan Wolfgang Anselmino)
Photo: Ann-Marie Rounkle

*Basement Bunker: A Queen in the Yellow Room on the Table
1*, 2003
Photo, Cibachrome on aluminium, 183 × 122
Belvedere, Vienna (permanent loan Wolfgang Anselmino)
Photo: Ann-Marie Rounkle

Basement Bunker: A Queen in the Yellow Room on the Table 2, 2003
Photo, Cibachrome on aluminium, 183 × 122
Belvedere, Vienna (permanent loan Wolfgang Anselmino)
Photo: Ann-Marie Rounkle

Fear of Mannequins (Wig Heads, Hollywood Boulevard), 1971
Photo, Cibachrome on aluminium, 183 × 122
Belvedere, Vienna (permanent loan Wolfgang Anselmino)

Fear of Mannequins (Wig Heads, Hollywood Boulevard), 1971
Photo, Cibachrome on aluminium, 183 × 122
Belvedere, Vienna (permanent loan Wolfgang Anselmino)

Jonathan Meese
TOTALADLER, Baby-CHEF der Kunst (das Ei des Columbussy),
2007
Bronze
165 × 238 × 233 cm
Edition 3 + 1 AP
Ragdan El-Akabi, Indigo Collection
Courtesy of Contemporary Fine Arts, Berlin

Hermann Nitsch
2 Schüttbilder der 40. Aktion, 1997
Each 200 × 300 cm
Courtesy of Atelier Hermann Nitsch

8. Symphonie für grosses Orchester und Chor performed on
June 25, 1990 at the MAK Vienna
4 scores, each 29.7 × 42 cm, on cardboard, 85 × 65 cm
Courtesy of Atelier Hermann Nitsch

1 screen with clips from actions
Courtesy of Atelier Hermann Nitsch

Oswald Oberhuber
Kunst ohne Künstler, 1969/ 2011
Collage
33 × 22.5 cm
Belvedere, Vienna

Wiener Schule, 1973
Mixed technique
60 × 50 × 4.5 cm
Belvedere, Vienna

Hermann Painitz
Entwurf für die Planierung der Alpen (Graz), 1969
Acrylic, Collage, Letraset on map
81 cm × 62 cm
Courtesy of Landesmuseum Niederösterreich, St. Pölten

Entwurf für die Planierung der Alpen (Glockner und Venediger), 1969
Acrylic, Collage, Letraset on map
59 cm × 62 cm
Courtesy of Landesmuseum Niederösterreich, St. Pölten

Entwurf für die Planierung der Alpen 5 (Wien), 1969
Acrylic, Collage, Letraset on map
35 cm × 50 cm
Courtesy of Landesmuseum Niederösterreich, St. Pölten

Entwurf für die Planierung der Alpen 6 (Wien), 1969
Acrylic, Collage, Letraset on map
35 cm × 50 cm
Courtesy of Landesmuseum Niederösterreich, St. Pölten

Entwurf für die Planierung der Alpen 8 (Wien), 1969
Acrylic, Collage, Letraset on map
35 cm × 50 cm
Courtesy of Landesmuseum Niederösterreich, St. Pölten

Entwurf für eine flache Welt, 1969
Acrylic, Collage, Letraset on map
50 cm × 35 cm
Courtesy of Landesmuseum Niederösterreich, St. Pölten

Planierung der Alpen (Vienna), 1969
Acrylic, Collage, Letraset on map
67 cm × 87 cm
Courtesy of Landesmuseum Niederösterreich, St. Pölten

Planierung der Alpen 4 (Graz), 1969
Acrylic, Collage, Letraset on map
35 cm × 50 cm
Courtesy of Landesmuseum Niederösterreich, St. Pölten

Planierung der Alpen 7 (Graz), 1969
Acrylic, Collage, Letraset on map
35 cm × 50 cm
Courtesy of Landesmuseum Niederösterreich, St. Pölten

Seb Patane
Patrons Paper 10/97, 2011
Silk screen print, ballpoint pen and crayon on model sheet
150 × 120 cm
Courtesy of the artist, Maureen Paley, London and Fonti,
Naples

Patrons Paper 4/97, 2011
Silk screen print, ballpoint pen and crayon on model sheet
150 × 120 cm
Courtesy of the artist, Maureen Paley, London and Fonti, Naples

Patrons Paper 11/92, 2011
Silk screen print, ballpoint pen and crayon on model sheet
150 × 120 cm
Courtesy of the artist, Maureen Paley, London and Fonti, Naples

Patrons Paper 2/98, 2011
Silk screen print, ballpoint pen and crayon on model sheet
150 × 120 cm
Courtesy of the artist, Maureen Paley, London and Fonti, Naples

Helga Philipp
o. T. (Objekt 70033), 1970
Silk screen print on acrylic glass, metal mirror
200 × 120 × 30 cm
Belvedere, Vienna (private donation)

Sitzmöbel, 1970
Measures variable
Belvedere, Vienna

Kinetisches Objekt and Sitzmöbel, 1970
Exhibition view Leben mit Kunst, Möbelhaus Ertl, Graz
Photo
16.3 × 24 cm
Inheritance Helga Philipp
Photo © Michael Leischner

Walter Pichler
Radikale Architektur : P/2008 Unterirdisches Gebäude mit ausfahrbarem Kern, 1963
Tin, cement
48 cm, ø 54 cm
Courtesy Tiroler Landesmuseum Ferdinandeum, Innsbruck

P/351 Unterirdisches Gebäude mit ausfahrbarem Kern, 1963
Pencil, photo montage on card board
19.7 cm × 25.5 cm
Courtesy Tiroler Landesmuseum Ferdinandeum, Innsbruck

P/354 Ausgang einer unterirdischen Stadt, 1964
China ink, collage on paper
21 × 29.7 cm
Courtesy Tiroler Landesmuseum Ferdinandeum, Innsbruck

P/355 Ausgänge einer unterirdischen Stadt, 1964
Pencil on transparent paper
21 × 29.5 cm
Courtesy Tiroler Landesmuseum Ferdinandeum, Innsbruck

P/549 Radikale Architekur I, 1963
China ink on transparent paper
21 × 29.6 cm
Courtesy Tiroler Landesmuseum Ferdinandeum, Innsbruck

P/558 Radikale Architektur I, 1963
Pencil on transparent paper
27,7 × 31 cm
Courtesy Tiroler Landesmuseum Ferdinandeum, Innsbruck

Marjetica Potrč
Monumental and Personal Modernism, 2002
9 sketches
Pencil and felt pen on paper
Each 29.5 × 20.9 cm, framed each 50 × 42 cm
Courtesy of the Generali Foundation, Vienna

Jason Rhoades
Mi Saga, U Saga (Emmanuelle Saga), 2005
Multimedia installation: Emmanuelle Flatwork, Perfect World Bench (polished aluminium tubes, cement), neon, chandlier, aluminium tubes, clamps, speakers, Wailing Wall (metall table, fibre glass camel toe, plastic, PeaRoeFoam, neon, Plexiglas, electric current), book (*1724 Birth of the Cunt*, 2004)
360 × 370 × 420 cm
Courtesy of Thyssen-Bornemisza Art Contemporary, Vienna

Thiago Rocha Pitta
Heritage, 2007
16 Film stills
C-Print
Each 27,5 cm × 37 cm
Edition: 5 + AP
Courtesy of the artists and Andersens Contemporary, Copenhagen

Gerwald Rockenschaub
2002
Black and white paint on 8 MDF tops
334 × 1000 cm (each 167 × 250 cm)
Courtesy of Georg Kargl Fine Arts, Vienna

Constanze Ruhm
My_Never_Ending_Burial_Plot, 2010
Photographers: Lukas Heistinger, Matthias Herrmann
3 C-prints/aluminium concealed
102 × 82 cm framed
Edition: 1/3 + 2 e.a.
Belvedere, Vienna

Gerhard Rühm
Reizwortzeichnungen, 2010
3 sheets: *Hoffnungsschimmer, Familien- and Traueranzeigen,
Wachstum gezielt steuern*
Collage, Pencil on paper
Each 40 × 30 cm
Courtesy of the artists

Fasen, 1957
3 sheets (idiogrammes)
Each 21 × 27.9 cm
Courtesy of the artists

Markus Schinwald
Dictio Pii, 2001
Film (35 mm) on DVD, 16'
Belvedere, Vienna

Jörg Schlick/Günter Brus
Parmiggiani-Report, 2004
China ink- and fine liner sketch, acrylic on polysterol
99.5 × 99.5 cm
Courtesy of ARTELIER CONTEMPORAY, Graz
Galerie Christian Nagel, Berlin

Selbst-Report, 2004
China ink- and fine liner sketch, acrylic on polysterol
99.5 × 99.5 cm
Courtesy of ARTELIER CONTEMPORAY, Graz
Galerie Christian Nagel, Berlin

Schlick-Report, 2004
China ink- and fine liner sketch, acrylic on polysterol
99.5 × 99.5 cm
Courtesy of ARTELIER CONTEMPORAY, Graz
Galerie Christian Nagel, Berlin

Munch-Report, 2004
China ink- and fine liner sketch, acrylic on polysterol
99.5 × 99.5 cm
Courtesy of ARTELIER CONTEMPORAY, Graz
Galerie Christian Nagel, Berlin

Christoph Schlingensief
Lungenbild (SEIN), 2008
from: *Eine Kirche der Angst vor dem Fremden in mir*, 2008
X-ray on textile
c. 200 × 297 cm
Courtesy of Thyssen-Bornemisza Art Contemporary, Vienna

Hase Fett, 2008
from: *Eine Kirche der Angst vor dem Fremden in mir*, 2008
Installation: wood, margarine, rabbit fur, ladder, metal top,
tape recorder, measuring cups
Dimensions site-specifially variable
Courtesy of Thyssen-Bornemisza Art Contemporary, Vienna

Cello TV, 2008
from: *Eine Kirche der Angst vor dem Fremden in mir*, 2008
Installation: 3 screens with videos, mixed media
Courtesy of Thyssen-Bornemisza Art Contemporary, Vienna

Gregor Schneider
Haus u r, Rheydt 1985 – today (Nacht – Video), 1996
Video PAL, 26' 12"
Courtesy of Galerie Luis Campaña, Berlin

Esther Stocker
Exhibition display *Utopia Gesamtkunstwerk*, 2012
Latex dispersion on wood, black felt carpet
Belvedere, Vienna

SUPERFLEX
The Financial Crisis (Session I-IV), 2009
Production: Propeller Group (Ho Chi Minh City)
Presented by Frieze Film, supported by Channel 4
Collaboration: Bo Groth Christensen (hypnotist), Tuan An-
drew Nguyen (production/direction), Matt Lucero (production
assistent), Ha Thuc Phu Nam (camera), Alan Hayslip (sound),
Nick Fernandez (cut)
1 channel-RED-film production, PAL 16:9, 12' 25"
Courtesy of Nils Staerk Gallery, Copenhagen and the artist

Una Szeemann
Montewood Hollyverità, 2003
Paint, stereo
Video 25' 59"
Courtesy of the artist

Peter Weibel
Das gequälte Quadrat, 1975
glass, iron, shirr
Per glass top: 74 × 90 cm
Courtesy of mumok, museum moderner kunst stiftung ludwig
wien

Franz West
Lemure, 2001
Aluminium coated
269 × 92 × 70 cm
Courtesy of Gernot Schauer Collection

WochenKlausur
Medizinische Versorgung Obdachloser, Vienna 1993
Community Survival Cabin, Plymouth 2011
Courtesy of the artists

Fritz Wotruba
Scenography and costumes for *Ring des Nibelungen. Ein Büh-
nenfestspiel aufzuführen in drei Tagen und einem Vorabend*
by Richard Wagner/Deutsche Oper Berlin 1967
Richard Wagner *Das Rheingold*, 2nd and 4th image:
Freie Gegend auf Bergeshöhen
Wallpaper, various dimensions
Courtesy of Fritz Wotruba Privatstiftung Vienna
Photo: Rotholz, Berlin © Fritz Wotruba Privatstiftung Vienna

Scenography and costumes for *Ring des Nibelungen. Ein Büh-
nenfestspiel aufzuführen in drei Tagen und einem Vorabend*
by Richard Wagner/Deutsche Oper Berlin 1967
Richard Wagner *Siegfried*, 1st image: *Wald*
Wallpaper, various dimensions
Courtesy of Fritz Wotruba Privatstiftung Vienna
Photo: Rotholz, Berlin © Fritz Wotruba Privatstiftung Vienna

Scenography and costumes for *Ring des Nibelungen. Ein Büh-
nenfestspiel aufzuführen in drei Tagen und einem Vorabend*
by Richard Wagner/Deutsche Oper Berlin 1967
Richard Wagner, *Götterdämmerung*, 4th image: *Uferraum.
Vor der Halle der Gibichungen*
Wallpaper, various dimensions
Courtesy of Fritz Wotruba Privatstiftung Vienna
Photo: Harry Croner © Fritz Wotruba Privatstiftung Vienna

Scenography and costumes for *Ring des Nibelungen. Ein Büh-
nenfestspiel aufzuführen in drei Tagen und einem Vorabend*
by Richard Wagner/Deutsche Oper Berlin 1967
Richard Wagner *Siegfried*, 2nd image: *Tiefer Wald*
Wallpaper, various dimensions
Courtesy of Fritz Wotruba Privatstiftung Vienna
Photo: Harry Croner © Fritz Wotruba Privatstiftung Vienna

Scenography and costumes for *ing des Nibelungen. Ein Büh-
nenfestspiel aufzuführen in drei Tagen und einem Vorabend*
by Richard Wagner/Deutsche Oper Berlin 1967
Model *Halle der Gibichungen*
Gesso, clay model
Courtesy of Fritz Wotruba Privatstiftung Vienna

Heimo Zobernig
ohne Titel, 1993
Pressboard, wood, cotton, aluminium foil/styrofoam, steel, etc
Circa 250 × 400 × 600 cm
Courtesy of Galerie Meyer Kainer, Vienna

Marc Adrian
Großes Sylvesterbild, 1977
Verre eglomise montage
190 × 145 cm
Belvedere, Vienna (permanent loan private collection)
Photo © Belvedere, Vienna/Markus Guschelbauer
© VBK, Vienna 2012

Klaus Auderer
Groundzerosystems: Baghdad 2003, Phnom Penh 2005
Colour pigment print
111 × 167 cm
Volume 2 + 1
Courtesy of Galerie Sabine Knust, Munich
Photo © Klaus Auderer

Josef Bauer
Installation mit Ecken-A, 1969
Courtesy of the artists
Photo © Josef Bauer
© VBK, Vienna 2012

Joseph Beuys
7000 Eichen (Die Erste der 7000 Eichen), 1982–1987
performance
Photo: Dieter Schwerdtle/© documenta archive
© VBK, Vienna 2012

Monica Bonvicini
We Finally Built Walls, 2010
Wood construction, 30 safety glass panels, black enamel paint
379 cm × 1207.5 cm × 6.8 cm (dimensions variable)
Courtesy of the artist and Galerie Max Hetzler, Berlin
Photo © def image
© VBK, Vienna 2012

Christian Boltanski/Ilya Kabakov/Jean Kalman
Der Ring – Fünfter Tag. Der Tag danach, 1999
A project by the Hebbel theatre, Berlin, and Theater der Welt
Portfolio, 29 sheets, (card board folder, 39 colour photographs, 1 poster)
Belvedere, Vienna
Photo © Martina Schmücker/David Zink Yi
Christian Boltanski, Ilya Kababov© VBK, Vienna 2012

Marcel Broodthaers
Musée d'art moderne, Département des Aigles, 1969
Print, invitation
17.5 × 11.5 cm
Generali Foundation, Vienna
Photo © Generali Foundation, Vienna
© VBK, Vienna 2012

Daniel Buren
Fiche technique, 1972
Acrylic on red and white fabric
142 × 137.5 cm
Belvedere, Vienna/Permanent loan Dr. Ernst Ploil
Photo © Belvedere, Vienna/Lea Titz
© VBK, Vienna 2012

Tom Burr
Derailed 2, 2005
Plywood, zinc hinges, paint, carpet
106 × 60 × 259 cm
Courtesy of the artist and Galerie Neu, Berlin
Photo © Lepkowski Studios, Berlin

Ernst Caramelle
ohne Titel, 1986
TV-Screens, wood, wine
194.5 × 124 × 39 cm
Rudi Molacek Collection, Vienna
Photo © Belvedere, Vienna/Markus Guschelbauer

Bernhard Cella
Salon für Kunstbuch im 21er Haus, since 2011
(ongoing project)
Sculpture
Courtesy of Belvedere, Vienna and the artist
Photo © Bernhard Cella

Cityrama II
Wolf Vostell, Stefan Wewerka, Galerie Dumont
Einladung zu „Cityrama II", 1962
25.7 × 19 cm
Courtesy of mumok, museum moderner kunst stiftung ludwig wien, previously Hahn Collection, Cologne
Photo © mumok, museum moderner kunst stiftung ludwig wien

Heinz Emigholz
Model for a *Endless House* (1959) by Frederick Kiesler
in *Two Projects by Frederick Kiesler* (Austria/Germany 2006/09)
HDV 4:3, 16"
©Heinz Emigholz/Amour Fou, Vienna

VALIE EXPORT
Restringierter Code, 1979
Performance, video performance
(Performance 1979, Städtische Galerie im Lenbachhaus,
Munich)
Photo: Michael Schuster/© the artist and Charim Galerie,
Vienna
© VBK, Vienna 2012

Claire Fontaine
I, 2009
Film still
HDV, 16:9, 4' 20"
Courtesy of the artist and T293, Naples/Rome

Peter Friedl
Bilbao Song, 2010
Film still
Video installation 16:9, 5'53", loop
Courtesy of the artist and Galerie Meyer Kainer, Vienna

gelatin
B-Thing (from the series *World Trade Center*), 2000
Photography (Fujiflex)
40 × 60 cm
Belvedere, Vienna (State funding for Galleries)
Photo © gelatin

Isa Genzken
empire vampire III, 19, 2004
Plastic, metal, glass, fabric, lacquer, paper, wood
320 × 100 × 75 cm
Courtesy of Thyssen-Bornemisza Art Contemporary, Vienna
Photo © Jens Ziehe/Photo courtesy of neugerriemschneider,
Berlin

Liam Gillick
Mirrored Image: A Volvo Bar, 2008
Dyed hessian, wood, vinyl texts, script, actors
25 elements in five colours: 10 elements each 240 × 120 ×
10 cm, 15 elements each 120 × 120 cm × 10 cm, overall in-
stallation size variable
Installation view at Liam Gillick, *One long walk … Two short piers
… (Ein langer Spaziergang … Zwei kurze Stege)*, Kunst- und Aus-
stellungshalle der Bundesrepublik Deutschland, Bonn, 2010
Photo © David Ertl/Photo courtesy by the artist and Esther
Schipper

Franz Graf
Exhibition view *DERR SCHRECKEN JEDOCH VERMEERTE
MEIN INTERESSE*, Bawag Contemporary, 2011
Photo © Oliver Ottenschläger/Photo courtesy BAWAG Con-
temporary
© VBK, Vienna 2012

Thomas Hirschhorn
Tool Family, 2007
Wood, cardboard, board of agglomerate, models, brown and
transparent adhesive tape, various tools, tools enlarged, book
enlarged, foil of yellow transparent sheet, prints, integrated
text
290 × 290 × 290 cm
Courtesy of the artist and ARNDT Berlin
Photo © Bernd Borchardt
© VBK, Vienna 2012

Julia Hohenwarter
Catwalk, 2009
Sculpture
Wood, dispersion paint
Belvedere, Vienna
Photo © Julia Hohenwarter

Hans Hollein/Walter Pichler
Poster draft for the exhibition *Architektur* at
Galerie nächst St. Stephan, 1963
China ink on paper, 45 × 55 cm
Courtesy of Hans Hollein/Walter Pichler

**Inspection Medical Hermeneutics
(Pavel Pepperstein/Sergei Anufriev)**
PARAMEN # 16, 1994
Acrylic paint on canvas
65 × 50 cm
Courtesy of Galerie Kamm, Berlin
Photo © Jens Ziehe

Christian Jankowski
Telemistica, 1999
Video, 22"
Exhibition view Galerie Meyer Kainer, 2000
Courtesy of Galerie Meyer Kainer

Tillman Kaiser
Innenblick Kirche, 2011
Card board, china ink, glass, butterfly wings, iron
200 × 129 × 61 cm
Belvedere, Vienna
Photo © Markus Krottendorfer

Ian Kiaer
Grey Cloth Project: Glashaus, 2005
Work on paper, cardboard, coloured acrylic sheet, acrylic rod
Work on paper: 49 × 64 cm; model: 25 × 30 × 22 cm
Installation view Tanya Bonakdar Gallery, New York
Collection of Gregory R. Miller and Michael Weiner, New York
Photo © Fabian Birgfeld, PhotoTECTONICS /Photo courtesy
the artist and Tanya Bonakdar Gallery, New York

Friedrich Kiesler
Scan of *Manifeste du Corréalisme (L'Architecture d'Aujourd'hui,
No. 2, special edition, June 1949)*

Martin Kippenberger
Alt Wien, Großplakat, 1991
Poster, 8 piece,
Each 84.1 × 118.9 cm
Private collection
Photo © Estate Martin Kippenberger, Galerie Gisela Capitain,
Cologne

Mahony
o. T. (Marginale), 2011
Various objects, different materials, several sizes
Courtesy of the artists and Galerie Emanuel Layr

Gordon Matta-Clark
Bronx Floors: Floor Above, Ceiling Below, 1972
3 black & white photographs, framed, 21.5 × 28 cm
Photo © Belvedere, Vienna/permanent loan Dr. Ernst Ploil

Ralo Mayer
And turns and turns and I turn pages. (...) / *"ÜBERSETZUNG
UND VERRAT"*, 2009/12
Film still
Co-channel HD-video with sound (40"), Fresnel lens, acrylic
glass
Based on the novel *The Ninth Biospherian* and the film proj-
ect with the same name, which was developed in cooperation
with Oliver Gemballa
Courtesy of the artists
Photo © Belvedere, Vienna

Paul McCarthy
Basement Bunker: Painting Queens in the Red Carpet Hall 3
Photo, Cibachrome on aluminium
183 × 122 cm
Belvedere, Vienna/permanent loan Wolfgang Anselmino
Photo: Ann-Marie Rounkle
Repro photo © Markus Guschelbauer

Jonathan Meese
TOTALADLER, Baby-CHEF der Kunst (das Ei des Columbussy),
2007
Bronze
165 × 238 × 233 cm
Edition 3 + 1 AP
Ragdan El-Akabi, Indigo Collection
Courtesy of Contemporary Fine Arts, Berlin
Photo © Jochen Littkemann
© VBK, Vienna 2012

Hermann Nitsch
Schüttbild der 40. Malaktion, 1997
200 × 300 cm
Courtesy of Atelier Hermann Nitsch
© VBK, Vienna 2012

Oswald Oberhuber
Kunst ohne Künstler, 1969/2011
Collage
33 × 22.5 cm
Belvedere, Vienna
Photo © Belvedere, Vienna/Markus Guschelbauer

Hermann Painitz
Entwurf für die Planierung der Alpen (Graz), 1969
Acrylic, collage, Letraset on map
81 × 62 cm
Landesmuseum Niederösterreich, St. Pölten
Photo © Peter Böttcher
© VBK, Vienna 2012

Seb Patane
Patrons Paper 4/97, 2011
Screen print, ballpoint pen and colour pencil on printed paper
150 × 120 cm
Courtesy of the artist, Maureen Paley, London and Fonti,
Naples
Photo © the artist, Maureen Paley, London and Fonti, Naples

Helga Philipp
Kinetisches Objekt und Sitzmöbel, 1970
Exhibition view Leben mit Kunst, Möbelhaus Ertl, Graz
Inheritance Helga Philipp
Photo © Michael Leischner

Marjetica Potrč
Monumental and Personal Modernism, 2002
Pencil and felt pen on paper
9 sketches (1 of 9)
each 29.5 × 20.9 cm, framed each 50 × 42 cm
Courtesy of Generali Foundation, Vienna
Photo © Generali Foundation, Vienna

Jason Rhoades
Mi Saga, U Saga (Emmanuelle Saga), 2005
Emmanuelle flatwork, Perfect World Bench (polished aluminium tubes, concrete), several neon phrases, two chandeliers,
aluminium tubes, clamps, speakers, Wailing Wall (plastic, metal table, fibreglass camel toe, PeaRoeFoam, neon, Plexiglas,
electrical wiring), and book (*1724 Birth of the Cunt*, 2004)
360 × 370 × 420 cm
Courtesy of Thyssen-Bornemisza Art Contemporary, Vienna
Photo © Landesmuseum Joanneum/Niki Lackner

Thiago Rocha Pitta
Heritage, 2007
Film still as c-print
66.5 × 100 cm
Courtesy of the artist and Andersens Contemporary,
Copenhagen

Gerwald Rockenschaub
Exhibition view *no red tape*, Georg Kargl Fine Arts, 2002
Courtesy of Georg Kargl Fine Arts, Vienna
Photo © Jens Preusse

Constanze Ruhm
My_Never_Ending_Burial_Plot, 2010
C-print/aluminium laminated
102 × 82 cm framed
Edition: 1/3 + 2 e.a.
Photographer: Lukas Heistinger
Belvedere, Vienna
Repro photo© Belvedere, Vienna/Guschelbauer/Titz

Gerhard Rühm
Wachstum gezielt steuern (from the series
Reizwortzeichnungen), 2010
40 × 30 cm
Collage, pencil on paper
Courtesy of the artists

Markus Schinwald
Dictio Pii, 2001
Film still
Film (35 mm) on DVD, 16"
Belvedere, Vienna (State funding for Galleries)
© VBK, Vienna 2012

Jörg Schlick/Günter Brus
Parmiggiani-Report (from the series *Langspielkreise*), 2004
China ink and fine liner sketches, acrylic on polystyrene
99.5 × 99.5 cm
Courtesy of ARTELIER CONTEMPORAY, Graz
Galerie Christian Nagel, Berlin

Installation view Galerie Christian Nagel Cologne, 2004
Photo © Simon Vogel/Photo courtesy Galerie Christian Nagel
Cologne/Berlin/Antwerpen

Christoph Schlingensief
Hase Fett, 2008
from: *Eine Kirche der Angst vor dem Fremden in mir*, 2008
Wood, margarine, hare fur, ladder, metal plate, cassette
recorder
Dimensions site specific
Courtesy of Thyssen-Bornemisza Art Contemporary, Vienna
Photo © Roman Mensing (artdoc.de)

Gregor Schneider
Haus u r, Rheydt 1985 – today (Nacht – Video), 2009
Photo © Gregor Schneider
© VBK, Vienna 2012

Esther Stocker
geometrisch betrachtet, 2008
Wood, dispersion paint
939 × 3416 × 448 cm
Exhibition view museum moderner kunst stiftung ludwig wien
Photo © Michael Goldgruber

Drafts for exhibition display
Utopia Gesamtkunstwerk, 2011
Mixed technique
29.7 × 42 cm
Belvedere, Vienna

SUPERFLEX
The Financial Crisis (Session I–IV), 2009
Film still
1 channel-RED-film projection, PAL 16:9, 12' 25"
Courtesy of Nils Staerk Gallery, Copenhagen and the artist

Una Szeemann
Montewood Hollyverità, 2001
Photography (Fuji Super Gloss Paper)
100 × 75 cm
Courtesy of the artist
Photo © Simon Chaput

Peter Weibel
Das gequälte Quadrat, 1975
glass, iron, shirr
Glass top: 74 × 90 cm
Courtesy of mumok, museum moderner kunst stiftung ludwig
wien
Photo © mumok, museum moderner kunst stiftung ludwig wien

Franz West
Lemure, 2001
Aluminium painted
269 × 92 × 70 cm
Sammlung Gernot Schauer
Photo © Belvedere, Vienna/Markus Guschelbauer

WochenKlausur
Medizinische Versorgung Obdachloser, Vienna 1993
Photo © WochenKlausur
Courtesy of the artists

Fritz Wotruba
Scenography and costumes for *Ring des Nibelungen. Ein Büh-
nenfestspiel aufzuführen in drei Tagen und einem Vorabend*
by Richard Wagner/Deutsche Oper Berlin 1967
Richard Wagner *Siegfried*, 2nd image: *Tiefer Wald*
Wallpaper, various dimensions
Courtesy of Fritz Wotruba Privatstiftung Vienna
Photo: Harry Croner © Fritz Wotruba Privatstiftung Vienna

Heimo Zobernig
ohne Titel, 1993
Floor, dividers, stairs, tables, chairs, multi-functional packing
table, refrigerator, various coffee cooking facilities, dishes,
three plastic tubs with water, etc
Several measures
*Project Unité, Art, Architecture, Design, Le Corbusier's Unité
d'Habitation*, Firminy 1993
Photo © Archiv HZ
© VBK, Vienna 2012

Essays

Gustav Klimt
The Beethovenfrieze, detail of the front wall, 1901/02
Belvedere, Vienna

Gustav Klimt
The Beethovenfrieze, 1901/02
Courtesy of ÖNB/ Vienna 283862 B
Photo: Moritz Nähr

Niki de Saint Phalle
Hon, 1966
Courtesy of Moderna Museet-Stockholm
(Photo Hans Hammarskiöld)

Jan Pietersz Saenredam
The Cave of Plato, 1604
Copperplate engraving
Courtesy of Kunstsammlungen der Veste Coburg

John Tenniel
Alice Finding Tiny Door Behind The Curtain, in:
Carroll, Lewis: *Alice in Wonderland*, New York:
The Heritage Press 1941, p. 11

*If in spite of our thorough research any individual illustrations
have not been correctly attributed or acknowledged, we offer
our apologies and would appreciate any information that will
allow us to rectify the matter in future editions.*

This catalogue is published on the occasion of the exhibition *Utopia Gesamtkunstwerk* at 21er Haus, Vienna, January 20—May 20 2012

Editors: Agnes Husslein-Arco, Harald Krejci und Bettina Steinbrügge

Publication Management: Ute Stadlbauer
Design: Christof Nardin/ Bueronardin
Translation/Copy-Editing: Ian Miltner, Lisa Rosenblatt, Catherine Brooke Penaloza-Patzak
Lithography: Pixelstorm, Vienna
Print: Ueberreuter Print GmbH

Authors work descriptions:
Véronique Aichner (VA), Nina Herlitschka (NH) , Harald Krejci (HK), Bettina Steinbrügge (BS)

Reprint: pp. 30–36 Boris Groys—Designers of the unconscious and their audience. (in: Boris Groys, Total Art of Stalinism, pp. 113–120)
Translation © Charles Rougle 1992
© Verso, London, 2011

© 2012 Belvedere, Vienna, Authors and Verlag der Buchhandlung Walther König, Köln

© VBK, Vienna 2012 for Marc Adrian, Josef Bauer, Joseph Beuys, Monica Bonvicini, Christian Boltanski, Ilya Kabakov, Marcel Broodthaers, Daniel Buren, VALIE EXPORT, Franz Graf, Thomas Hirschhorn, Jonathan Meese, Hermann Nitsch, Hermann Josef Painitz, Markus Schinwald, Gregor Schneider, Heimo Zobernig
All rights reserved.

Cover Image: Helga Philipp, *Kinetisches Objekt und Sitzmöbel*, 1970, Inheritance Helga Philipp
Photo © Michael Leischner

Published by
Verlag der Buchhandlung Walther König, Köln
Ehrenstr. 4, 50672 Köln
Tel. +49 (0) 221 / 20 59 6-53
Fax +49 (0) 221 / 20 59 6-60
verlag@buchhandlung-walther-koenig.de

Bibliographic information published by the Deutsche Nationalbibliothek
The Deutsche Nationalbibliothek lists this publication in the Deutsche Nationalbibliografie; detailed bibliographic data are available in the Internet at http://dnb.d-nb.de

Printed in Austria

Distribution:
Switzerland
AVA Verlagsauslieferungen AG
Centralweg 16
CH-8910 Affoltern a.A.
Tel. +41 (44) 762 42 60
Fax +41 (44) 762 42 10
verlagsservice@ava.ch

UK & Eire
Cornerhouse Publications
70 Oxford Street
GB-Manchester M1 5NH
Fon +44 (0) 161 200 15 03
Fax +44 (0) 161 200 15 04
publications@cornerhouse.org

Outside Europe
D.A.P. / Distributed Art Publishers, Inc.
155 6th Avenue, 2nd Floor
USA-New York, NY 10013

ISBN: 978-3-86335-140-3